THE HISTORY OF
CHARLES
XII

KING OF SWEDEN

François-Marie Arouet de Voltaire

THE HISTORY OF
CHARLES
XII

KING OF SWEDEN

Translated by Antonia White

BARNES
&NOBLE
BOOKS
NEW YORK

This edition published by Barnes & Noble, Inc.,
by arrangement with The Folio Society Limited.

1993 Barnes & Noble Books

ISBN 1-56619-189-0
Printed and bound in the United States of America

M 9 8 7 6 5 4 3 2 1

Contents

Dissertation   27

BOOK I   31
Abridged history of Sweden up to Charles XII. His education;
his enemies. Character of the Tsar Peter Alexeiovitch. Very
curious particulars concerning this prince and the Russian
nation. Russia, Poland and Denmark unite against Charles XII.

BOOK II   51
Prodigious and sudden change in the character of Charles XII.
At the age of eighteen he wages war against Denmark, Poland
and Russia; ends the war with Denmark in six weeks; defeats
eighty thousand Russians with eight thousand Swedes and
invades Poland. Description of Poland and its government.
Charles wins several battles and is master of Poland, where he
prepares to nominate a king.

BOOK III   87
Stanislas Leczinski elected King of Poland. Death of the
cardinal-primate. Fine retreat of General Schulenburg. Foundation of St Petersburg. Battle of Fraustadt. Charles enters
Saxony. Peace of Alt-Ranstadt. Augustus abdicates and yields
the crown to Stanislas. General Patkul, the tsar's plenipotentiary, is broken on the wheel and quartered. In Saxony Charles
receives ambassadors from all the princes; he goes alone to
Dresden to see Augustus before leaving.

BOOK IV   117
Charles leaves Saxony, pursues the tsar and penetrates deep
into the Ukraine. His losses; his wound. Battle of Poltava.
Consequences of this battle. Charles forced to flee to Turkey.
His reception in Bessarabia.

Contents

BOOK V   140
State of the Sublime Porte. Charles stays near Bender. His
occupations. His intrigues with the Porte. His plans. Augustus
regains his throne. The King of Denmark invades Sweden. All
Charles's other realms are attacked. The tsar celebrates his
triumph in Moscow. Battle of the Prut. History of the tsarina,
the peasant girl who became empress.

BOOK VI   166
Intrigues in the Sublime Porte. The Khan of Tartary and the
Pasha of Bender try to force Charles to leave. He defends
himself with forty servants against an army. He is captured
and treated as a prisoner.

BOOK VII   189
The Turks transfer Charles to Demirtash. King Stanislas is
captured at the same time. Bold action of M. de Villelongue.
Revolution in the Seraglio. Fighting in Pomerania. Altona
burnt by the Swedes. Charles at last leaves to return to his
dominions. His strange mode of travelling. His arrival at
Stralsund. Charles's misfortunes. Peter the Great's success.
His triumph in St Petersburg.

BOOK VIII   212
Charles marries his sister to the Prince of Hesse. He is besieged
in Stralsund and escapes to Sweden. Enterprises of Baron Görtz,
his prime minister. Projects for a reconciliation with the tsar
and an invasion of England. Charles besieges Frederikshald in
Norway. He is killed. His character. Görtz is beheaded.

APPENDIX: Voltaire's replies to certain allegations of inac-
curacy made against *The History of Charles XII*.   241

Letter from M. de Voltaire, 25 April 1733   243

Notes on La Motraye's *Remarques*   246

Letter to Marshal Schulenburg   259

Contents

Letter to the *Journal des savants*   263

Letter to M. Nordberg   267

The Necessity of Doubt   272

Important Statement   278

Dissertation on *The History of Charles XII*

THERE are very few sovereigns whose personal history need have been written. Nearly all princes have been flattered or maligned to no purpose: the memory of only a very small number of them survives, and this number would be smaller still were only the just ones remembered.

The princes who have the most right to immortality are those who have done some good to mankind. Thus, as long as France exists, Frenchmen will remember Louis XII's love for his people; they will excuse the great faults of Francis I for the sake of his patronage of the arts and sciences; they will bless the memory of Henry IV, who conquered his heritage by dint of vanquishing and pardoning; they will praise the magnificence of Louis XIV, who protected the arts to which Francis I had given new life.

The memory of bad princes survives for an opposite reason; men remember them as they do floods, fires and plagues.

Between the tyrants and the good kings, but more akin to the former, are the conquerors: these have a dazzling reputation, and people are avid to know the minutest details of their lives. Such is the wretched weakness of men that they admire those who have done evil brilliantly, and are often more inclined to talk of the destroyer of an empire than of him who founded it.

As for all the other princes, who have been illustrious neither in peace nor in war, and who have been famed neither for great vices nor for great virtues, as their life furnishes no example either to be imitated or shunned, it is not worthy to be remembered. How many of all those emperors of Rome, Germany or Russia, how many of all those sultans, caliphs, popes and kings deserve that their name should be found anywhere but in chronological tables which merely need to record their dates?

There is a common level among princes as among other men; nevertheless the rage for writing has reached such a point that, no sooner has a sovereign expired, than the public is inundated with volumes in the form of memoirs, biographies and anecdotes of his court. Hence the books multiply so formidably that if a man were to live a hundred years and spend all of them reading them, he would not have time to peruse everything that has been published in Europe, on history alone, for the past two centuries.

This itch to transmit irrelevant details to posterity and to rivet the eyes of future centuries on everyday events arises from a weakness very common to those who have lived at some court and who have had the misfortune to have had some part in public affairs. They regard the court in which they have lived as the most splendid there has ever been; the king they have known as the greatest monarch; the affairs in which they have been involved as the most important in the history of the world. They imagine that posterity will see all this with the same eyes.

Because a prince starts a war, because his court is troubled with intrigues, because he buys the friendship of one of his neighbours and sells his own to another, because he finally makes peace with his enemies after some victories and some defeats, his subjects, fired by the excitement of current events, imagine they are living in the most remarkable era since the creation. What happens? This prince dies; entirely different measures are introduced after him; the intrigues of his court, his mistresses, his ministers, his generals, his wars and he himself are forgotten.

During all the years that Christian princes have endeavoured to deceive each other and made wars and alliances, thousands of treaties have been signed, thousands of battles fought and innumerable splendid or infamous deeds performed by them. When all this mass of events and details is presented to posterity they nearly all cancel each other out; the only ones who survive are those who have produced great revolutions or those who, because they have been described by some excellent writer, are rescued from the crowd, like portraits of obscure men painted by great masters.

We might well, therefore, have banished the thought of adding this personal history of Charles XII, King of Sweden, to the multitude of books with which the public is overwhelmed, had not this prince and his rival, Peter Alexeiovitch, a much greater man than he, been universally admitted to be the most remarkable characters who have appeared for more than twenty centuries. But we have not decided to write this life merely for the petty satisfaction of recording extraordinary facts; we have thought that it might be useful to some princes to read this book, should it chance to fall into their hands. Certainly there is no sovereign who ought not to be cured of the madness of conquering by reading the life of Charles XII. For where is the sovereign who could say: 'I have more courage, more virtues, a stronger mind, a robuster body, a better understanding of warfare, and better troops than Charles XII?' And if, with all these advantages, this king was so unfortunate, what can other princes, who have the same ambition, with less talents and resources, hope for?

We have composed this history from the accounts of well-known persons, who spent several years at the court of Charles XII and Peter the Great, Emperor of Russia, and who, having retired to a free country long after the death of these princes, had no interest in disguising the truth. It is based on memoirs furnished by Monsieur Fabrice, who lived on familiar terms with Charles XII for seven years; Monsieur de Fierville, the French ambassador, and Monsieur de Villelongue, a colonel in the Swedish army, and even by Poniatowsky.

We have not set down a single fact on which we have not consulted eye-witnesses of unimpeachable veracity. This is why this history will be found to be very different from the chronicles which have been published hitherto under the name of *Life of Charles XII*. If we have omitted several small combats fought between Swedish and Russian officers, it is because we had no intention of writing the history of these officers, but only that of the King of Sweden. We have even chosen to write only of the most interesting events in his life. We are convinced that the history of a prince is not the record of everything he did but of what he did worthy of being transmitted to posterity.

We must warn the reader that many things which were true when we wrote this history in 1728 are already ceasing to be so today. For example, trade is beginning to be less neglected in Sweden. The Polish infantry is better disciplined and more accustomed to obeying orders than it was then. When one reads a history one must always bear in mind the time at which the author wrote it. A man who read only Cardinal de Retz would take the French for madmen entirely addicted to civil war, faction and folly. A man who read only the history of the splendid years of Louis XIV would say: 'The French are born to obey, to conquer and to cultivate the arts.' Another who saw the memoirs of the first years of Louis XV would observe nothing in our nation but laxity, extreme greed for self-enrichment, and too much indifference to all the rest. The Spaniards of today are no longer the Spaniards of Charles the Fifth but may be so in a few years. The English no more resemble Cromwell's fanatics than the monks and monsignori with which Rome is peopled resemble the Scipios. I do not know whether the Swedes might suddenly have troops as formidable as those of Charles XII. One says of a man: 'He was brave on such a day'; in speaking of a nation one should say: 'It seemed so under such a government and such a year'.

If some prince and some minister find some disagreeable truths in this work, let them remember that, being public men, they owe the public an account of their actions; that it is at this price they purchase their greatness; that history is a witness, not a flatterer; and that the only way to oblige men to speak well of us is to act well.

BOOK I

SWEDEN and Finland compose a kingdom about two hundred of our leagues broad and three hundred long. It extends from south to north from roughly latitude 55° to latitude 70°, and has a rigorous climate with almost no spring or autumn. Winter prevails there for nine months of the year; the heat of summer follows suddenly on excessive cold, and it freezes as early as October, with none of those imperceptible gradations which bring in the seasons elsewhere and make the change gentler. In recompense, nature has given this rude climate a serene sky and pure air. The summer, nearly always hot and sunny, produces flowers and fruit in a very short space of time. The long nights of winter are alleviated by dawns and twilights which last proportionately longer as the sun does not withdraw so far from Sweden; and the light of the moon, which is obscured by no cloud there, is further increased by the reflection of the snow which covers the ground, and very frequently by illuminations in the sky resembling zodiacal light, makes it as possible to travel by night in Sweden as by day. The cattle there are smaller than in southern countries, for lack of pastures. The men there are taller; the serenity of the sky makes them healthy; the rigour of the climate makes them strong; they live long when they do not weaken themselves by the immoderate use of strong liquors and wines, which the northern nations seem to like all the more because nature has denied them to them.

The Swedes are well-made, robust, agile and capable of enduring the greatest hardships, hunger and poverty. They are born warriors, full of pride and more brave than industrious, having long neglected trade which is the only thing which could give their country what it lacks, and which they do little to cultivate even nowadays. It is said that it was from Sweden, of which a part is still called Gotland, that those hordes of Goths poured down who inundated Europe and wrested it from the Roman Empire, which had been its usurper, tyrant and legislator for five hundred years.

The northern countries were more densely populated then than they are nowadays because their religion allowed the inhabitants to give more citizens to the state by having several wives, and because these wives themselves incurred no reproach except for laziness and sterility, and were as hard-working and robust as the men, they bore children earlier and remained fecund longer. But Sweden, with what remains to it today of Finland, now has no more than four million inhabitants. The country is barren and poor. Scania is its only province which grows wheat. There are not more than nine million of our *livres* in minted money in the entire country. The public bank, which is the oldest in Europe, was introduced from necessity because, payments being made in copper and iron coins, transport was too difficult.

Sweden was still free until the middle of the fourteenth century. During this long space of time the government changed more than once; but all the innovations were in favour of liberty. Their chief magistrate had the name of king, a title which, in different countries, is given to very different powers; for, in France and Spain, it signifies an absolute ruler, and in Poland, Sweden and England, the head of a republic. This king could do nothing without the senate; and the senate depended on the diet which was frequently convoked. The representatives of the nation in these great assemblies were nobles, bishops and town deputies; in time even the peasants, a section of the people unjustly despised elsewhere, and enslaved in almost all the north, were admitted to them.

About the year 1492, this nation, so jealous of its liberty, and which is still proud of having subjugated Rome thirteen centuries ago, was put under the yoke by a woman and by a nation less powerful than the Swedes.

Margaret of Valdemar, the Semiramis of the North, Queen of Denmark and Norway, conquered Sweden by force and by cunning, and made a single kingdom out of these three vast states. After her death, Sweden was torn by civil wars; she shook off the yoke of the

Danes and resumed it; sometimes she had kings, sometimes administrators. About the year 1520, she was oppressed in a horrible manner by two tyrants: one was Christian II, King of Denmark, a monster composed of vices without a single virtue; the other an Archbishop of Upsala, the Primate of the Kingdom, who was as barbarous as Christian. One day, the two of them acting in concert caused the consuls and magistrates of Stockholm, together with ninety-four senators, to be arrested and had them massacred by executioners, on the pretext that they were excommunicated by the pope for having defended the rights of the state against the archbishop.

While these two men, united for the purpose of oppression but disunited when it came to sharing the spoils, were exerting the most tyrannical despotism and exacting the cruellest vengeance, a new event changed the face of the north.

Gustavus Vasa, a young man descended from the ancient kings of the country, emerged from the forests of Dalecarlia where he had been in hiding, and came to deliver Sweden. He was one of those noble spirits which nature so rarely fashions, with all the qualities necessary for commanding men. His tall stature and impressive appearance gained him adherents as soon as he showed himself. His eloquence, to which his imposing looks added force, was all the more persuasive for being spontaneous; his genius planned enterprises which the common herd thinks foolhardy but which, in the eyes of great men, are merely bold; his indefatigable courage made them succeed. He was intrepid, but prudent, of a gentle disposition in a ferocious age, in fine, according to what is said of him, as virtuous as a party leader can be.

Gustavus Vasa had been Christian's hostage and unlawfully held prisoner. Escaped from his prison, he had wandered, disguised as a peasant, in the mountains and woods of Dalecarlia. There he had been reduced to the necessity of working in the copper mines in order to live and to hide himself. Buried in these subterranean regions he dared to contemplate dethroning the tyrant. He revealed his identity to the peasants; he appeared to them a man of a higher species, whom ordinary men felt naturally inclined to obey. In a short time he turned these raw peasants into trained soldiers. He attacked Christian and the archbishop and, having won several victories, drove both of them out of Sweden; after which the council of state justly elected him king of the land he had liberated.

He was hardly established on the throne before he attempted a more difficult enterprise than military conquest. The real tyrants of the state were the bishops, who owned nearly all the wealth of Sweden and used it to oppress her subjects and make war on her kings. This power was all the more terrible, because the ignorance of the people rendered it sacrosanct. He punished the Catholic religion for the crimes of its ministers. In less than two years he made Sweden a Lutheran country, by the superiority of his diplomacy even more than by his authority. Having thus conquered this kingdom, as he said, by overcoming the Danes and the clergy he reigned happy and unchallenged to the age of sixty, and died full of glory, leaving his family and his religion on the throne.

One of his descendants was that Gustavus-Adolphus known as Gustavus the Great. This king conquered Ingria, Livonia, Bremen, Verden, Vismar and Pomerania, not to mention more than a hundred places in Germany, surrendered by Sweden after his death. He shook the throne of Ferdinand II. He protected the Protestants in Germany, abetted in this by the intrigues of Rome itself, which feared the power of the emperor even more than that of heresy. It was he who, by his victories, effectively contributed to the downfall of the House of Austria: an enterprise of which all the glory is attributed to Cardinal Richelieu, who had the art of making himself a reputation, whereas Gustavus restricted himself to doing great things. He was about to carry the war beyond the Danube and perhaps to dethrone the emperor when he was killed, at the age of thirty-seven, at the battle of Lützen, which he won against Wallenstein, bearing with him to the grave the name of the 'Great', the regrets of the north, and the esteem of his enemies. His daughter Christina, born with a rare genius, preferred conversing with scholars to reigning over a nation interested only in warfare. She made herself as illustrious by quitting the throne as her ancestors had by conquering or strengthening it. The Protestants slandered her, as if one could not have great virtues without believing in Luther, and the popes exulted too much over the conversion of a woman who was only a philosopher. She retired to Rome, where she spent the rest of her days in the midst of the arts she loved, and for which she had renounced an empire at the age of twenty-seven.

Before abdicating she advised the Swedish Council of State to elect in her place her cousin Charles-Gustavus, the tenth of that name, son of the Count Palatine, the Duke of Zweibrücken. This king added fresh conquests to those of Gustavus-Adolphus: he first invaded Poland, where he won the famous battle of Warsaw, which lasted three days. He waged a long and successful war against the Danes, besieged their capital, reunited Scania to Sweden, and assured, at least for a time, the possession of Sleswig to the Duke of Holstein. Subsequently, having suffered some defeats and made peace with his enemies, he turned his ambition against his subjects. He conceived the plan of establishing arbitrary power in Sweden, but he died, like Gustavus the Great, at the age of thirty-seven, before being able to achieve this despotic aim, which his son Charles XI realized to the full.

Charles XI, a warrior like all his ancestors, was more absolute than they. He abolished the authority of the senate, which was declared the senate of the king, not of the kingdom. He was frugal, vigilant and hard-working, so that he might have been loved had not his despotism reduced his subjects' feelings for him to one alone: fear.

In 1680, he married Ulrica-Eleonora, daughter of Frederick III, King of Denmark, a virtuous princess, who was worthy of more confidence than her husband showed in her. From this marriage was born (27 June 1682) King Charles XII, perhaps the most extraordinary man who has ever lived on earth, who united in himself all the great qualities of his forebears, and who had no other defect or misfortune except to have surpassed them all. It is of him we propose to write here all that we have learnt for certain about his character and his deeds.

The first book he was made to read was the work of Samuel Puffendorf in order that he might be early acquainted with his states and those of his neighbours. The first foreign language he learnt was German, which he spoke ever after as well as his mother tongue. At the age of seven he could control a horse. The violent exertions in which he delighted, and which revealed his martial inclinations, early built him up a vigorous constitution, capable of sustaining the fatigues which his temperament imposed on him.

Although gentle in his childhood, he had an inflexible stubborn-ness: the only way to make him yield was to put him on his mettle; by appealing to his pride one could make him do anything. He had an aversion to Latin, but as soon as he was told that the King of Poland and the King of Denmark understood Latin, he very quickly learnt it. People used the same method to induce him to learn French: but, as long as he lived, he obstinately refused to speak it, even with the French ambassadors who knew no other language.

As soon as he had some knowledge of Latin, he was made to translate Quintus Curtius: the liking he took to this book was inspired very much more by its subject than by its style. One day the tutor who was expounding this author to him asked him what he thought of Alexander: 'I think,' said the prince, 'that I wish I could be like him.' 'But he lived only thirty-two years,' the tutor told him. 'Ah!' he replied, 'is that not enough when one has conquered kingdoms?' These replies were duly reported to his father the king, who exclaimed: 'Here is a boy who will be worthier than myself, and who will go further than Gustavus the Great.' One day he was in the king's apartment, amusing himself by looking at two maps, one of a town in Hungary taken from the emperor by the Turks and the other of Riga, the capital of Livonia, a province conquered by Sweden a century earlier. At the bottom of the map of the Hungarian town were these words, adapted from the Book of Job: 'God gave it to me and God has taken it away from me: blessed be the name of the Lord.' The young prince, having read these words, promptly took a pencil and wrote at the bottom of the map of Riga: 'God gave it to me and the devil shall not take it away from me.'* Thus, even in the most trivial acts of his childhood, his indomitable nature often allowed a glimpse of those traits which characterize remarkable men and which indicated what he was one day to be.

He was eleven when he lost his mother. This princess died (5 August 1693) of a malady induced, it is said, by the distresses her husband caused her and her efforts to conceal them.† Charles XI had despoiled a great number of his subjects of their goods by a species

---

* Two French ambassadors to Sweden have told me this fact.

† Père Barre, a canon regular of St Geneviève, has copied this whole passage in his 'History of Germany', Volume VII, but he applies it to a Count of Würtemberg.

of judicial court called the Chamber of Liquidations, established solely on his authority. A host of citizens, nobles, merchants, farmers, widows and orphans, ruined by this chamber, thronged the streets of Stockholm and came daily to the palace to utter vain protests. The queen helped these unfortunates with everything she possessed: she gave them her money, her jewels, her furniture, even her clothes. When she had nothing left to give them, she threw herself at her husband's feet in tears and implored him to have pity on his subjects. The king replied solemnly: 'Madam, we took you to give us children, and not to give us advice.' From then on, he treated her with a harshness which shortened her days.

He died four years after her (16 April 1697) in the forty-second year of his age and the thirty-seventh of his reign, when the Empire, Spain and Holland on one side, and France on the other, had just asked him to act as mediator in settling their quarrels, and he had already begun the work of making peace between these powers.

He bequeathed to his fifteen-year-old son a secure throne, respected beyond the bounds of Sweden, subjects who were poor, but warlike and obedient, together with finances in good order, managed by capable ministers.

At his accession, Charles XII found himself not only absolute and uncontested master of Sweden and Finland, but he still reigned over Livonia, Karelia and Ingria; he possessed Wismar, Viborg, the islands of Rügen and Ösel, the most important part of Pomerania, and the Duchies of Bremen and Verden, all conquests of his ancestors and assured to his crown by long possession and guaranteed by the solemn treaties of Münster and Oliva, supported by the terror of the Swedish armies. The Peace Treaty of Ryswick, begun under the auspices of the father, was concluded under those of the son: from the moment he began to reign he was the mediator of Europe.

The Swedish laws fixed the majority of kings at fifteen: but Charles XI, autocratic in everything, made a will delaying that of his son till eighteen. By this arrangement, he furthered the ambitious designs of his mother, Hedwig-Eleonora, the widow of Charles X. This princess was appointed, by her son, to be the young king's guardian and regent of the realm in conjunction with a council of five.

The regent had taken part in public affairs during the reign of the king her son. She was advanced in years, but her ambition, greater than her physical or mental powers, made her hope she would long enjoy the pleasures of authority under the king her grandson. She kept him as much as possible out of public affairs. The young prince spent his time hunting, or occupied himself in reviewing the troops, sometimes even drilling with them; these amusements seemed only natural to a high-spirited youth of his age. There was no sign of discontent in his behaviour which might have alarmed the regent; and this princess flattered herself that these distractions would make him incapable of application, so that she would be able to govern longer.

One day in the November of the year of his father's death, when he had just been reviewing several regiments, Piper, one of the councillors of state, who was with him, observed that the king appeared to be sunk in a deep reverie. Piper said to him: 'May I take the liberty of asking your Majesty what he is thinking about so seriously?' 'I am thinking,' replied the prince, 'that I feel worthy to command these brave fellows: and I wish that neither they nor I should receive orders from a woman.' Piper instantly seized the opportunity of making a great fortune. He himself had not enough influence to dare to undertake the dangerous enterprise of ousting the queen from the regency and advancing the king's majority; he proposed this negotiation to Count Axel Sparre, a spirited man who was seeking to increase his prestige; he flattered him by telling him what the king had confided to him. Sparre believed him, undertook the whole responsibility, and henceforth worked only for Piper. The councillors of the regency were soon persuaded. They vied with each other to hasten on the execution of this plan in order to curry favour with the king.

They went in a body to the queen, who was not expecting such a declaration. The assembly of the diet was then in session. The councillors of the regency submitted the proposal to it; there was not a single vote against it; the measure was carried through at a speed nothing could check; so that three days after Charles XII had expressed a wish to reign, the States General had handed the government over to him. The power and influence of the queen vanished in a moment. From then on she led a private life, more suitable to her age, though less so to her temperament. The king was crowned on the following 24th of December. He made his entrance into Stockholm on a chestnut horse shod with silver, carrying the sceptre and wearing the crown, to the acclamations of the whole populace, idolatrous of anything new and ever ready to cherish great hopes of a young prince.

The Archbishop of Upsala is the only person authorized to perform the coronation ceremony: this is almost the only one of so many rights which his predecessors arrogated to themselves that he still retains. After having, according to custom, anointed the prince, he held up the crown so as to place it on his head: Charles snatched it from the archbishop's hands and crowned himself, gazing haughtily at the prelate. The crowd, always impressed by a grand gesture, applauded the king's action. Even those who had groaned most under the despotism of the father let themselves by carried away into praising this sign of arrogance in the son which was a portent of further tyranny.

As soon as Charles was master, he entrusted the management of state affairs to Councillor Piper, who soon became his Prime Minister in all but name. A few days later he made him a count, which is an eminent distinction in Sweden, and not an empty title which can be assumed by men of no importance, as in France.

The first years of the king's rule gave a far from favourable impression of him: it seemed that he had been more impatient to reign than worthy to do so. He had not, indeed, any dangerous passion, but people saw nothing in his behaviour but the impetuosity of the youth and stubbornness. He seemed haughty and lacking in application. The ambassadors who were at his court even took him for a mediocrity, and depicted him as such to their masters.* Sweden had the same opinion of him; no one knew his character; he did not know it himself, until the storms that suddenly brewed up in the north gave his hidden talents an opportunity to display themselves.

Three powerful princes, wishing to take advantage of his youth, conspired, almost simultaneously, to ruin him. The first was his cousin, Frederick IV, King of Denmark; the second Augustus, Elector of Saxony and King of Poland; the third and most dangerous was Peter the Great, Tsar of Russia. We must explain the origin of

* The original letters attest this.

these wars, which produced such great events, beginning with Denmark.

Charles XII had two sisters, the elder of whom had married the Duke of Holstein, a courageous and gentle young prince. The duke, oppressed by the King of Denmark, came to Stockholm with his wife to throw himself on Charles's mercy and ask his help, not only as his brother-in-law but as the king of a nation which had an unappeasable hatred of the Danes.

The ancient house of Holstein, merged into that of Oldenburg, had mounted the throne of Denmark in 1449 by election. All the kingdoms of the north were then elective. That of Denmark soon became hereditary. One of its kings, Christian III, had an affection for his brother Adolphus and a concern for his welfare almost un-exampled among princes. He did not wish to leave him without a dominion but he could not dismember his own states. He therefore decided to share with him the Duchies of Holstein-Gottorp and Sleswig, by a most peculiar agreement, in which it was settled that the descendants of Adolphus should govern Holstein conjointly with the Kings of Denmark; that these two duchies should belong to them in common, and that the king could make no innovation without the duke, nor the duke without the king. So strange a union, of which there had nevertheless already been an example in the same royal house for some years, was a source of quarrels between the Danish branch and that of Holstein-Gottorp, the king always endeavouring to oppress the dukes, and the dukes to be inde-pendent. It had cost the last duke his liberty and his realm. He had recovered both at the Conference of Altona in 1689, through the intervention of Sweden, England and Holland, guarantors of the execution of the treaty. But, as a treaty between sovereigns is often only a submission to necessity until the stronger can overcome the weaker, the quarrel between the new King of Denmark and the young duke revived more venomously than ever. While the duke was in Stockholm, the Danes were already perpetrating acts of hostility in the land of Holstein and secretly allying themselves with the King of Poland in order to overcome the King of Sweden himself.

Frederick Augustus, Elector of Saxony, whom neither the nego-tiations and eloquence of the Abbé de Polignac nor the great qualities of the Prince de Conti, his rival to the throne, had been able to prevent being elected King of Poland two years earlier, was a prince even better known for his courage and courtesy than for his incredible physical strength. His court was the most brilliant in Europe after that of Louis XIV. No prince was more generous, gave more, or accompanied his gifts with more grace. He had bought half the votes of the Polish nobility, and forced the other half by the advance of a Saxon army. He believed it necessary to have his troops in Poland in order to establish himself more firmly on the throne, but he needed a pretext to keep them there. He destined them to attack the King of Sweden in Livonia, on an occasion we shall now relate.

Livonia, the most beautiful and fertile province of the north, had formerly belonged to the Knights of the Teutonic Order. The Russians, the Poles and the Swedes had disputed the possession of it. The Swedes had annexed it for nearly a hundred years and it had finally been officially ceded to them by the Peace of Oliva.

The late king, Charles XI, had treated the Livonians as harshly as his other subjects. He had deprived them of their privileges and of part of their estates. Patkul, unhappily famous for his tragic death, was deputed by the Livonian nobility to carry the complaints of the province to the throne. He made a speech to his master that was respectful but strong and full of that manly eloquence which disaster produces when it is combined with daring. But kings too often regard these public speeches only as empty formalities which they usually go through without paying attention to them. However, Charles XI, who could dissemble his feelings when he was not giving way to his violent fits of temper, tapped Patkul lightly on the shoulder: 'You have spoken for your country like a brave man,' he said. 'I respect you for it; continue.' But a few days later, he had him declared guilty of treason and condemned to death. Patkul, who had been in hiding, took to flight. He carried his grievances into Poland. Later on, he was admitted into the presence of King Augustus. Charles XI was dead, but Patkul's sentence remained in force, and his grievances persisted. He represented to the Polish monarch how easy it would be for him to conquer Livonia; a desperate people, eager to shake off the yoke of Sweden; a boy king, incapable of defending himself. These suggestions were well received by a prince who was already tempted by the idea of this conquest.

Augustus, at his coronation, had promised to endeavour to recover the provinces which Poland had lost. He thought that, by invading Livonia, he would both please the republic and strengthen his power; but he was mistaken in both these ideas which seemed so plausible. Everything was soon ready for a sudden invasion, without his even first deigning to resort to the idle formality of declarations of war and manifestos. The storm-cloud was thickening at the same time in the quarter of Russia. The monarch who governed it deserves the attention of posterity.

Peter Alexeiovitch, Tsar of Russia, had already made himself redoubtable by the battle he had won against the Turks in 1697, and by the capture of Azov which had given him command of the Black Sea. But it was by deeds more astonishing than victories that he was seeking the appellation of *Great*. Muscovy, or Russia, embraces the north of Asia and of Europe and extends fifteen hundred leagues from the frontiers of China to the borders of Poland and Sweden. But Europe knew scarcely anything of this vast country before the advent of the Tsar Peter I. The Muscovites were less civilized than the Mexicans when they were discovered by Cortez; the people, born slaves of masters more barbarous than themselves, wallowed in ignorance, in the lack of all technical skills and in the indifference to this lack which stifled all industry. An ancient law, sacrosanct to them, forbade them, under pain of death, to leave their country without the permission of the patriarch. This law, made to remove opportunities of realizing their servitude, pleased a nation which, in the depths of its ignorance and poverty, disdained all commerce with foreign nations.

The Russian era began at the creation of the world. At the beginning of the last century they reckoned it had taken place 7207 years ago, without being able to give a reason for this date. Their new year began on the 13th of our September. They alleged, as a reason for fixing that day, that God had probably created the world in autumn, when the fruits of the earth are ripe. Thus the only semblances of knowledge that they had were grossly erroneous; none of them suspected that autumn in Russia might be spring in another country where the climate was the opposite. It was not long since they had wanted to burn the secretary of a Persian ambassador in Moscow who had predicted an eclipse of the sun.

They were even ignorant of the use of figures; for calculating, they used beads strung on wire. There was no method of counting money in all the financial departments, including the treasury of the Tsar.

*Their religion was, and still is, that of the Greek Christians but mingled with superstitions, to which they were all the more strongly attached the more extravagant they were and the more galling their yoke. Few Muscovites dared eat pigeon because the Holy Ghost is depicted in the form of a dove. They regularly observed four Lents a year, and, during these periods of abstinence, they dared not use eggs or milk in their diet. God and St Nicholas were the objects of their worship, and immediately after them, the tsar and the patriarch. The authority of this last was as boundless as their ignorance. He pronounced death sentences and inflicted the most cruel tortures, and there was no possibility of appeal against his judgement. Twice a year, he rode in state through the streets, followed by all his clergy; the tsar, on foot, held his horse's bridle, and the people prostrated themselves before him like the Tartars before their Grand Lama. People went to confession but only in the case of the greatest crimes; then it seemed necessary to them to get absolution but not to repent. They believed the blessing of their 'popes' made them pure in the sight of God. Thus, having been to confession, they felt no remorse in continuing to rob and murder; what is a deterrent to other Christians was to them an encouragement to sin. They were scrupulous about not drinking milk on a fast-day, but fathers of families, priests, women and girls got drunk on brandy on feast-days. Nevertheless people quarrelled about religion in this country as elsewhere; the greatest dispute was whether laymen should make the sign of the cross with two fingers or three. A certain Jacob Nursuff, in the preceding reign, had incited a revolt in Astrakhan on the subject of this dispute. There were even fanatics, just as in those civilized countries where everyone is a theologian, and Peter, who always pushed justice to the length of cruelty, had some of those poor wretches, known as *vosko-Jesuits*, burnt at the stake.

The tsar had many other subjects in his vast empire who were not Christians. The Tartars, who inhabit the western shore of the

---

* All this passage is copied word for word by the Genevievian Barre, in his *History of Germany*, Vol. IX, page 75 and following ones.

Caspian Sea and the Sea of Azov, are Mahomedans. The Siberians, the Ostiaks and the Samoyeds, who live in the frozen north, were savages, some of whom were idolaters and the rest did not have even the idea of a god; nevertheless the Swedes who were exiled among them as prisoners found their conduct more civilized than that of their previous Russian gaolers. Peter Alexeiovitch had received an education which tended to increase the barbarism of that part of the world still more. His nature made him take an immediate liking to foreigners, before he knew in what way they could be useful to him. Le Fort, as we have said elsewhere, was the first instrument he employed to change the face of Russia. His powerful genius, which a barbarous education had repressed but been unable to destroy, developed almost instantaneously. He resolved to be a man, to command men, and to create a new nation. Many princes before him had renounced crowns because they were weary of the burden of the cares of state, but none had ceased to be king in order to learn to rule better: this was what Peter the Great did.

He left Russia in 1698, having reigned only two years, and went to Holland, disguised under a common name, as if he were a servant of this same Le Fort, whom he was sending as ambassador extraordinary to the States-General. Arrived in Amsterdam, he enrolled himself among the carpenters employed by the East Indies department of the admiralty and worked in the shipyard like the other carpenters. In the intervals of his labour, he learnt the branches of mathematics that could be of practical use to a prince, the sciences of fortification and navigation and the art of drawing plans. He went into the craftsmen's workshops and examined all they manufactured: nothing escaped his observation. From there he went to England, where he perfected himself in the science of shipbuilding; back once more in Holland, he took note of everything which could be advantageous to his own country. Finally, after two years of travels and toils which no man but he would have voluntarily imposed on himself, he reappeared in Russia, bringing with him the arts of Europe. A multitude of craftsmen of all kinds followed him there. For the first time, great Russian ships were seen on the Black Sea, in the Baltic and the Atlantic. Buildings of noble and symmetrical architecture were erected in the midst of the Muscovite huts. He established schools, academies, printing-works and libraries; the towns were civilized; clothes and customs changed little by little, although with difficulty. The Muscovites gradually came to know the meaning of organized society. Even superstitions were abolished; the patriarch was deprived of all authority, and the tsar proclaimed himself the religious head of state. This last move, which would have cost a less absolute prince his throne and his life, succeeded almost without opposition, and assured him the success of all the other innovations.

After having humbled an ignorant and barbarous clergy, he dared to try to educate it; in doing so he risked making it redoubtable, but he thought himself powerful enough not to fear it. He had theology and philosophy taught in the few remaining monasteries, though it is true that this theology was still typical of the uncivilized era from which Peter Alexeiovitch had forced his country to emerge. A trustworthy man has assured me that he was present at a public debate where the subject under discussion was whether smoking was a sin; the adjudicator claimed that it was permissible to intoxicate oneself with brandy, but not to smoke, because Holy Writ says that what comes out of a man's mouth defiles him, but what goes into it does not.

The monks were not pleased with Peter's reforms. Hardly had the tsar set up printing-works than they used them to discredit him: they published a treatise declaring him to be Antichrist; their proofs were that he shaved off the beards of living men and that the bodies of dead ones were dissected in his academy. But another monk, who wished to make his fortune, refuted this book and demonstrated that Peter was not Antichrist, because the number 666 was not in his name. The author of the libel was broken on the wheel and that of the refutation was made Bishop of Rezan.

Above all, the reformer of Russia passed a wise law which puts many civilized countries to shame; it forbade any man in the service of the state, any citizen established in business and, above all, any minor, to enter a monastery.

This prince realized how important it was that subjects who might be useful should not be allowed to devote themselves to a life of idleness nor to dispose of their liberty for ever at an age when they cannot dispose of the least part of their fortune. Nevertheless the skill of the monks daily evaded this law, made for the benefit of humanity, as if the monks in fact profited by peopling the cloisters at the expense of the country.

The tsar not only subjected the church to the state, after the example of the Turkish sultans, but, being a greater politician, he destroyed a Pretorian Guard similar to the Janissaries; he accomplished, in a short time, what the Turks had attempted in vain; he disbanded the Russian Janissaries, known as the Streltzy, who had a powerful hold over the tsar. This armed force, more formidable to its masters than to its neighbours, consisted of about thirty thousand infantrymen, of whom half remained in Moscow and the other half were stationed on the frontiers. A soldier in the Streltzy received only four roubles a year pay, but privileges or abuses amply compensated him. Peter first formed a company of foreigners, in which he enrolled himself and did not disdain to begin by being a drummer and performing all the duties of one, so much was the nation in need of good examples! He became an officer by degrees. Little by little, he created new regiments, and finally, feeling himself master of disciplined troops, he disbanded the Streltzy Guards, who did not dare disobey his orders.

The cavalry was almost what the Polish cavalry is now, and what the French was in the days when the kingdom of France was only an aggregation of feudal domains. The Russian nobles mounted themselves at their own expense and fought without discipline, sometimes with no other weapons than a sabre or a bow; they were incapable of being commanded, and consequently of winning battles.

Peter the Great taught them to obey by his example and by severe corporal punishments; for he had served as a private and a junior officer, and, as tsar, he rigorously punished the Boyars, that is the nobles, who claimed that the privilege of the nobility was not to serve the State except in their own way. He established a regular corps of artillery and took five hundred bells from the churches to melt down for cannons. He had thirteen thousand cast-iron cannons in the year 1714. He also created corps of dragoons, a fighting force very suitable to the native talent of the Russians and to their small breed of horse. Today, in 1738, Russia has thirty regiments of dragoons, each a thousand men strong, and well maintained.

It was he who established hussars in Russia. Finally, he even had a school of engineers, in a country where no-one before him had known the elements of geometry.

He was a good engineer himself, but he excelled principally in all the maritime arts; he was a good ship's captain, an able pilot, a good sailor and an expert carpenter. His proficiency in these skills was all the more estimable because he had been born with an extreme fear of water. In his youth, he had been unable to cross a bridge without quaking and used to close the wooden shutters of his carriage; his courage and genius overcame this instinctive weakness.

He had a fine port built near Azov, at the mouth of the Don; he intended to harbour galleys there, but later, thinking these long, light, flat ships could be successfully used in the Baltic, he had more than three hundred of them built in his favourite city of St Petersburg; he showed his subjects how to build them of fir and how to navigate them. He had even learnt surgery and he had been known, in case of need, to tap a person suffering from dropsy. He was an expert mechanic and used to instruct the workmen.

The financial resources of the tsar were meagre in relation to the vast size of his kingdom; he never had more than a revenue of twenty-four million, reckoning the mark at about fifty *livres* as we do today, and as perhaps we shall not do tomorrow; but to be able to do great things in one's country is to be very rich. It is not the scarcity of money, but of men and talents that makes an empire weak.

The population of Russia is not large, although the women are fertile and the men robust. Peter himself, in civilizing his states, unfortunately helped to depopulate them. Frequent recruitment for wars, which for a long time were unsuccessful, the transplantation of whole peoples from the shores of the Caspian Sea to those of the Baltic, where they were worn out with hard labour, and ravaged by diseases (three quarters of the children in Russia died from smallpox which is more dangerous in those regions than elsewhere); in short, the sad consequences of a government which long remained savage and barbarous even in its civilizing activities are the reason why this great part of the continent still has vast empty wastes. At present, Russia is reckoned to contain five hundred thousand families of the landed gentry, two hundred thousand of those employed in administration, a little more than five million bourgeois and peasant ones who pay some kind of tax, and six hundred thousand men in the provinces conquered by Sweden; the Cossacks of the Ukraine and the Tartars, vassals of Russia, do not amount to more than two million: in fact, it has been discovered that these vast realms contain no more than fourteen million people,* that is to say a little more than two thirds of the inhabitants of France.

Tsar Peter, in addition to reforming his country's customs, laws and army, thereby giving it a new image, also wished it to become a great trading nation, since trade both enriches the state and benefits the whole world. He undertook to make Russia the trading centre of Asia and Europe. He wished to join the Dnieper, the Volga and the Don by canals, of which he drew up the plans, and to open up new routes from the Baltic to the Black Sea and the Caspian and from these two seas to the Arctic Ocean.

The port of Archangel, icebound for nine months of the year and accessible only by a long and dangerous channel, was ill-suited to his new requirements. As early as 1700, he had planned to build a port on the Baltic, which would become the trading station of the north, and a city which would be the capital of his empire.

He was already seeking a sea-route from the north-east to China, and the artefacts of Peking and Paris were to embellish his new city.

On land, a road seven hundred and fifty-four versts long, cut through marshes which had to be filled in, was constructed to lead from Moscow to his new city. The majority of his plans were carried out during his own reign, and the two empresses who succeeded him one after the other carried them even further when they were practicable and abandoned only those that proved impossible.

He spent as much time as his wars permitted in travelling about his states; but he travelled as a legislator and natural philosopher, everywhere examining nature, seeking to correct or improve it, personally sounding the depths of rivers and seas, ordering the construction of locks and canals, visiting shipyards, having mines sunk, testing metals, ensuring that accurate maps were drawn and working on these himself.

The imperial city of St Petersburg, which he built in a wilderness,

* This was written in 1727: the population has since been increased by conquests, by civilization, and by the anxiety to attract foreigners.

today contains sixty thousand houses and now boasts a brilliant court and all the amenities of a civilized capital.

He built the port of Kronstadt on the Neva, forts in the Ukraine and Siberia and dockyards at Archangel, St Petersburg and Astrakhan; he also built arsenals and hospitals. He made all his houses small and in poor taste, but the public buildings he erected were impressively large and magnificent.

The sciences, which elsewhere had developed slowly through centuries, were already perfected when he introduced them into his kingdom. He created an academy on the model of the famous societies of Paris and London: the Delisles, the Bulfingers, the Bernouillis and the celebrated Wolf, an excellent scholar versed in all branches of philosophy, were summoned at great expense to St Petersburg. This academy still exists, and is at last producing some Russian philosophers.

He compelled the young nobles of his realm to travel in order to educate themselves and bring back to Russia the polish they had acquired abroad. I have met young Russians who are extremely witty and knowledgeable. This is how a single man has changed the greatest empire in the world. It is appalling that this reformer of men should have lacked the principal virtue, humanity. Many virtues as he had, he was bestial in his pleasures, ferocious in his behaviour and barbarous in his vengeance. He civilized his subjects, but was a savage himself. He frequently carried out his sentences on criminals with his own hands, and once, at a drunken banquet, he displayed his skill at cutting off heads. In Africa there are sovereigns who shed the blood of their subjects with their own hands, but these monarchs are regarded as barbarians. The execution of a son, whom it was necessary to correct or to disinherit, would render Peter's memory odious, did not the good he did his subjects almost make one forgive his cruelty to his own flesh and blood.

Such was the Tsar Peter; and his great projects were still no more than outlined when he joined forces with the kings of Poland and Denmark against a boy whom they all despised. The founder of Russia wished to be a conqueror; he believed he could win an easy victory, and that so well-planned a war would be useful to his other plans. The art of war was a new art which must be demonstrated to his people.

Moreover, in order to carry out all his ideas, he needed a port on the east of the Baltic. He needed the province of Ingria, which lies to the north-east of Livonia; the Swedes were its masters and he would have to wrest it from them. His predecessors had had rights over Ingria, Estonia and Livonia; it seemed a propitious time to re-establish these rights which had been lost for a hundred years and annihilated by treaties. He therefore concluded an alliance with the king of Poland in order to wrest from the young Charles XII all those lands which lie between the Gulf of Finland, the Baltic Sea, Poland and Russia.

BOOK II

THUS three powerful monarchs were threatening the boy-king Charles XII. The rumours of these preparations threw Sweden into consternation and alarmed the council. The great generals were dead; there was reason to fear the worst under a young king who had hitherto given a bad impression of himself. When he attended the council meetings, he almost invariably put his feet on the table and leant back, looking bored and indifferent, apparently taking no part in the proceedings.

The council held a debate, at which he was present, on the country's dangerous situation. Some councillors were proposing to avert the storm by negotiation when suddenly the young prince sprang to his feet with the determined, self-confident air of a leader who has decided on a course of action. 'Gentlemen,' he said, 'I have resolved never to start an unjust war but never to end a legitimate one except by defeating my enemies. I have made up my mind; I shall go out and attack the first who declares himself, and, when I have conquered him, I hope to inspire some fear in the others.' These words astonished the old councillors; they stared at each other without daring to reply. Finally, amazed to have such a king and ashamed to be less hopeful than he, they received his orders to go to war with enthusiasm.

They were even more surprised when they saw him suddenly renounce all the most innocent diversions of youth. From the moment he began to prepare himself for war, he launched on an entirely new way of life from which he never afterwards deviated. Fired by the idea of Alexander and Caesar, he proposed to imitate everything in both these conquerors except their vices. He renounced all pomp and splendour, all sports and relaxations, and reduced his meals to the utmost frugality. He had been fond of ostentation in dress; henceforth he never wore anything but the uniform of a common soldier. He had been suspected of a passion for a woman at his court; whether this was true or not, it is certain that he renounced women for ever, not only for fear of being dominated by them, but to set an example to his soldiers, whom he wished to keep under the strictest discipline; perhaps even more from the vanity of being the only king who could master a craving so difficult to repress. He also resolved to abstain from wine for the rest of his life. Some people have told me that he took this decision in order to subjugate the whole of his nature and add another virtue to his heroism; but the majority have told me that he wished thereby to punish himself for an excess he had committed, and for having insulted a woman at the dinner-table in the presence of his [grand] mother. If that is so, this self-condemnation and this privation which he imposed on himself all his life are a no less admirable form of heroism.

He began by promising aid to his brother-in-law, the Duke of Holstein. Eight thousand men were immediately sent into Pomerania, the neighbouring province to Holstein, to strengthen the duke against the attacks of the Danes. The duke needed them; his states had already been ravaged, his castle of Gottorp captured, and his town of Tönning was being so relentlessly besieged that the King of Denmark had come there in person in order to enjoy what he believed to be certain victory. This spark was beginning to set the empire ablaze. On one side, the Saxon troops of the King of Poland, those of Brandenburg, Wolfenbüttel and Hesse-Cassel, were marching to join the Danes. On the other, the eight thousand men of the King of Sweden, the troops of Hanover and Celle and three Dutch regiments were coming to the aid of the duke.* While the little country of Holstein was thus the theatre of war, two fleets, one English and one Dutch, appeared in the Baltic Sea. England and Holland were the guarantors of the Treaty of Altona, which the Danes had broken; they hastened to come to the aid of the oppressed Duke of Holstein because their commercial interests were opposed to any increase of the King of Denmark's power. They knew

* Copied word for word by Père Barre, Vol. X, p. 293 *et seq.*

that the Dane, being master of the Sound, would impose heavy dues on the trading nations as soon as he was strong enough to treat them with impunity. This interest had long committed the English and Dutch to keeping the balance of power between the princes of the north as equal as they could; they joined forces with the young King of Sweden, who seemed bound to be overwhelmed by so many united enemies, and came to his aid for the same reason these were attacking him, because they thought him incapable of defending himself.

He was on a bear hunt when he received the news that the Saxons had invaded Livonia; his method of hunting these animals was as unusual as it was dangerous. The only weapons used were forked sticks behind a net suspended from trees. An enormous bear made straight for the king who, after a long struggle, overwhelmed it with the aid of the net and his stick. It must be owned that when one's mind dwells on such adventures, on the prodigious strength of King Augustus and the journeys of the tsar, one might think oneself back in the days of Theseus and Hercules.

He set out for his first campaign on the 8th of May, new style, in the year 1700. He left Stockholm, never again to return to it. A vast crowd of people accompanied him to the port of Karlskrona, wishing him well, shedding tears, and applauding him. Before leaving Sweden, he set up a defence council in Stockholm, composed of several senators. This committee was to take charge of everything concerning the fleet, the troops and the fortification of the country. The body of the senate was to be provisionally in charge of all the rest of the affairs of the kingdom. Having thus made some arrangement for the administration of his realm, his mind was free to concentrate entirely on the war. His fleet was composed of forty-three ships; the one he boarded, named the *King Charles*, was the largest ever seen [in Sweden] and carried a hundred and twenty guns; Count Piper, his Prime Minister, and General Rehnskiöld embarked on it with him. He joined the fleets of the allies. The Danish fleet avoided a battle and left the three combined fleets free to approach near enough to Copenhagen to bombard it.

It is known for certain that it was the king himself who then suggested to General Rehnskiöld that they should make a raid and besiege Copenhagen by land while it was blockaded by sea.

Rehnskiöld was astonished by a proposal which showed as much strategic skill as courage in a young prince with no military experience. Soon everything was ready for the raid; orders were given to embark five thousand men who were on the coast of Sweden, and these were added to the troops they had on board. The king left his large ship and boarded a lighter frigate: they began by sending off three hundred grenadiers in little boats. Among these, small flat-bottomed boats carried faggots, chevaux-de-frise and entrenching tools; five hundred picked men followed in other boats; after them came the king's warships, with two English and two Dutch frigates which were to support the raid by bombarding the city.

Copenhagen, the capital of Denmark, is situated in the isle of Zealand, in the midst of a beautiful plain; to the north-west lies the Sound and to the east the Baltic Sea, where the King of Sweden then was. At the sight of the unexpected advance of the enemy's ships which threatened an invasion, the inhabitants, dismayed by the inactivity of their fleet and the activity of the Swedish one, wondered apprehensively where the blow would fall. Charles's fleet stopped opposite Humblebek, seven miles from Copenhagen. The Danes promptly assembled their cavalry at this spot. The infantry were posted behind deep trenches, and such artillery as they were able to move there was directed against the Swedes.

The king was about to leave his frigate in order to take his place in the first boat, at the head of his guards, when he saw that the French ambassador, who was standing at his elbow, was preparing to follow him. 'Your Excellency,' he said to him in Latin (for he would never speak French), 'you have no quarrel with the Danes; pray go no further.' 'Sire,' replied the Comte de Guiscard in French, 'the King my master ordered me to reside at your majesty's court; I trust you will not drive me from it today when it has never been so brilliant.' So saying, he gave his hand to the king, who leapt into the boat, and followed him into it with Count Piper.* They advanced under cover of the cannon-fire from the ships supporting the raid. Charles XII, impatient at not landing fast enough, leapt from his boat into the sea, sword in hand and up to his waist in water; his ministers, the French ambassador, the officers and soldiers promptly followed his example and waded to the shore, in spite of a volley of

* Copied word for word by Père Barre, Vol. X, p. 396.

musket-shots from the Danes. The king, who had never in his life heard the sound of musket-fire, asked Major-General Stuart, who was standing beside him, what was this little whistling sound he kept hearing. 'It is the noise of the bullets they are firing at you,' the major told him. 'Good,' said the king, 'henceforth that shall be my music.' At that very moment, the major who was explaining the noise of the bullets, received one in his shoulder, and a lieutenant fell dead at the king's other side.

Troops attacked in their trenches are usually beaten, because the attackers always have an impetus which the defenders cannot have, and because awaiting the enemy in one's lines is often an admission of one's weakness and of the other's superiority. The Danish cavalry and infantry fled after a feeble resistance. The king, having captured their trenches, threw himself on his knees to thank God for the first success of his arms. He then and there ordered redoubts to be erected facing the town and himself marked out the site for a camp. At the same time, he sent his ships back to Scania, a part of Sweden near Copenhagen, to fetch nine thousand reinforcements. Everything conspired to serve Charles's impetuous will. The nine thousand men were on the shore, ready to embark, and, the very next day, a favourable wind brought them to him.

All this had been done in full view of the Danish fleet, which had not dared to advance. Copenhagen, intimidated, promptly sent envoys to the king to implore him not to bombard the town. He received them on horseback, at the head of his regiment of guards: the envoys threw themselves on their knees before him: he made the town pay four hundred rix-dollars and ordered all kinds of provisions to be conveyed to the camp, for which he faithfully promised to pay. The provisions were brought to him, because they were obliged to obey; but no one in the least expected that the conquerors would deign to pay; those who brought them were highly surprised to be paid promptly and generously, even by the lowest ranks of the army. For a long time a discipline had prevailed among the Swedish troops which had contributed no little to their victories: the young king still further increased its severity. A soldier would not have dared to refuse to pay for what he bought, still less to go looting or even leave the camp. Moreover, he gave orders that his troops were not to despoil the dead after a victory without his permission and he had no difficulty in making them obey this rule. Prayers were always said twice a day in his camp, at seven in the morning and four in the afternoon; he never failed to be present at them, and to give his soldiers an example of piety which always impresses men when they do not suspect hypocrisy in it. His camp, whose occupants were more civilized than those of Copenhagen, had everything in abundance; the peasants preferred to sell their provisions to the Swedes, their enemies, rather than to the Danes, who did not pay them so well. The inhabitants of the town were even obliged on more than one occasion to come to the King of Sweden's camp to seek the provisions that were lacking in their markets.

The King of Denmark was then in Holstein, where he seemed to have gone only in order to raise the siege of Tönning. He saw the Baltic covered with enemy ships and a young conqueror, already master of Zealand, about to take possession of the capital. He issued a proclamation throughout his realm that those who took up arms against the King of Sweden would be given their liberty. This announcement carried great weight in a country, formerly free, where now all the peasants, and even many of the townsfolk, were serfs. Charles sent a message to the King of Denmark saying that he was only making war in order to oblige him to make peace; that he had only to decide whether to render justice to the Duke of Holstein or to see Copenhagen destroyed and his kingdom put to fire and sword. The Dane was only too happy to deal with a conqueror who prided himself on justice. A congress was convened in the town of Travendal, on the frontiers of Holstein. The King of Sweden had no intention of allowing the diplomatic skill of ministers to drag out the negotiations interminably: he wanted the treaty to be concluded as swiftly as his invasion of Zealand. In fact, it was concluded on the 5th of August, to the advantage of the Duke of Holstein, who was indemnified for all the expenses of the war, and freed from oppression. The King of Sweden wanted nothing for himself; he was satisfied to have succoured his ally and humiliated his enemy. Thus Charles XII, at the age of eighteen, began and ended this war in less than six weeks.

Precisely at the same time, the King of Poland was besieging the town of Riga, the capital of Livonia, and the tsar was advancing from the east at the head of nearly a hundred thousand men. Riga was defended by the old Count Dahlberg, a Swedish general, who, at the age of eighty, combined the fiery spirit of a young man with the experience of sixty campaigns. Count Flemming, later minister of Poland, a great warrior and statesman, and the Livonian, Patkul, were both vigorously conducting the siege under the eyes of the king; but, in spite of several advantages the besiegers had gained, the experience of old Count Dahlberg rendered their efforts useless, and the King of Poland despaired of taking the city. Finally, he seized an honourable opportunity of raising the siege. Riga was full of merchandise belonging to the Dutch. The States-General ordered their ambassador to King Augustus to make representations to him about this. The King of Poland needed no pressing. He consented to raise the siege rather than cause the least inconvenience to his allies, who were not in the least surprised by this eagerness to oblige them, of whose true motive they were well aware.

There thus remained nothing more for Charles to do to complete his first campaign except to march against his rival for glory, Peter Alexeiovitch. His animosity towards him was kindled all the more because there were still three Russian ambassadors in Stockholm who had just sworn the renewal of an inviolable peace. He, who prided himself on strict probity, could not understand how a legislator like the tsar could make a mockery of what ought to be so sacred. The young prince, himself the soul of honour, did not think there was a different morality for kings and for private individuals. The Emperor of Russia had just published a manifesto, which he would have done better to suppress. He alleged, as a reason for the war, that he had not been paid sufficient honour when he had visited Riga *incognito* and that provisions had been sold to his ambassadors at too high a price. These were the grievances for which he was ravaging Ingria with eighty thousand men.

He appeared before Narva, at the head of this great army, on the 1st of October, in weather more severe in this region than it is in January in Paris. The tsar, who, in similar seasons, used sometimes to ride four hundred miles to visit some mine or canal in person, spared his troops no more than himself. He knew, moreover, that the Swedes, from the days of Gustavus-Adolphus, were as used to making war in the depths of winter as in summer; he wished to accustom his Russians also to ignore the seasons and to make them one day at least equal to the Swedes. Thus, at a time when snow and ice force other nations, in temperate climes, to suspend hostilities, Peter was besieging Narva, thirty degrees from the Pole, and Charles XII was advancing to its relief. The tsar had no sooner arrived before the town than he hastened to put into practice what he had recently learnt on his travels. He marked out his camp, fortified it on all sides, threw up redoubts at intervals and himself dug the first trench. He had given the command of his army to the Duke of Croy, a German, an able general, but ill supported by the Russian officers. The tsar himself chose to hold only the rank of an ordinary lieutenant in his own army, so as to set an example of military obedience to his nobles, who had hitherto been as undisciplined as the disorderly rabble of ill-armed serfs they were accustomed to lead. It was not surprising that the man who had deliberately become a carpenter in Amsterdam in order to have a fleet should deliberately become a lieutenant at Narva in order to teach his people the art of war.

The Russians are robust, indefatigable, and perhaps as courageous as the Swedes, but it requires time to season troops and discipline to make them invincible. The only regiments of which anything could be hoped were commanded by German officers, but there were very few of them. The rest were savages, torn from their forests, clad in the skins of wild beasts, some armed with bows and arrows and others with clubs. Few had muskets, none had ever seen a regular siege, and there was not a single good gunner in the entire army. A hundred and fifty cannon, which should have reduced the little town of Narva to rubble, had hardly made a breach in its walls, while its artillery was hourly mowing down whole lines of men in the trenches. Narva was almost unfortified, and Baron Horn, who commanded it, had not a thousand regular troops, yet this vast army had besieged it for six weeks without being able to reduce it.

It was already the 15th of November when the tsar learnt that the King of Sweden, having crossed the sea with two hundred troopships, was advancing to the relief of Narva. There were not more than twenty thousand Swedes, but superiority of numbers was the tsar's only advantage. Far from despising his enemy, he used his utmost skill to crush him. Not content with eighty thousand men, he proposed to oppose him with yet another army, and to halt him at every stage. He had already sent for thirty thousand men, who were advancing from Pleskov by forced marches. He then took a step which would have made him contemptible, if a legislator who had done such great things could ever be deemed so. He left the camp, where his presence was needed, to go out to meet this new body of troops, which was perfectly capable of reaching its destination without him. By doing this, he gave the impression of being afraid of fighting, even in an entrenched camp, a young and inexperienced prince who might be going to attack him.

However that may be, he planned to hem Charles XII in between two armies. Nor was that all: a detachment of thirty thousand men from the camp before Narva was posted a league from the town, on the Swedish king's route; twenty thousand Streltsky were further along the same road and five thousand more formed an advance guard. Charles would have to fight his way through all these troops before reaching the camp, which was fortified by a rampart and a double ditch. The King of Sweden had landed at Pernaw, on the Gulf of Riga, with about sixteen thousand infantry and a little more than four thousand cavalry. From Pernaw he had made a forced march to Reval, followed by all his cavalry, but only four thousand of his infantry. He continued to advance, without waiting for the rest of his troops. Soon he found himself, with only his eight thousand men, confronting the enemy's outposts. He did not hesitate to attack them, one after the other, without giving them time to realize what a small number they had to contend with. The Russians, seeing the Swedes advancing on them, thought they had a whole army to fight. The advance guard of five thousand men, which was guarding a mountain pass where a hundred resolute men could have halted an entire army, fled at the first approach of the Swedes. The twenty thousand men who were behind, seeing their comrades fleeing, were seized with panic and fled themselves, creating disorder in the camp when they arrived back. All the posts were taken in two days, and what, on other occasions, would have been reckoned three victories did not delay the king's march for one hour. At last he appeared, with his eight thousand men, wearied by so long a march, before a camp of eighty thousand Russians, defended by a hundred and fifty cannon. He allowed his troops only the briefest rest before giving orders for an immediate attack.

The signal was two shots and the battle-cry, the German words meaning 'With God's help'. A general officer pointed out to the king the great danger of such an attack. 'What!' he exclaimed. 'Do you suppose that, with my eight thousand brave Swedes, I cannot crush eighty thousand Russians?' A moment later, fearing that he had sounded boastful, he ran after this officer: 'Do you not agree with me?' he said. 'Have I not two advantages over the enemy? One is that their cavalry will be useless to them; the other, that in such a cramped space, their great numbers will only hamper them. So I shall really be stronger than they.' The officer thought it wiser to agree and, at midday on the 30th November 1700, they marched against the Russians.

As soon as their cannon had breached the trenches, the Swedes advanced with fixed bayonets. Behind them, a furious snowstorm drove straight into the faces of the enemy. For half-an-hour the Russians allowed themselves to be killed without quitting the outer edge of the trenches. The king was attacking the right of the camp, where the tsar's quarters were; he hoped to meet him in person, not knowing that the emperor had gone to meet those forty thousand reinforcements who were due to arrive shortly. At the first discharge of the enemy's musketry, the king received a bullet in the chest, but it was a spent bullet which lodged harmlessly in the folds of his black cravat. His horse was killed under him. Monsieur de Sparre told me that the king leapt nimbly on to another horse, saying: 'These fellows make me do my drill,' and continued to fight and give orders with the same presence of mind. After three hours' fighting, all the trenches had been taken by storm. The king pursued the enemy's right flank to the river Narva with his left wing, if one can so describe four thousand men who were pursuing forty thousand. The bridge broke under the fugitives, and, in a moment, the river was covered with corpses. The rest, in despair, returned to their camp without knowing where they were going; they found some huts, behind which they took cover, and from there they defended themselves for a while because they had no means of escape. Finally their generals, Dolgorouky, Golovkin and Federovitch came and surrendered to the king and laid down their arms at his feet. While they were doing so, the Duke of Croy, the commander of the army, arrived to surrender himself, along with thirty officers.

Charles received all these important prisoners with as much graciousness and civility as if he were doing the honours to his guests at a court fête. He wished to keep only the generals. All the junior officers and the soldiers, after being disarmed, were conducted to the river Narva, where they were provided with boats to cross it, so that they could return to their homeland. Meanwhile night was approaching, and the Russian right wing was still fighting. The Swedes had lost no more than six hundred men; eighteen thousand Russians had been killed in their trenches, a great number had been drowned and many had crossed the river. Nevertheless there still remained enough in the camp to exterminate the Swedes to the last man. But it is not the number of the slain but the panic of those who survive which loses battles. The king took advantage of what little daylight remained to capture the enemy's artillery. He took up a good position between their camp and the town; there he slept for a few hours on the ground, wrapped in his cloak, waiting for day-break, when he could fall on the enemy's left wing, which was not yet entirely routed. At two o'clock in the morning, General Vede, having heard how graciously the king had received the other generals, and how he had dismissed all the junior officers and privates, sent an envoy to ask Charles to grant him the same favour. The conqueror informed him that he had only to approach at the head of his troops and lay down his arms and standards. This general soon appeared with his Russians, who numbered some thirty thousand. The officers and soldiers marched bare-headed through the ranks of less than seven thousand Swedes. The soldiers, as they passed before the king, threw their muskets and swords on the ground, and the officers laid the standards and regimental colours at his feet. He sent this whole multitude back across the river without retaining a single prisoner. Had he kept them, the number of prisoners would have been at least five times greater than that of the conquerors.

He then entered Narva in triumph, accompanied by the Duke of Croy and the other Russian general officers: he ordered their swords to be returned to them, and knowing that they had no money and the merchants of Narva would not lend them any, he sent a thousand ducats to the Duke of Croy and five hundred to each of the Russian officers who could not sufficiently express their admiration for this treatment which was more generous than they had even conceived possible. A report of the victory of Narva was immediately drawn up to send to Stockholm and to Sweden's allies, but the king, with his own hand, cut out everything which was too flattering to himself and too insulting to the tsar. His modesty could not prevent several medals being struck in Stockholm to commemorate these events. Among others, one showed him on one side on a pedestal to which a Russian, a Dane and a Pole were chained; on the reverse was Hercules, armed with his club treading on Cerberus and inscribed: *Tres uno contudit ictu.* [He crushed three with a single blow.]

Among the prisoners taken at the battle of Narva was one who furnished a notable example of the revolutions of fortune. This was the eldest son and heir of the King of Georgia, the Czarafis Artfchelou; this title of czarafis signifies prince, or son of the czar, among all the Tartars as in Russia, for the word *czar* or *tsar* meant king among the ancient Scythians, from whom all these peoples are descended, and is not derived from the *Caesars* of Rome, so long unknown to these barbarians. His father Mitteleski, ruler of the most beautiful part of the lands which lie between the mountains of Ararat and the eastern shores of the Black Sea, had been driven from his kingdom by his own subjects in 1688 and had chosen to throw himself on the mercy of the Emperor of Russia rather than have recourse to the Turks. This king's nineteen-year-old son had taken part in Peter the Great's expedition against the Swedes and had been captured in battle by some Finnish soldiers who had already stripped him and were about to kill him, when Count Rehnskiöld rescued him from their hands. Having supplied him with clothes, he presented him to his master. Charles sent him to Stockholm, where this unfortunate prince died a few years later. When the king saw him depart, he could not refrain from uttering aloud, in front of his officers, a spontaneous reflection on the strange fate of an asiatic prince, born at the foot of the Caucasus, who was going to live as a prisoner among the snows of Sweden. 'It is,' he said, 'as if I were one day to be a prisoner among the Tartars in Crimea.' These words made no impression at the time, but later they were remembered only too well when they had proved to be prophetic.

The tsar was advancing by forced marches with the army of forty thousand Russians, reckoning to surround his enemy on all sides. Half-way, he learnt of the battle of Narva and the dispersal of his entire camp. He realized that, with his forty thousand inexperienced and undisciplined men, it would be foolhardy to attack a victor who had just destroyed eighty thousand of their like in an entrenched camp. He retraced his steps, convinced of the necessity of disciplining his troops as well as civilizing his subjects. 'I know,' he said, 'that the Swedes will go on beating us for a long time, but, in the end, they themselves will teach us how to beat them.' Moscow, his capital, was panic-stricken by the news of this defeat. Such was the pride and ignorance of the Russians that they believed they had been defeated by a superhuman power and that the Swedes were sorcerers. This opinion was so universal that public prayers were ordered to be said to St Nicholas, the patron of Russia. This prayer is too curious to be left unrecorded. Here it is:

O thou who art our perpetual consoler in all our adversities, great, infinitely powerful Saint Nicholas, by what sin have we offended thee in our sacrifices, genuflections, prostrations and thanksgivings that thou shouldst have thus abandoned us. We implored thy assistance against these terrible, insolent, furious, appalling, invincible destroyers when, like lions and bears who have lost their young, they attacked us, terrified us, wounded us and slew us by the thousand, we who are thy people. Since it is impossible that this could have happened without sorcery and magic, we implore thee, O great Saint Nicholas, to be our champion and standard-bearer, to deliver us from this host of sorcerers, and to drive them far from our frontiers, with the reward they deserve.

While the Russians were complaining of their defeat to St Nicholas, Charles XII was giving thanks to God and preparing himself for fresh victories.

The King of Poland fully expected that his enemy, having conquered the Danes and the Russians, would soon fall on him. He allied himself more closely than ever with the tsar. These two princes arranged an interview in order to decide on a common policy. They met at Birzen, a little town in Lithuania, without any of those formalities which only delay matters and for which, in their situation, they were in no mood. The princes of the north meet each other with a familiarity which is not yet the custom in the south of Europe. Peter and Augustus spent a fortnight together, indulging in riotous dissipation, for the tsar, who wished to reform his people, never managed to control his own dangerous addiction to debauchery.

The King of Poland promised to furnish the tsar with fifty thousand German troops, which were to be hired from various princes, and which the tsar was to pay. The latter, on his side, was to send fifty thousand Russians into Poland to learn the art of war, and promised to pay King Augustus three million rix-dollars within two years. Had this treaty been carried out, it might have been fatal to the King of Sweden; it was a sure and ready way of making the Russians efficient soldiers and perhaps of forging fetters for part of Europe.

Charles XII set himself the task of preventing the King of Poland from reaping the benefit of this alliance. After spending the winter near Narva, he appeared in Livonia, near that very town of Riga which Augustus had besieged in vain. The Saxon troops were posted along the river Dvina, which is very wide at this point; their duty was to prevent Charles, who was on the opposite bank, from crossing it. The Saxons were not commanded by their prince, who was ill at the time, but by Marshal Steinau; commanding under him were Prince Ferdinand, Duke of Courland, and that same Patkul, who was defending his country against Charles XII with his sword, after having maintained its rights against Charles XI, with his pen, at the risk of his life. The King of Sweden had had large boats built on a new model, with very high bows which could be raised and lowered like drawbridges. When raised, they protected the troops they carried; when lowered they served as a landing-stage. He also made use of another device. Having noticed that the wind was blowing from the north, where he was, to the south, where the enemy was encamped, he ordered a quantity of wet straw to be set on fire, so that the thick smoke should drift across the river and prevent the Saxons from seeing what his troops were doing. Under cover of this cloud he launched boats filled with yet more smoking straw, so that the cloud grew denser and denser and, driven by the wind into the eyes of the enemy, made it impossible to know whether the king were crossing or not. Nevertheless he was already on his way, thanks to this stratagem for whose planning and execution he alone was responsible. Half-way across, he said to General Rehnskiöld: 'You see! The Dvina is going to be as kind to us as the sea of Copenhagen – take my word for it, general, we shall beat them!' In a quarter of an hour he reached the other bank and was mortified to be only the fourth to leap ashore. He immediately had his cannon landed and drew up his line of battle without the enemy, blinded by the smoke, being able to offer any opposition beyond a few shots fired at random. When the wind had dissipated the fog, the Saxons saw that the King of Sweden was already marching on them.

Marshal Steinau did not lose a moment; as soon as he saw the Swedes, he charged them with the main body of his cavalry. The violent impact of this troop, falling on the Swedes just as they were forming their battalions, threw them into confusion. They broke ranks and were pursued right into the river. After a moment, the King of Sweden rallied them in mid-stream, issuing his orders as calmly as if he were holding a review. His soldiers, marching in more serried ranks than before, then repulsed Marshal Steinau and advanced into the plain. Steinau realized that his soldiers had been taken by surprise; like an able general, he made them withdraw to a dry place, flanked by a marsh and a wood where his artillery was. The advantage of the terrain and the time he had given the Saxons to recover from their shock revived all their courage. Charles did not hesitate to attack them; he had fifteen thousand men with him; Steinau and the Duke of Courland had about twelve thousand and no artillery except a single unmounted cannon. The battle was fierce and bloody. The duke had two horses killed under him; he thrice penetrated into the middle of the king's guard, but, when he was finally unhorsed by a blow from a musket-butt, disorder broke out in his army, which no longer disputed the victory. His cuirassiers dragged him, with difficulty, bruised and half-dead, from under the horses that were trampling on him.

After his victory, the King of Sweden hastened on to Mittau, the capital of Courland. All the towns of that duchy surrendered to him unconditionally; it was a triumphal journey rather than a conquest. He proceeded without a check to Lithuania, subduing everything in his way. He felt great satisfaction, as he frankly admitted, when he entered the town of Birzen, where the King of Poland and the tsar had plotted his downfall a few months earlier.

It was here that he conceived the plan of dethroning the King of Poland by the agency of the Poles themselves. One day, when he was sitting there at table, silent and completely absorbed in this plan, and eating and drinking with his usual abstemiousness, a German colonel who was present at his dinner, said, loud enough for him to hear, that the meals that the King of Poland and the tsar had eaten at that same table were somewhat different from those of his majesty. 'Yes,' said the king, rising to his feet, 'and it will be easier for me to upset their digestions.' Having conceived this plan, he immediately prepared, with the combination of a little diplomacy and his military strength, to implement it.

Poland, part of the ancient realm of Sarmatia, is a little larger than France; its population is smaller than that of France but greater than that of Sweden. Its people have been Christians only for some seven hundred and fifty years. It is strange that the language of the Romans, who never entered this country, is not commonly spoken nowadays anywhere but in Poland; everyone there speaks Latin, even the servants. This large country is very fertile, but this makes the natives all the less industrious.* The workmen and merchants one sees in Poland are Scots, Frenchmen and, above all, Jews. They have nearly three hundred synagogues, and are multiplying at such a rate that they will eventually be expelled from Poland as they have been from Spain. They buy wheat, cattle and other local produce at the cheapest possible price from the peasants, market them in Danzig and Germany, and sell them dear to the nobles who are willing to pay high prices to satisfy their craving for the only kind of luxury they know and care for. Thus this country, watered by magnificent rivers and rich in pasture and salt-mines, remains poor, in spite of its abundance, because the populace is enslaved and the nobility arrogant and idle.

Its government is the most faithful copy of the ancient Celtic and Gothic one which has been superseded or modified everywhere else. It is the only state which still calls itself a republic, but is ruled by an elected king.

Every nobleman has the right to vote in the election of a king

* Copied by Père Barre, Vol. IX.

and to become king himself. This greatest of privileges is, however, subject to the greatest abuses: the throne is nearly always put up for auction, and, as a Pole is seldom rich enough to buy it, it has often been sold to foreigners. The nobility and clergy defend their liberty against their king, and deprive the rest of the people of theirs. The masses are enslaved, so fated is the majority of mankind everywhere to be subjugated in one way or another to the minority! There, the peasant does not sow for himself but for his lord, to whom he, his field and the labour of his hands belong, and who can sell him and kill him as he does his cattle. Every nobleman is answerable only to himself. He can be tried for a criminal offence only by the whole body of his peers and he cannot be arrested until after he has been found guilty, hence he is hardly ever punished. Many of them are poor; these hire themselves out as servants to the richer ones for whom they are willing to perform the most menial tasks. They would rather serve their equals than enrich themselves by trade, and, even while rubbing down their masters' horses, proudly call themselves electors of kings and destroyers of tyrants.

Anyone seeing a king of Poland in all his royal pomp and majesty might think him the most absolute monarch in Europe; in fact, he is the least so. The Poles really do make that contract with him which is supposed to be made in other nations between sovereign and subjects. The King of Poland, at his actual coronation, by swearing the *pacta conventa* [covenanted agreement], dispenses his subjects from their oath of obedience should he break the laws of the Republic.

He appoints all state officials and confers all titles. Nothing is hereditary in Poland, except estates and noble rank. The son of a count palatine and the son of a king have no claim to the dignities of their father, but there is this great difference between the king and the republic; the king cannot revoke an appointment once he has made it and the republic has the right to deprive him of his crown if he transgresses the laws of the state.

The nobles, jealous of their liberty, often sell their votes, but seldom their affections. Scarcely have they elected a king than they fear his ambition and begin to conspire against him. Those to whom he has given high positions, from which he cannot degrade them, often become his enemies instead of remaining his loyal supporters.

Those who are attached to the court are hated by the rest of the nobility; this means there are always two parties, an inevitable, and even necessary, division in countries where people wish to have kings and, at the same time, preserve their liberty.

Matters concerning the nation are regulated by the States-General, which they call Diets. These diets are composed of the body of the senate and several nobles; the senators are the counts palatine and the bishops; the second chamber is composed of the deputies of the local diets of each palatinate. These great assemblies are presided over by the Archbishop of Gniesen, the Primate of Poland, who acts as regent during the interregnums and is the highest person in the land after the king. He is almost invariably the only cardinal in Poland because, as the Roman purple gives its recipient no precedence in the senate, any bishop who became a cardinal would be obliged either to sit according to his senatorial rank or to renounce the solid rights of the dignity he possesses in his own country in order to maintain the pretentious claims of a foreign title.

The laws of the land require these diets to be held alternately in Poland and Lithuania. The deputies often settle their business, sabre in hand, like the ancient Sarmatians from whom they are descended, and sometimes even, unlike the Sarmatians, to whom this vice was unknown, when they are drunk. Every noble deputed to these States-General enjoys the right the Roman tribunes had of vetoing the laws of the senate. A single nobleman has only to say 'I protest', to veto the unanimous resolutions of all the rest; if he then leaves the place where the diet is being held, it has to be dissolved.

The remedy they apply to the troubles created by this law has even more dangerous results. Poland is seldom without two factions. Unanimity in the diets being thus impossible, each party forms confederacies in which decisions are taken on a majority vote with no regard to the protests of the minority. These assemblies, which are illegal, but sanctioned by custom, are held in the king's name, although often without his consent and against his interests, rather as the League in France used the name of Henry III in order to overpower him, and as the English parliament which sent Charles I to the scaffold began by putting the name of that prince at the head of all the resolutions it took to ruin him. When the troubles are over, it is then the business of the general diets either to confirm or annul the acts of these confederacies. A diet can even alter everything done by the preceding one, for the same reason that, in monarchic states, a king can abolish the laws of his predecessor, and his own.

The nobles, who make the laws of the republic, are also its military strength. On great occasions, they muster on horseback, and can form a corps of over a hundred thousand men. This great army, called 'Pospolite', is difficult to mobilize and ill-organized; the difficulty of obtaining victuals and fodder makes it impossible for it to keep together long. It lacks discipline and experience, but the love of liberty which animates it always makes it formidable.

This army of nobles may be defeated or dispersed, or even kept in bondage for a time, but it soon shakes off the yoke; its members compare themselves to reeds which the storm beats down but which stand up again when the wind stops blowing. It is for this reason that they have no fortified towns; they wish to be the only ramparts of their republic. They never allow their king to build fortresses for fear he should use them to oppress them more than to defend them. Their country lies quite open, except for two or three frontier towns. If, during their civil or foreign wars, they determine to sustain a siege, earthworks have to be hastily thrown up, half-ruined old walls repaired and half-choked ditches enlarged, but the town is captured before the defences are completed.

The Pospolite is not permanently kept ready to guard the country; its cavalry is only mustered by order of the diets, or sometimes, in cases of extreme danger, merely by that of the king.

Poland's regular defence-force is an army which is maintained at the republic's expense. It is composed of two bodies under two different generals. The first body is the Polish one, and is thirty thousand strong; the second, the Lithuanian, numbers twelve thousand. The two generals are independent of each other: although nominated by the king, they are responsible only to the republic and have supreme authority over their troops. The colonels are absolute masters of their regiments; it is their business to provision them as best they can and to pay them. But, being seldom paid themselves, they ravage the country and ruin the farmers to satisfy their hunger and that of their soldiers.* The Polish lords live in

---

* Passage copied by Père Barre. We shall cite no more of his plagiarisms; it is too much of a nuisance for the publisher.

more magnificent style in these armies than they do in the towns; their tents are more splendid than their houses. The cavalry, which makes up two-thirds of the army, is almost entirely composed of noblemen; it is remarkable for the beauty of the horses and the richness of their accoutrements.

The cavalrymen never march without being accompanied by grooms who lead their horses, which are caparisoned with bridles adorned with silver plates and studs, embroidered saddles, gilt and sometimes solid silver stirrups, and long trailing saddle-cloths, like those used by the Turks, whose magnificence the Poles imitate as far as possible.

In contrast to this superbly equipped cavalry, the infantry at that time was dilapidated, ill-clad and ill-armed; it did not even wear any kind of uniform; at least this was so up to 1710. These foot-soldiers, who look like Tartar gipsies, endure hunger, cold, fatigue and all the hardships of war with an amazing stoicism. The characteristics of the ancient Sarmatians, their ancestors, can be seen in the Polish soldiers; the same lack of discipline, the same fury in attack, the same readiness to flee and to return to the fray, the same savage carnage when they are victorious.

The King of Poland had at first assumed that these two armies would fight for him, that the Polish Pospolite would spring to arms at his orders, and that all these forces, united to those of his Saxon subjects and his Russian allies, would make such a vast array that the small Swedish force would not dare to confront it. But he found himself suddenly deprived of these aids by the very pains he had taken to have them all at once.

Accustomed to absolute power in his hereditary dominions, he was perhaps too ready to believe that he could govern Poland like Saxony. At the beginning of his reign, he had aroused hostile feelings towards him; his first acts had angered the party which had been opposed to his election and alienated nearly all the rest. The Poles resented seeing their towns filled with Saxon garrisons and their frontiers with troops. This nation, far more eager to preserve its freedom than to attack its neighbours, did not regard King Augustus's war against Sweden and the invasion of Livonia as being of any advantage to the republic. A free country is seldom deceived about its true interests. The Poles felt that if this war, undertaken without their consent, were unsuccessful, their country, open on all sides, would fall a prey to the King of Sweden; and, if it were successful, they would be subjugated by their own king, who would then be master of Livonia as well as Saxony and thereby enclose Poland between these two countries. Faced with the alternative of becoming slaves to the king they had elected or being ravaged by the justly angered Charles XII, they raised a unanimous protest against this war which they regarded as declared more against themselves than the King of Sweden. They saw the Saxons and the Russians as instruments to be used to enslave them. Soon, learning that the King of Sweden had overcome everything that stood in his way and was advancing into the heart of Lithuania with a victorious army, their rage against their sovereign burst out all the more freely because he was being defeated.

Lithuania, at the time, was divided between two parties, that of the Princes Sapieha and that of Oginski. The private quarrels which had created these two factions had developed into a civil war. The King of Sweden won the Princes Sapieha over to his side, and Oginski, ill-supported by the Saxons, saw his party almost annihilated. The Lithuanian army, which these troubles and lack of money had reduced to small numbers, was partly dispersed by the conqueror. The few troops who sided with the King of Poland were split up into little bands of fugitives who wandered through the countryside, living on plunder. In Lithuania, Augustus was confronted with the impotence of his party, the hatred of his subjects and an enemy army led by an enraged, victorious and implacable young king.

There was indeed an army in Poland, but, instead of consisting of thirty-six thousand men, as prescribed by law, it consisted of less than half that number. Not only was it ill-armed and ill-paid, but its generals had not yet decided which side to take.

The king might have resorted to ordering the nobility to follow him, but he dared not expose himself to a refusal, which would have revealed his weakness and thereby increased it.

In this state of trouble and uncertainty, all the palatinates pressed the king to summon a diet, just as, in times of crisis in England, all parties of the state present addresses to the king to ask him to convoke a parliament. Augustus had more need of an army

than of a diet, where the actions of kings are criticized. Nevertheless, he was obliged to convoke one, in order not to antagonize the
nation irrevocably. It was therefore appointed to meet on the 2nd
of December 1701. He soon realized that Charles XII had at least as
much influence in the diet as he himself had. Those who supported
the Sapiehas, the Lubomirskis and their friends, Count Leczinski,
the treasurer to the crown, who owed his fortune to King Augustus,
and above all the partisans of the Princes Sobieski, were all secretly
on the side of the King of Sweden.

The most important of these partisans and the King of Poland's
most dangerous enemy was Cardinal Radjouski, Archbishop of
Gniesen, the primate of the realm and the president of the diet. He
was a crafty, double-faced man, completely dominated by an
ambitious woman, whom the Swedes called 'Madam Cardinal', and
who incessantly incited him to involve himself in intrigues and
factions. King John Sobieski, Augustus's predecessor, had begun by
making him Bishop of Varmia and Vice-Chancellor of the kingdom.
Radjouski, while still only a bishop, obtained a cardinal's hat
through the favour of this same king. This dignity soon opened the
way to the primacy, so that, combining in his person all the tokens
of eminence that impress men, he was in a position to set about his
many political intrigues with impunity.

After the death of King John, he exerted his influence to put
Prince James Sobieski on the throne, but the violent hatred the
people had felt for the father, great as he was, made them repudiate
the son. The cardinal-primate then joined forces with the Abbé de
Polignac, the French ambassador, to give the crown to the Prince de
Conti who was, indeed, elected. But money and the Saxon troops
defeated his negotiations. He finally allowed himself to be drawn
into the party which crowned the Elector of Saxony, and waited
patiently for an opportunity of creating dissension between the
nation and its new king.

The victories of Charles XII, protector of Prince James Sobieski,
the civil war in Lithuania, and the growing hostility of the public
at large to King Augustus made the cardinal-primate think that the
time had come when he could send Augustus back to Saxony and
throw the way to the throne open to the son of King John. This
prince, formerly the innocent object of the hatred of the Poles, was

beginning to become their idol, now that it was King Augustus whom they hated, but he dared not, at that time, conceive the idea of so great a revolution; nevertheless the cardinal was, step by step, secretly laying the foundations for it.

At first he seemed to wish to reconcile the king with the republic. He sent circular letters, ostensibly dictated by the spirit of concord and charity, but, in reality, a well-worn and well-known trap into which men still fall. He wrote a touching letter to the King of Sweden, beseeching him in the name of Him whom all Christians worship, to grant peace to Poland and her king. Charles XII replied to the cardinal's intentions rather than his words. However, he remained in the Grand-Duchy of Lithuania with his victorious army, declaring that he had no wish to disturb the diet, that he was making war against Augustus and the Saxons, not the Poles, and that, far from attacking the republic, he had come to liberate it from oppression. These letters and replies were for public consumption. Behind the scenes emissaries went continually to and fro from the cardinal to Count Piper and secret meetings were held in that prelate's house: as a result of these private negotiations, the diet decided to take action. It proposed to send an embassy to Charles XII, and it unanimously demanded of their own king to stop calling in Russian troops and to send his Saxon ones back to their own country.

Augustus's misfortunes had already brought about what the diet demanded of him. The alliance secretly concluded with the tsar at Birzen had become as meaningless as it had at first seemed formidable. He was far from being in a position to send the tsar the fifty thousand men he had promised to raise in the empire. The tsar himself, Poland's dangerous neighbour, was in no hurry to exert all his power in aid of a divided kingdom from which he hoped to reap some spoils. He contented himself with sending twenty thousand Russians into Lithuania, who did more harm there than the Swedes. They fled everywhere before the conqueror, ravaging the farms of the Poles, until, pursued by the Swedish generals and finding nothing left to pillage, they returned in bands to their own country. As for the remnants of the Saxon army defeated at Riga, King Augustus sent them back to winter and bring themselves up to strength in Saxony, in the hope that this sacrifice, forced on him as it was, might pacify the enraged Polish nation and win it back to him.

The war then gave place to a series of intrigues. The diet was split into almost as many factions as there were palatines. One day King Augustus dominated it, the next, his opponents. Everyone clamoured for freedom and justice but no one had any idea what freedom and justice meant. Time was wasted in plotting in secret and haranguing in public. The diet did not know what it wanted or what it ought to do. Large assemblies have almost never taken wise decisions in times of civil commotion because their factious members are usually bold and their well-intentioned ones timid. The diet broke up in confusion on the 17th February 1702, after three months of intrigues and indecision. The senators, that is the palatines and bishops, remained in Warsaw. The Polish Senate has the right to make provisional laws, which the diet seldom annuls, and this smaller body, being used to dealing with practical affairs, debated much more quietly and reached a decision sooner.

They decreed that an ambassador should be sent to the King of Sweden, as the diet had proposed, and that the Pospolite should take up arms and hold itself in readiness for any emergency. They made several regulations designed to quieten the troubles in Lithuania, but still more to diminish the authority of their king, though it was less to be feared than that of the Swedish one.

Augustus, however, preferred to accept harsh laws from his conqueror, rather than from his subjects. He decided to sue the King of Sweden for peace, and wished to negotiate a secret treaty with him. He had to conceal this move from the senate, which he regarded as a still more intractable enemy. The business needed to be handled delicately, so he entrusted it to the Countess of Koenigsmark, a high-born Swedish lady, with whom he was at that time in love. She was the sister of that unfortunate Count of Koenigsmark, the murdered lover of Princess Sophia-Dorothea of Brunswick, and the mother of Maréchal de Saxe who commanded the armies in France with so much success and glory. This lady, world-famed for her wit and beauty, was more capable than any minister of successfully conducting a negotiation. Moreover, as she had property in Charles XII's dominions and had spent a long time at his court, she had a plausible excuse for going to see this prince. She therefore went to the Swedish camp in Lithuania and first approached Count

Piper, who too rashly promised her an audience with his master. The countess, among the charms which made her one of the most attractive women in Europe, had the extraordinary talent of being able to speak the languages of several countries she had never seen, as fluently and idiomatically as a native. Sometimes she even amused herself by writing French verses, which might have been taken to have been written by someone born at Versailles. She composed some for Charles XII, which deserve to be recorded for posterity. She introduced the gods of mythology who all praised the various virtues of Charles XII. The poem ended thus:

> *Enfin chacun des dieux, discourant à sa gloire*
> *Le plaçait par avance au temple de mémoire;*
> *Mais Vénus ni Bacchus n'en dirent pas un mot.**

So much wit and charm were lost on a man like the King of Sweden. He obstinately refused to see her. She took to trying to waylay him during his frequent rides. One day, she did succeed in meeting him in a very narrow path; she alighted from her carriage as soon as she saw him, but the king merely bowed to her, and without saying a single word, promptly turned his horse and rode away. The only satisfaction the Countess of Koenigsmark received from her diplomatic mission was the conviction that she was the only person of whom the King of Sweden was afraid.

The King of Poland was then obliged to throw himself on the mercy of the senate. Through the medium of the Count Palatine of Marienburg he made two propositions to it: one, that he should be left in command of the republican army, which he would pay two quarters in advance out of his own pocket; the other, that it would allow him to bring twelve thousand Saxons back to Poland. The cardinal-primate's reply was as adamant as the King of Sweden's refusal. He told the Count of Marienburg, in the name of the assembly, 'that it had decided to send an embassy to Charles XII, and that it did not advise him to bring back the Saxons'.

In this extremity, the king wished to preserve at least the semblance of royal authority. He sent one of his chamberlains to enquire

---

* Finally, each of the gods who so eloquently belauded his glory awarded him in advance a niche in the temple of fame: but neither Venus nor Bacchus uttered a word. *Trs.*

of Charles when and how his Swedish majesty would receive the
embassy of the king his master and the republic. Unfortunately he
forgot to ask the Swedes for a safe-conduct pass for this chamberlain.
The King of Sweden had him put in prison instead of granting him
an audience, saying that he was expecting to receive an embassy
from the republic, but nothing from King Augustus. This breach of
international law was justifiable only on the principle that might is
stronger than right.

Leaving garrisons behind in some of the Lithuanian towns,
Charles then advanced beyond Grodno, a town famous in Europe for
the diets which are held there, but badly built and worse fortified.

A few miles beyond Grodno, he met the embassy of the republic,
which was composed of five senators. They wished first of all to
arrange the ceremonial formalities to be observed, but the king
ignored their ideas of protocol. They demanded that the republic
should be referred to as *Most Serene* and that the king's carriages and
those of his senators should be sent to meet and transport them. The
replay was that the republic would be called *Illustrious* and not *Most
Serene*; that the king never used a carriage; that he had a great many
officers with him, but no senators; that a lieutenant-general would be
sent to meet them and that they would arrive on their own horses.

Charles XII received them in his own tent, with some display of
military pomp, and listened to their speeches which were full of
caution and ambiguity. It was evident that they feared Charles XII
and disliked Augustus, but that they were ashamed to depose their
own elected king at the order of a foreigner. Nothing was decided,
and in the end Charles XII gave them to understand that he would
settle the matter in Warsaw.

His march was preceded by a manifesto which the cardinal and
his party published throughout Poland in eight days. In this document Charles invited all the Poles to unite their vengeance to his,
and claimed to make them see that their interests were identical
with his. They were, nevertheless, very different, but the manifesto,
backed by a large party, by the confusion of the senate, and by the
approach of the conqueror, made a great impression. People realized
the necessity of recognizing Charles for Protector, since this was
what he wished to be, and also that they were only too lucky that
he should be content with this title.

The senators opposed to Augustus openly publicized the manifesto under his very eyes. The few who adhered to him remained silent. Finally, when Charles was known to be approaching by forced marches, they all took fright and prepared to leave. The cardinal was one of the first to quit Warsaw; the majority fled precipitately, some to their estates to await the outcome of events, others to go and rally their friends. No one remained with the king but the imperial and Russian ambassadors, the papal legate and a few bishops and palatines attached to his cause. He had to flee, and nothing had yet been decided in his favour. Before leaving, he held a hurried counsel with the handful of senators who still represented the senate. However zealous they were to serve him, they were Poles; they had all conceived such a violent aversion to the Saxon troops that they dared not grant him the freedom to bring in more than six thousand of them to defend him; they also voted that these six thousand men should be commanded by the Polish generalissimo and sent back immediately after the peace. The armies of the republic they left at his disposal.

As a result, the king left Warsaw, too weak against his enemies and little satisfied even with his own party. He promptly issued his orders for the Pospolite and the republican armies to assemble, but these forces were no more than empty names. There was nothing to be hoped for in Lithuania which was occupied by the Swedes. The Polish army, reduced to a handful of troops, lacked weapons, provisions and the will to fight. The majority of the nobles, intimidated, irresolute or disaffected, remained on their estates. In vain, the king, authorized by the law of the land, ordered all the nobles to mount horse and follow him, under pain of death; it was beginning to become questionable whether they ought to obey him. His great resource lay in the troops of his electorate, where the uncompromisingly absolute form of government left him in no fear of disobedience. He had already secretly sent for twelve thousand Saxons who were hastily advancing. He also brought back eight thousand whom he had promised to the emperor in the imperial war against France and whom he was obliged to recall owing to his dire situation. To introduce so many Saxons into Poland was to turn everyone against him and to violate the law made by his own party, which allowed him only six thousand; but he well knew that, if he were victorious, they would not dare to complain, and that, if he were defeated, they would not forgive him for having brought in even the six thousand. While these soldiers were arriving company by company, and he was going from palatinate to palatinate to assemble the nobles who were loyal to him, the King of Sweden at last arrived before Warsaw on the 5th of May 1702. The gates were opened to him at the first summons. He dismissed the Polish garrison, disbanded the town guard, established sentry-posts every-where, and ordered all the inhabitants to come and surrender all their weapons; but, content with disarming them and not wishing to embitter them, he only demanded a tribute of a hundred thousand francs. King Augustus was at that time assembling his forces at Cracow; he was much surprised when the cardinal-primate appeared there. Perhaps this man wished to maintain his respectability to the last and to dethrone his king with outward decorum; he gave him to understand that the King of Sweden seemed disposed to make a reasonable compromise and humbly begged permission to go and see Charles XII. Augustus granted what he could not refuse; in other words, free licence for the prelate to injure him.

The cardinal-primate departed straightway to see the King of Sweden to whom he had not yet dared present himself. He saw this prince at Prague, near Warsaw, but with none of the ceremony which had marked the reception of the ambassadors of the republic. He found the conqueror wearing a uniform of coarse blue cloth with brass buttons, jack-boots and buff elbow-length gauntlets, in a room with no hangings. With him were the Duke of Holstein, his brother-in-law, Count Piper, his prime minister, and several officers. The king came forward a few steps to meet the cardinal and they stood conferring together for a quarter-of-an-hour. Charles cut the discussion short by saying aloud: 'I will not grant the Poles peace until they elect another king.' The cardinal, who was expecting this declaration, promptly made it known to all the palatinates, assuring them of the extreme displeasure he said it caused him and at the same time of the necessity of complying with the conqueror's conditions.

At this news, the King of Poland realized that he must either lose his throne or keep it by a battle. He drew on all his resources for this great decisive action. All his Saxon troops had arrived from the frontiers of Saxony; the nobles of the Palatinate of Cracow, where he still was, flocked to offer him their services. He himself urged each of his nobles to remember their oaths of fealty; they promised to shed their last drop of blood for him. Fortified by their aid and by the troops which bore the name of 'the army of the crown', he set out for the first time to seek the King of Sweden in person. As the latter was himself advancing towards Cracow, he soon found him.

The two kings met face to face on the 13th of July 1702 in a vast plain near Clissau, between Warsaw and Cracow. Augustus had nearly twenty-four thousand men; Charles XII only twelve thousand. The battle began with an exchange of artillery fire. At the first volley, which was fired by the Saxons, the Duke of Holstein, a most courageous and virtuous young prince, who was commanding the Swedish cavalry, was hit in the loins by a cannon-ball. The king enquired whether he was dead; on being told that he was, he said not a word. He shed a few tears and hid his face in his hands for a moment; then, suddenly, urging his horse to a full gallop, he charged into the midst of the enemy at the head of his guards.

The King of Poland did all that could be expected of a prince who was fighting for his crown. Three times he personally rallied his troops to the charge, but he was fighting only with his Saxons; the Poles, who formed his right wing, all fled as soon as the battle began, some from terror, some from disaffection. Charles XII's good fortune prevailed. He won a complete victory; the enemy camp, the standards, the artillery, and even Augustus's war-chest were all left in his hands. He did not stop on the battlefield, but marched straight to Cracow, pursuing the King of Poland who was fleeing before him.

The citizens of Cracow were rash enough to shut their gates to the conqueror; he battered them down. The garrison did not dare fire a single shot; they were chased with sticks and whips right into the castle, which the king entered with them. As a single artillery officer was daring to prepare to fire a cannon, Charles rushed up to him and snatched the fuse from him; the commandant flung himself at the king's feet. Three Swedish regiments were billeted in the citizens' houses and the town taxed a contribution of a hundred thousand rix-dollars. Count Stenbock, who was appointed governor of the town, heard a rumour that treasure had been hidden in the tombs of the Polish kings who are buried in the church of St Nicholas in Cracow. He had the tombs opened, but nothing was found but the gold and silver ornaments which belonged to the churches; the conquerors took part of these, and Charles XII even sent a gold chalice to a church in Sweden, which would have raised the Polish catholics against him, could anything have prevailed over their terror of his army.

He left Cracow, determined to pursue King Augustus relentlessly, but a few miles beyond the city, his horse fell and he broke his thigh. He had to be carried back to Cracow, where he lay in bed for six weeks in the hands of the surgeons. This accident gave Augustus a breathing-space. He promptly spread it about in Poland and the empire that Charles XII had died of his fall. This false news, which, for a little while, was believed, produced universal astonishment and perplexity. In this brief interval Augustus assembled, first at Marienburg, then at Lublin, all the orders of the realm which were already convened at Sandomir. There was a large crowd present, for few of the palatinates refused to send their deputies. He won back nearly everyone's support by handsome gifts, promises and that affability which is essential to absolute monarchs to make themselves popular and to elective ones to maintain their throne. The diet was soon undeceived about the false news of the Swedish King's death, but the impetus it had already given to this great body persisted and it let itself be carried away by it; all the members swore to remain faithful to their sovereign, so easily are men in the mass persuaded to change their opinions! The cardinal-primate himself, still pretending to be attached to King Augustus, came to the Diet of Lublin; he kissed the king's hand, and had not the slightest scruple about taking the oath with the rest. This oath consisted in swearing that one had never attempted and never would attempt anything against Augustus. The king dispensed the cardinal from the first part of the oath, and he blushed as he swore to the rest. The decision reached by this diet was that the Republic of Poland should maintain an army of fifty thousand men, at the expense of the state, for the service of its sovereign; that the Swedes should be given six weeks to declare whether they wanted peace or war, and the same period allowed to the Princes Sapieha, the first authors of the troubles in Lithuania, to come and ask pardon of the King of Poland.

But, while these deliberations were going on, Charles XII, who had recovered from his injury, was sweeping on, carrying all before him. Still firmly determined to force the Poles to depose their king themselves, he convened, through the intrigues of the cardinal-primate, a new assembly in Warsaw to oppose the one in Lublin. His generals pointed out to him that its discussions might drag on indefinitely and in the end prove abortive; that meanwhile the Russians were daily fighting the troops he had left in Livonia and Ingria, and, in the frequent battles which took place in these provinces between the Russians and the Swedes, the latter were not always the victors; in short, that his presence might soon be necessary there. Charles, as stubbornly immovable in his ideas as he was impetuous in his actions, replied: 'If I have to stay here fifty years, I will not leave until I have dethroned the King of Poland.'

He left the Warsaw assembly to wrangle with the Lublin one in speech and writing and to find some justification for its proceedings in the laws of the realm, laws which are always ambiguous and interpreted by each party to suit itself, and which only success renders indisputable. He himself, having increased his victorious army by six thousand cavalry and eight thousand infantry he had received from Sweden, marched against the remnants of the Saxon army he had defeated at Clissau, and which had had time to rally and swell its ranks while his riding accident had kept him in bed. This army retreated before his advance and retired into Prussia, to the north-west of Warsaw, with the river Bug between it and its enemies. Charles swam across it at the head of his cavalry, while the infantry went to find a ford higher up. On the 1st of May 1703, he caught up with the Saxons at a place called Pultusk. They were commanded by General Steinau and numbered about ten thousand. The King of Sweden, in his hasty march, had not brought more with him, convinced that he needed even less. The terror of his military prowess was so great that half the Saxon army fled at his approach without giving battle. General Steinau stood his ground for a moment with a couple of regiments; the next, he himself was swept away in the general flight of his army which scattered before it had been beaten. The Swedes took less than a thousand prisoners and killed less than six hundred men, having had more trouble in pursuing the Saxons than in defeating them.

Augustus, left with nothing but the remnants of his universally defeated Saxons, hastily retired to Thorn, an old city situated on the Vistula, in the kingdom of Prussia, which is under Polish protection. Charles promptly prepared to besiege it. The King of Poland, not thinking himself safe there, withdrew, and hurried to every place in Poland which had not been overrun by the Swedes and where he could still assemble a few soldiers. However, Charles, advancing with such impetuous haste, swimming across rivers, and galloping forward with his foot-soldiers riding pillion behind his cavalrymen, had not been able to bring any artillery with which to besiege Thorn; he was obliged to wait for some to arrive from Sweden by sea.

While waiting, he stationed himself a few miles from the town, and often approached too close to the rampart in order to reconnoitre it. On these dangerous excursions, the plain blue uniform he always wore was useful to him in a way that had never occurred to him; it prevented him from looking conspicuous and being picked out as a personal target for the enemy's muskets. One day, having approached very near indeed with one of his generals, named Liewen, who was wearing a blue uniform* trimmed with gold braid, he feared that this general was too clearly visible, and ordered him to get behind him. Such a generous impulse was so natural to him that he did not even stop to think that he was exposing his own life to obvious danger in order to save his subject's. Liewen, realizing too late that he had been wrong to wear a conspicuous uniform, which exposed those with him to danger too, and fearing equally for the king, wherever he stood, hesitated whether he ought to obey; as he was momentarily arguing with himself, the king seized him by the arm, thrust himself in front of him and covered him. At that very instant, a volley of cannon-fire, coming from the side, struck the general dead on the very spot the king had just left. The death of this man, definitely killed instead of him, and because he had tried to save him, contributed not a little to strengthening his life-

---

* In the first editions we had given this officer a scarlet uniform, but the chaplain Nordberg has so convincingly proved that it was blue that we have corrected this error.

long conviction of predestination and made him believe that fate, which had preserved his life in such an extraordinary way, was reserving him for accomplishing greater things.

Everything was going well with him; he was as successful in his negotiations as on the battlefield. He was, as it were, present in the whole of Poland, for his Commander-in-Chief Rehnskiöld was in the heart of this state with a large army corps. Nearly thirty thousand Swedes under various generals, scattered to the north and east on the frontiers of Russia, withstood the attempted assaults of the entire Russian empire, and Charles himself was in the west, at the other end of Poland, at the head of the flower of his troops.

The King of Denmark, bound by the Treaty of Travendal, which he was not powerful enough to break, remained silent. This extremely prudent monarch did not dare openly express his resentment at seeing the King of Sweden so close to his dominions. Further away, towards the south-west, between the Elbe and the Weser, the strongly-garrisoned Duchy of Bremen, the last remaining territory acquired by the former Swedish conquests, still left the way to Saxony and the empire open to the new conqueror. Thus, from the German Ocean almost to the mouth of the Dnieper, that is, throughout the breadth of Europe, and up to the gates of Moscow all was in consternation and a total revolution seemed imminent. Charles's ships, in complete control of the Baltic, were employed in transporting the prisoners he had taken in Poland to his own country. Sweden, calm in the midst of these great upheavals, was enjoying a profound peace and exulting in the glory of its king without having to bear the burden of its cost, for his victorious troops were paid and maintained at the expense of the vanquished.

While the rest of the north was reduced to cowed silence before the armed might of Charles XII, the town of Danzig had the audacity to offend him. Fourteen frigates and forty transport ships were bringing the king a reinforcement of six thousand men, as well as the artillery and munitions needed to complete the siege of Thorn. It was necessary for this fleet to sail up the Vistula. At the mouth of this river stands Danzig, a rich free city, which, together with Thorn and Elbing, enjoys the same privileges in Poland as the imperial cities do in Germany. Its liberty had been attacked in turn by the Danes, Sweden and various German princes, and it had only preserved it because of the mutual jealousy of these powers. On behalf of the king, Count Stenbock, one of the Swedish generals, summoned an assembly of the civic authorities, and demanded passage for the troops and some of the munitions. The magistrates, with an imprudence common in those who are dealing with someone stronger than themselves, dared neither refuse him nor definitely grant his demands. General Stenbock compelled them by force to give him more than he had demanded: a contribution of forty thousand crowns was even levied on the town as a penalty for its rash refusal. Finally, the reinforcements, artillery and munitions, having arrived before Thorn, the siege was begun on the 22nd of September.

Robel, the governor of the town, defended it for a month with a garrison of five thousand. At the end of that time, he was forced to surrender unconditionally. The soldiers of the garrison were made prisoners of war and despatched to Sweden. Robel, after being disarmed, was taken before the king. This prince, who never lost an opportunity of honouring merit in his foes, gave him a sword with his own hand, made him a present of a considerable sum of money, and dismissed him on parole. But the town, which was small and poor, was condemned to pay forty thousand pounds, an excessive contribution for it.

Elbing, a town built on an arm of the Vistula, which had been founded by the Teuton Knights and was also annexed to Poland, did not learn from the mistake of the Danzigers. It hesitated too long about allowing the Swedes passage and was more severely punished for it than Danzig. Charles entered it, on the 31st of December, at the head of four thousand men with fixed bayonets. The terrified inhabitants threw themselves on their knees in the streets, imploring his mercy. He had them all disarmed, billeted his soldiers on the townsfolk and then, having summoned the chief magistrate, demanded a contribution of two hundred and sixty thousand crowns to be paid that very day. He also seized the two hundred pieces of cannon of the town and an enormous quantity of gunpowder. Winning a battle would not have won him such rich spoils. All these successes were the harbingers of the dethronement of King Augustus.

Scarcely had the cardinal sworn to attempt nothing against his king, than he repaired to the diet at Warsaw, still on the pretence of making peace. He arrived, talking of nothing but concord and obedience, but accompanied by soldiers raised on his own estate. Finally, he threw off his mask, and, on the 14th of February 1704, he declared, in the name of the assembly, *Augustus, Elector of Saxony, unfit to wear the crown of Poland.* The diet then unanimously proclaimed that the throne was vacant. The King of Sweden's wish, and consequently that of this diet, was to give Prince James Sobieski the throne of his father King John. James Sobieski was then at Breslau in Silesia, waiting impatiently for the crown his father had worn. One day he was out hunting, a few leagues from Breslau, with his brother Prince Constantine, when thirty Saxon horsemen, secretly sent by King Augustus, suddenly emerged from a nearby wood, surrounded the two princes and carried them off. Relay horses had been saddled in readiness and, mounted on these, they were promptly conveyed to Leipzig, where they were confined under close guard. This coup upset the plans so carefully laid by Charles, the cardinal and the Warsaw assembly.

Fortune, which makes game of crowned heads, decreed that, almost at the very same moment, King Augustus was on the point of being captured himself. He was at table, three leagues from Cracow, relying, for eating his dinner undisturbed, on an advance guard posted some distance away, when General Rehnskiöld suddenly appeared, after having abducted this guard. The King of Poland had only just time to mount his horse and gallop away. General Rehnskiöld pursued him for four days, ready to capture him any minute. The king fled as far as Sandomir, with the Swedish general still in hot pursuit, and it was only by extraordinary good luck that Augustus escaped.

During all this time, King Augustus's party and the cardinal's were abusing each other as traitors to the country. The army of the crown was divided between these two factions. Augustus, finally forced to accept Russian aid, repented not having appealed for it sooner. Desperately seeking reinforcements, he had been going from pillar to post, now hurrying to Saxony, where his resources were drained dry, now back again to Poland, where no one dared serve him. Meanwhile the victorious King of Sweden, the effective ruler of Poland, proceeded calmly to implement his plans for its future.

Count Piper, whose political acumen was as great as his master's military genius, now suggested to Charles XII that he should assume the Polish crown himself. He pointed out how easy it would be for him to do so, with a victorious army, and a powerful party in the heart of a kingdom which he had already subdued. He tempted him with the title of Defender of the Reformed Faith, a designation very gratifying to Charles's ambition. It would be easy, he said, to do in Poland what Gustavus Vasa had done in Sweden: establish Lutheranism there and break the chains of a people enslaved by the nobility and the clergy. Charles was momentarily tempted, but military glory was his idol. He sacrificed his own interest to it, as well as the pleasure it would have given him to wrest Poland from the pope. He told Count Piper that he found it more gratifying to give kingdoms away than to acquire them, and added, with a smile: 'You were born to be the minister of an Italian prince.'

Charles was still near Thorn, in that part of Prussia which belongs to Poland; from there he could both keep an eye on what was happening in Warsaw and hold the neighbouring powers in check. Prince Alexander, the brother of the two Sobieskis, came to him to demand vengeance. Charles promised it all the more readily because it seemed easy and because he would also be revenging himself. But, being impatient to give Poland a king, he proposed to Prince Alexander that he should mount the throne which fortune seemed determined to prevent his brother from occupying. He did not expect the offer to be refused, but Prince Alexander replied that nothing would ever induce him to profit by the misfortune of his elder brother. The King of Sweden, Count Piper, and all his friends, in particular the young Palatine of Posnania, Stanislas Leczinski, urged him to accept the crown, but he was adamant. The neighbouring princes learnt with amazement of this almost incredible refusal and did not know which to admire more, a King of Sweden, who, at the age of twenty-three, could give away the crown of Poland, or Prince Alexander who had refused it.

BOOK III

YOUNG Stanislas Leczinski was then deputed by the Assembly of Warsaw to go and give the King of Sweden an account of several differences that had arisen among its members since the abduction of Prince James. Stanislas had a prepossessing face, suggesting a nature at once courageous and gentle, together with that air of honesty and frankness which is the greatest of all outward attractions and gives more weight to a man's words than the most persuasive eloquence. Charles was struck by the sagacity with which he spoke of Augustus, of the assembly, of the cardinal-primate, and of the different interests which divided Poland. King Stanislas did me the honour of telling me that he said, in Latin, to the King of Sweden: 'How can we hold an election, if Prince James and Prince Constantine are prisoners?' and that Charles replied: 'How can the Republic be freed without an election?' This conversation was the one and only intrigue which put Stanislas on the throne. Charles deliberately prolonged the conversation in order the better to assess the young deputy's abilities. After their private talk, he said publicly that he had never seen a man more fitted to reconcile all parties. He immediately made enquiries about Leczinski's character. He learned that he was extremely courageous, and inured to hardship; that he always slept on a kind of straw pallet, and required no servant to attend to his personal wants; that he was not only economical, but temperate in eating and drinking, a rare characteristic in those regions. In addition, he was adored by his vassals and was, perhaps, the only lord in Poland who had some real friends at a time which recognized no other ties than those of self-interest and political factions. This character, which had something in common with his own, made Charles come to a final decision. After their meeting, he remarked aloud: 'That is a man who will always be my friend.' People soon realized that those words meant: 'That is the man who will be king.'

When the Primate of Poland learnt that Charles XII had nominated the Palatine Leczinsky, much in the way Alexander had nominated Abdolonymes, he hastened to the King of Sweden to try and make him change his mind, for he wanted the crown to go to one of the Lubomirskis. 'But what have you against Stanislas Leczinski?' asked the conqueror. 'He is too young, sire,' said the primate. The king replied tartly: 'He is about my own age,' turned his back on the prelate, and promptly despatched Count Horn to intimate to the Warsaw Assembly that it must elect a king within five days and that it must elect Stanislas Leczinski. Count Horn arrived on the 7th of July and fixed the election for the 12th, just as he might have ordered a battalion to strike camp. The cardinal-primate, frustrated of the fruit of so many intrigues, returned to the assembly, where he did his utmost to ensure the failure of an election in which he had no part. But the King of Sweden himself arrived incognito in Warsaw, so he had to keep silent. All the primate could do was to absent himself from the election; he was reduced to an ineffective neutrality, being unable to oppose the conqueror and unwilling to support him.

On Saturday the 12th of July 1704, the day fixed for the election, the diet met at three o'clock in the afternoon at Colo, where it had been arranged for this ceremony to take place. The Bishop of Posen, who presided at the diet instead of the cardinal-primate, arrived, followed by the noblemen of the party. Count Horn and two other generals attended the ceremony as ambassadors extraordinary from Charles to the republic. The session lasted till nine o'clock in the evening, when the Bishop of Posen ended it, by declaring in the name of the diet that Stanislas was elected King of Poland. All those who had voted for him threw their caps in the air and the noise of their cheers drowned the cries of the opponents.

The cardinal-primate and those who had wished to remain neutral gained nothing by staying away from the election; the very next day they all had to come and pay homage to the new king; their greatest mortification was that they were obliged to follow him to the King of Sweden's quarters. This prince paid the sovereign he had just created all the honours due to a king of Poland, and, to add weight to his new dignity, gave him money and troops.

Charles XII immediately left Warsaw to go and complete the conquest of Poland. He had ordered his army to meet him before Leopold, the capital of the great Palatinate of Russia, a place important in itself and still more so for the riches it contained. It was thought that it would hold out for a fortnight, on account of the fortifications King Augustus had erected round it. The conqueror besieged it on the 5th of September, and the next day took it by assault. Everyone who dared to resist was put to the sword. The victorious troops, now masters of the town, did not disperse in search of pillage, in spite of the rumoured treasures in Leopold. They ranged themselves in battle order in the main square. There what remained of the garrison came to surrender themselves as prisoners of war. The king proclaimed, to the sound of the trumpet, that all those inhabitants who had any goods belonging to King Augustus or his adherents must bring them in person before nightfall, under pain of death. Such stringent measures were taken to enforce this order that few dared disobey it: four hundred chests filled with gold and silver coins, plate and other things of value were brought to King Charles by their intimidated owners.

Almost on the very same day, something very different occurred to the newly enthroned King Stanislas. Some business which urgently required his presence had obliged him to remain in Warsaw. With him were his mother, his wife and two daughters and his new court, composed of the cardinal-primate, the Bishop of Posen, and some Polish grandees. They were guarded by six thousand Poles of the army of the crown, who had only recently entered his service and whose loyalty had not yet been put to the proof. General Horn, the governor of the town, had only fifteen hundred Swedes with him. Everything was perfectly peaceful in Warsaw, and Stanislas was reckoning on leaving in a few days' time to join Charles for the conquest of Leopold. Suddenly he learnt that a large army was approaching the town. It was led by King Augustus, who was making a fresh effort, and, by one of the finest marches ever made by a general, had avoided the King of Sweden and was descending on Warsaw with twenty thousand men in order to kidnap his rival.

Warsaw was unfortified, and the Polish troops who defended it were far from reliable. Augustus had spies in the town; if Stanislas remained, he was lost. He sent his family back to Posen, under the guard of the Polish troops he most trusted. In all this confusion, he thought he had lost his second daughter, but he found her again in a manger, in a neighbouring village where she had been left behind: he told me this story himself. It was this same child who was destined later, after many vicissitudes, to become Queen of France. Several noblemen took different roads; the new king himself went off to seek Charles XII. He learnt early to bear misfortunes, having been forced to leave his capital six weeks after he had been elected sovereign there.

Augustus entered the capital as an angry and victorious monarch. The inhabitants, already fleeced by the King of Sweden, were fleeced even more by Augustus. The cardinal's palace and all the town and country houses of the confederate lords, together with their goods and chattels, were ruthlessly plundered. The strangest thing about this short-lived revolution was that the papal legate who had come with Augustus, demanded in his master's name that the Bishop of Posen should be handed over to him as liable to trial by the Roman curia as a bishop who supported a prince placed on the throne by the military power of a Lutheran.

The Roman curia, which has always sought to increase its temporal power at the expense of the spiritual, had long ago established a kind of jurisdiction in Poland, with the papal legate at its head. The pope's ministers had never failed to use every favourable opportunity of extending their power, which was revered by the masses but always challenged by those who were wiser. They had abrogated to themselves the right to judge all ecclesiastical cases and, especially in troubled times, had usurped many other privileges, which they maintained until about 1728, when they were curtailed. Such abuses are never reformed until they have become utterly intolerable.

King Augustus, delighted to have a respectable pretext for punishing the Bishop of Posen and thereby pleasing the Roman curia, which, at any other time, he would have defied, delivered the Polish prelate into the hands of the nuncio. The bishop, after seeing his house pillaged, was taken by soldiers to the Italian minister, and sent to Saxony, where he died. Count Horn was subjected to continuous enemy fire in the castle where he had shut himself in; finally, the place could no longer hold out, and he surrendered himself as a prisoner of war, together with his fifteen hundred Swedes. This was the first battle Augustus won in his disastrously unfortunate campaign against the Swedes.

This last effort was the last flare-up of a dying fire. His troops, assembled in haste, were Poles, prepared to abandon him at the first setback, Saxon recruits who had never yet seen any fighting, and Cossack vagabonds, more efficient at plundering the vanquished than at winning battles; all of them trembled at the mere name of the King of Sweden.

This conqueror, accompanied by King Stanislas, went to meet his enemy at the head of the pick of his troops. Wherever he went, the Saxon army fled at his approach. Towns for thirty miles round sent him their keys; not a day passed without his gaining some new advantage. These successes became too familiar to Charles. He said it was more like going hunting than making war, and complained of not having to pay any price for victory.

For some time Augustus entrusted the command of his troops to Count Schulenburg, a very able general, who needed all his experience to lead a demoralized army. He was more concerned to safeguard his master's troops than to win battles, so he waged war against the two kings with a tactical skill which constantly frustrated their activities. He stole marches on them, blocked strategic thoroughfares and sacrificed some cavalry to give his infantry time to withdraw safely. He saved his troops by some glorious retreats, the only kind of glory it was possible to achieve in the face of such an enemy.

Hardly had he reached the Palatinate of Posen than he learnt that the two kings, whom he believed to be fifty leagues away, had covered these fifty leagues in nine days. He had only eight thousand infantry and a thousand cavalry; he had to hold his own against a superior army, the King of Sweden's reputation, and the natural fear which so many defeats inspired in the Saxons. He had always claimed, contrary to the opinion of the German generals, that infantry could resist cavalry in open country, even without *chevaux-de-frise*; he dared to test this theory that day against this victorious cavalry commanded by two kings and the pick of the Swedish generals. He took up such an advantageous position that he could not be surrounded. His first line knelt on the ground; it was armed with pikes and muskets, so that the tightly-serried soldiers presented the enemy's horse with a kind of rampart bristling with pikes and bayonets; the second line, bending forward a little over the shoulders of the first, fired over their heads, and the third, standing upright, fired simultaneously behind the other two. The Swedes charged with their usual impetuosity against the Saxons, but the latter awaited them without flinching; the musket shots and the formidable array of pikes and bayonets terrified the horses, which reared instead of advancing. This meant that the Swedes could only attack in disorder, while the Saxons defended themselves without breaking their ranks.

Having warded off the attack, Schulenburg drew up his men in a rectangular battalion, and, though he had received five wounds, he retired in good order in this formation, in the middle of the night, to the little town of Gurau, three leagues from the battlefield. He had hardly begun to draw breath there before the two kings suddenly appeared behind him.

Beyond Gurau, towards the river Oder, lay a thick wood, through which the Saxon general escaped with his exhausted infantry. The Swedes, undeterred, pursued him through this wood, advancing with difficulty through overgrown paths almost impassable to men on foot. The Saxons got through the wood only five hours before the Swedish cavalry. On the far side of the wood runs the river Parts, at the foot of a village named Rutsen. Schulenburg had sent a messenger by coach to assemble boats; he managed to cross the river with his troops, already diminished by half. Charles arrived just as Schulenburg reached the other bank. Never had a conqueror pursued his enemy so relentlessly. Schulenburg's reputation depended on escaping from the King of Sweden; the king's one thought was to enhance his own by capturing Schulenburg and what remained of his army. He lost no time in making his cavalry cross by a ford. The Saxons found themselves trapped between this river Parts and the great river Oder, which rises in Silesia and is already deep and rapid at this spot.

The defeat of Schulenburg seemed inevitable; nevertheless, after sacrificing a few soldiers, he crossed the Oder during the night and thus saved his army. Charles could not help saying: 'Today Schulenburg has beaten us.'

It was this same Schulenburg who was later General of the Venetians and to whom the republic has erected a statue in Corfu, for having defended this bulwark of Italy against the Turks. Only republics render soldiers such honours; kings merely give them rewards.

But this action, which made Schulenburg famous, was useless to King Augustus. This prince once again abandoned Poland to his enemies. He withdrew to Saxony, and ordered the fortifications of Dresden to be repaired with all haste, for he already feared, not without reason, for the capital of his hereditary states.

Charles could now regard the subjugation of Poland as complete; his generals in Courland, following his example, had just wiped out several small bodies of Russians who, since the great battle of Narva, had only appeared in guerrilla bands and waged war like Tartar vagabonds, pillaging, fleeing and reappearing only to flee again.

Wherever the Swedes were, they believed themselves certain to win, even though they were twenty to a hundred. In such propitious circumstances, Stanislas prepared for his coronation. Fortune, which had caused him to be elected in Warsaw, and had then driven him out of it, now recalled him thither to the acclamations of a crowd of nobles, whom the outcome of the war had attached to him. A diet was convened there; all the obstacles in his path were removed; only the Roman curia stood in his way.

It was natural that it should declare for King Augustus, who had renounced the protestant faith and become a catholic in order to ascend the throne, against Stanislas, who had been placed on the same throne by a great enemy of catholicism. Clement XI, who was then pope, sent briefs to all the Polish prelates, in particular the cardinal-primate, threatening them with excommunication if they dared to assist at the coronation of Stanislas, or to connive in any treasonable activity against the lawful king, Augustus.

If these briefs had reached the bishops who were in Warsaw, it was to be feared that a few would obey out of weakness and that the majority would take advantage of their contents to make more exacting conditions for their support in proportion as it became more necessary. Precautions had therefore been taken to prevent the pope's letters from being received in Warsaw. A Franciscan was secretly given the briefs to deliver by hand to the prelates. He gave one first to the suffragan bishop of Chelm; this prelate, who was greatly attached to Stanislas, took it to the king with its seal unbroken. The king sent for the friar and asked him how he had dared to undertake such a commission. The Franciscan replied that it was by order of his superior. Stanislas told him in future to take orders from his king, rather than from the General of the Franciscans, and promptly banished him from the city.

The same day the King of Sweden published an edict, forbidding all the secular and regular clergy in Warsaw, under pain of severe penalties, to meddle in political affairs. For further security, he had guards stationed at the gates of all the prelates' houses and forbade any foreigner to enter the town. He took upon himself the responsibility for these small severities so that Stanislas should not be at loggerheads with the clergy on his accession. He said that he found it relaxing after the fatigues of warfare to thwart the intrigues of the papal court, and that one fought against it with paper, whereas one had to attack other sovereigns with actual weapons.

The cardinal-primate was asked by Charles and Stanislas to perform the coronation ceremony. He did not think he ought to leave Danzig in order to anoint a king whom he had not wished to elect, but as his policy was to do nothing without a pretext, he wished to provide a legitimate excuse for his refusal. So, during the night, he had the papal brief nailed on the door of his own house. The Chief Magistrate of Danzig was highly indignant, and instigated a search for the culprits, who were never found. The primate pretended to be angry, but in fact was extremely pleased; he had a reason for not anointing the new king, and at the same time avoiding any trouble with Charles XII, Augustus, Stanislas and the pope. He died a few days later, leaving his country in appalling confusion, having succeeded, with all his intrigues, only in embroiling himself simultaneously with the three kings, Charles, Augustus and Stanislas, with the Polish republic, and with the pope, who had ordered him to come to Rome to give an account of his conduct. Still, as even politicians occasionally feel some remorse in their last moments, he wrote to King Augustus, when he was dying, to ask his forgiveness.

The coronation took place peacefully and with due pomp, on the 4th of October 1705, in the city of Warsaw in spite of its being the usual custom in Poland for kings to be crowned in Cracow. Stanislas Leczinski and his wife Charlotta Opalinska were anointed King and Queen of Poland by the Archbishop of Leopold, assisted by many other prelates: Charles XII was present incognito at this coronation ceremony, the only reward he reaped from his conquests.

Charles had subjugated Poland and given her a new king; Denmark no longer dared to harass him; the King of Prussia was seeking his friendship and King Augustus had retired to his hereditary states. Yet he still had an army to reckon with: the tsar, who was becoming daily more redoubtable. Peter had given Augustus feeble military aid in Poland, but he had created powerful diversions in Ingria.

He himself had begun not only to be a great soldier but to teach his Russians the art of war. His troops were becoming well disciplined; he had good engineers, an efficient artillery and many good officers; he knew the great art of maintaining army supplies. Some of his generals had learnt to fight well, and, when necessary, not to fight; what is more he had built up a fleet capable of holding its own against the Swedes in the Baltic Sea.

Taking advantage of this military strength, which only his genius could have created, and of the absence of the King of Sweden, he took Narva by assault on the 21st of August 1704, after a regular siege and after preventing its being helped by sea or land. The soldiers pillaged and ransacked the town, committing the most barbarous atrocities. The tsar rushed hither and thither to stop the wholesale disorder and murder; he himself snatched women from the hands of soldiers who were about to cut their throats after having raped them. He was even obliged to kill with his own hands some Russians who refused to listen to his orders. In the town hall of Narva, they still show the table on which he laid his sword when he entered it; and people still remember the words he addressed to the citizens assembled there: 'This sword is not stained with the blood of the inhabitants, but with that of the Russians which I have shed to save your lives.'

Had the tsar always displayed such humanity he would have

been the greatest of men. He aimed at something more than destroying cities; he was then in process of founding one, in the midst of his new conquests, not far from Narva itself. This was the town of St Petersburg, which he subsequently made his residence and trading centre. It is situated between Finland and Ingria, on a marshy island, around which the Neva divides itself into several branches before flowing into the Gulf of Finland. He himself drew the plan of the city, the fortress, the port, the quays which embellish it and the forts which defend its entrance. In 1703, this uncultivated desert island, which was a swamp in the short summer of those regions and a frozen lake in winter, which could be reached by land only by traversing pathless forests and deep bogs, and which had hitherto been inhabited only by wolves and bears, was filled with over three hundred thousand men whom the tsar had assembled from all parts of his realm. Peasants from the kingdom of Astrakhan and those who lived on the frontiers of China were transported to St Petersburg. Paths had to be hacked through forests, roads built, marshes drained and dikes erected before the foundations of the town could be laid. Nature was everywhere forcibly coerced into subjection. The tsar was stubbornly determined to people a region which did not seem intended for human habitation. Neither the floods which ruined his works, nor the barrenness of the soil, nor the ignorance of the workmen, nor even the death-rate among them which amounted to two hundred thousand in the early days could make him change his mind. The city was founded in spite of the obstacles set up by nature, by the character of the people involved in the task, and by an unfortunate war. By 1705 St Petersburg was already a town and its harbour was filled with ships. The emperor attracted foreigners to it by rich rewards, giving lands to some and houses to others, and by encouraging all the arts which could make life pleasant in that savage region. Above all, he had made St Petersburg safe against enemy attacks. The Swedish generals, who had often beaten his troops everywhere else, had not been able to inflict any damage on this growing colony. It remained peaceful in the midst of the war all round it.

The tsar, while thus creating new dominions for himself, still extended a helping hand to King Augustus, who was losing his own; he persuaded him through General Patkul, who had recently joined the Russian army and was then the tsar's ambassador in Saxony, to come to Grodno and confer with him once again about the unhappy state of his affairs. King Augustus came, accompanied by General Schulenburg, whose crossing of the Oder had made him famous in the North, and in whom he placed his last hope. The tsar arrived there, marching at the head of an army of seventy thousand men. The two monarchs made new plans of war. The dethroned King Augustus no longer feared angering the Poles by abandoning their country to the Russian troops. It was decided that the tsar's army should split up into several units in order to halt the King of Sweden at every step. It was during this interview that King Augustus revived the Order of the White Eagle, a feeble device to gain him the support of a few Polish lords, who wanted solid advantages rather than an empty honour which becomes ludicrous when it is bestowed on one by a prince who is king only in name. The conference of the two kings ended in an extraordinary way. The tsar suddenly departed, leaving his troops with his ally, to put down in person a rebellion which threatened to break out in Astrakhan. He had hardly left when King Augustus ordered Patkul to be arrested in Dresden. The whole of Europe was surprised that he should dare, contrary to international law, and apparently against his own interests, to imprison the ambassador of the only prince who protected him.

The secret reason for this act, according to what Maréchal de Saxe, the son of King Augustus, has done me the honour of telling me, was as follows. Patkul, proscribed in Sweden for having upheld the rights of his native Livonia, had been one of King Augustus's generals; but, since his proud and irascible spirit could ill tolerate the arrogance of General Flemming, the king's favourite, who was more irascible and imperious than himself, he had transferred to the service of the tsar, where he was now a general and Russian ambassador to the Saxon Court. Being a man of shrewd intelligence, he discovered that Flemming and the Chancellor of Saxony were proposing to make peace at any price with the King of Sweden. He promptly made a plan to forestall them, and to arrange some agreement between the tsar and Charles XII. The chancellor got wind of his project and obtained leave to arrest him. King Augustus told the tsar that Patkul was a perfidious wretch who had betrayed them both. He was, in fact, guilty only of having served his new master too well, but an ill-timed act of service is often punished as treachery.

.Meanwhile, on one side, the sixty thousand Russians, split up into several small bands, were burning and ravaging the estates of Stanislas's adherents; on the other, General Schulenburg was advancing with his new troops. But fortune favoured the Swedes, who routed these two armies in less than two months. Charles XII and Stanislas attacked the separate units of Russians one after the other, so swiftly that one Russian general was beaten before he heard of the defeat of his colleague.

No obstacle thwarted the conqueror; if there happened to be a river between him and the enemy, Charles and his Swedes swam across it. A Swedish detachment captured Augustus's baggage which contained two hundred thousand crowns in silver coin. Stanislas seized eight hundred thousand ducats belonging to Prince Menzikoff, a Russian general. Charles, at the head of his cavalry, made thirty leagues in twenty-four hours, each rider leading another horse to mount when his own was exhausted. The Russians, panic-stricken and reduced to a small number, fled in disorder to beyond the Dnieper.

While Charles was driving the Russians before him into the heart of Lithuania, Schulenburg at last re-crossed the Oder to offer battle to Field-Marshal Rehnskiöld, reputed the best of Charles XII's generals, who was called 'the Parmenio of the Alexander of the north'. These two illustrious generals, who seemed to share their masters' destiny, met not far from Pulits at a place called Fraustadt, a territory already fatal to Augustus's troops. Rehnskiöld had only thirteen battalions and twenty-two squadrons, amounting in all to some ten thousand men. Schulenburg had twice as many. It should be mentioned that there was a corps of six or seven thousand Russians in his army, men who had been long disciplined and on whom he relied as seasoned soldiers. This battle of Fraustadt took place on the 12th of February 1706; but this same General Schulenburg who, with four thousand men, had, in a way, beaten the King of Sweden, was utterly defeated by General Rehnskiöld. The battle did not last a quarter of an hour. The Saxons put up not a moment's resistance; the Russians threw down their arms as soon as they saw the Swedes; the panic was so sudden and the confusion so great that the victors found seven thousand loaded muskets which had been flung down on the battlefield without being fired. Never had a rout been swifter, more complete and more ignominious; yet never had a general disposed his forces better, as all the Swedish and Saxon officers admitted, than Schulenburg had at Fraustadt. They saw on that day how little human prudence can master events.

Among the prisoners was an entire regiment of Frenchmen. These unfortunate men had been captured by the Saxons at that famous battle of Hochstedt, so disastrous to Louis XIV. They had subsequently entered the service of King Augustus, who had formed them into a regiment of dragoons, under the command of a Frenchman of the Joyeuse family. The colonel was killed in the first, or rather the only, charge of the Swedes, and the entire regiment became prisoners of war. On that very day, these Frenchmen asked if they might serve Charles XII, and they were taken into his service by an extraordinary fate which destined them to yet another change of conqueror and master.

As for the Russians, they begged for life on their knees, but they were brutally massacred more than six hours after the battle, to punish them for the atrocities of their compatriots, and to get rid of these prisoners whom the victors would not have known what to do with.

Augustus now found himself without resources: all he had left was Cracow, where he had shut himself up with two Russian regiments, two Saxon ones and a few troops of the crown army, whom he even feared might hand him over to the enemy; but his misfortune reached its height when he learnt that, on the 1st of September 1706, Charles XII had at last entered Saxony.

He had crossed Silesia without even deigning to warn the Court of Vienna. Germany was thrown into consternation; the Diet of Ratisbon, which represents the empire, but whose resolutions are often as ineffective as they are solemn, declared the King of Sweden an enemy of the empire if he crossed the Oder with his army: this very declaration decided him to march into Germany all the sooner.

At his approach people abandoned their villages and fled in all directions. He dealt with them as he had done with the inhabitants of Copenhagen. He had it proclaimed everywhere that he had only come to grant peace; that all those who returned to their homes and paid the taxes he ordered would be treated as his own subjects, and the others relentlessly pursued. This announcement by a prince who had never been known to break his word made all those who had fled in terror come flocking back to their homes. He set up his camp at Alt-Ranstadt, near the plain of Lützen, the battlefield famous for the victory and death of Gustavus-Adolphus. He went to see the place where this great man had been killed, and when he had been shown the spot, he said: 'I have tried to live as he did, perhaps one day God will grant me as glorious a death.'

From this camp, he ordered the Estates of Saxony to hold a session and to send him without delay the records of the electorate's finances. As soon as he had them in his possession and knew exactly how much Saxony could supply, he levied a tax on it of six hundred and twenty thousand rix-dollars a month. In addition to this contribution, the Saxons were obliged to provide every Swedish soldier with two pounds of meat, two pounds of bread, two pots of beer, and fourpence a day, as well as fodder for the cavalry. Having thus fixed the contributions, the king inaugurated a new policy to protect the Saxons from any offensive behaviour by his soldiers; he ordered that, in all the towns where he had stationed a garrison, every householder on whom the soldiers were billeted, should give monthly certificates of their conduct, without which the soldier could not draw his pay. Moreover, inspectors went from house to house every fortnight, to inquire whether the Swedes had done any damage. They saw to it that the hosts were compensated and the culprits punished.

One knows what strict discipline Charles XII imposed on his troops; that they did not pillage towns taken by assault without permission, that they even pillaged in an orderly way, and desisted at the first command. The Swedes still boast today of the discipline they observed in Saxony, and yet the Saxons complained of the appalling ravages they committed; contradictions which it would be impossible to reconcile, did one not know how differently men see the same things. It would be very hard to believe that the victors did not sometimes abuse their privileges or the vanquished sometimes regard the slightest pilfering as barbarous brigandry. One day, when the king was riding near Leipzig, a Saxon peasant threw himself on his knees before him, imploring redress against a soldier who had just made off with what was destined for his family's dinner. The king summoned the soldier to him. 'Is it true,' he asked sternly, 'that you have robbed this man?' 'Sire,' said the soldier, 'I have not done him as much harm as you have done his master. You have taken a kingdom from him, and all I took from this yokel was a turkey.' The king gave the peasant ten ducats with his own hand and forgave the soldier for the sake of his bold and witty retort, saying: 'Remember, my friend, that if I have taken away a kingdom from King Augustus, I have taken none of it for myself.'

The great fair of Leipzig was held as usual; the merchants came to it in complete security; not a Swedish soldier was to be seen at the fair; the King of Sweden's army might have been in Saxony for no other purpose than to watch over the country's safety. Charles ruled over the whole electorate with as absolute power and in as undisturbed tranquillity as in Stockholm.

King Augustus, wandering about Poland, deprived both of his kingdom and his electorate, finally wrote a letter in his own hand to Charles XII to sue for peace. He secretly commissioned Baron Imhof to go and deliver the letter, along with Fingsten, the official spokesman of the privy council, delegating his full powers to both of them and giving them a free hand. 'Go,' he said, in so many words, 'and try and obtain reasonable and Christian terms for me.' He was reduced to the necessity of concealing his overtures for peace and not resorting to the mediation of any other prince, for being then in Poland at the mercy of the Russians, he had good reason to fear that the dangerous ally he was deserting would take revenge on him for submitting to the conqueror. His two plenipotentiaries arrived by night at Charles XII's camp and had a secret audience with him. The king read the letter. 'Gentlemen,' he told the plenipotentiaries, 'you shall have my reply in a moment.' He promptly retired to his study and wrote as follows:

I consent to grant peace on the following conditions, which I am not prepared to alter in any way whatever.

1) That King Augustus renounces the crown of Poland for ever, that he recognizes Stanislas as lawful king, and that he promises never to think of remounting the throne, even after the death of Stanislas.

2) That he repudiates all other treaties, in particular those he has made with Russia.

3) That he sends back the Princes Sobieski, with befitting honour, to my camp, and all prisoners he may have taken.

4) That he delivers up to me all the deserters who have gone over to his service, in particular Johan Patkul, and that he stops all proceedings against those who have left his service to enter mine.

He gave this paper to Count Piper, telling him to negotiate the rest with King Augustus's plenipotentiaries. They were horrified by the severity of these terms. They used what little skill one employs, when one is powerless, to try and mitigate their hardness. They had several conferences with Count Piper. That minister's only reply to all their suggestions was: 'Such is the will of my master, and he never changes his mind.'

While this peace was being secretly negotiated in Saxony, fortune seemed to put King Augustus in a position to obtain a more honourable one and to treat his conqueror on a more equal footing.

Prince Menzikoff, the generalissimo of the Russian armies, came to join him in Poland with thirty thousand men, at a time when he not only did not desire his help, but even feared it. He had with him some Polish and Saxon troops, amounting in all to six thousand men. Surrounded by the army of Prince Menzikoff, with only this small force to defend him, he had everything to fear if his negotiations were discovered. He saw himself simultaneously dethroned by his enemy and in danger of being taken prisoner by his ally. In this critical situation, the army found that one of the Swedish generals, named Meijerfelt, at the head of ten thousand men, was close at hand at Kalisz, near the Palatinate of Posnania. Prince Menzikoff urged King Augustus to engage them in battle. The king, greatly embarrassed, delayed on various pretexts, for, although he had three times as many troops as the enemy, there were four thousand Swedes in Meijerfelt's army and that was sufficient to make the outcome dubious. To provoke a battle with the Swedes during his negotiations for peace and lose it would be to dig his own grave; he therefore decided to send a trustworthy messenger to the enemy general to let him into the secret of these negotiations and to advise him to retreat. But this advice had the very opposite effect of the one he expected. General Meijerfelt thought it was a snare to intimidate him, and, on those grounds alone, he decided to risk the battle.

The Russians that day defeated the Swedes for the first time in a pitched battle. This victory, which King Augustus won almost in spite of himself, was complete: in the midst of his ill fortune, he made a triumphal entry into Warsaw, his former capital, now a ravaged and ruined city, prepared to receive the conqueror, whoever he might be, and to acknowledge the stronger man as its king. He was tempted to seize this moment of prosperity and proceed to Saxony to attack the King of Sweden with the Russian army. But, having reflected that Charles XII was at the head of a hitherto invincible Swedish army; that the Russians would abandon him at the very first rumour of the treaty he had begun to negotiate; that Saxony, his hereditary country, already drained of money and men, would be ravaged by the Russians as well as the Swedes; that the empire, occupied with the war against France, could not help him, and that he would be left stateless, penniless and friendless, he thought it better to yield to the conditions the King of Sweden imposed on him. These conditions became all the harder when Charles learnt that he had attacked his troops during the negotiations. His fury and the pleasure of still further humiliating an enemy who had just defeated him made him even more inflexible on all the articles of the treaty. Thus King Augustus's victory only served to make his situation more unfortunate; something which perhaps had never happened to anyone else.

He had just had the *Te Deum* sung in Warsaw when Fingsten, one of his plenipotentiaries, arrived from Saxony with this peace treaty which deprived him of his crown. Augustus hesitated, but he signed it, and then left for Saxony in the vain hope that his presence might soften the King of Sweden and that his enemy might remember the former alliances between their two houses, and their blood-relationship.

These two princes met each other for the first time at a place called Gutersdorf. Charles XII received his visitor, with marked lack of ceremony, in a room in Count Piper's living-quarters. He was wearing jack-boots and his usual coarse blue cloth uniform with brass buttons, with a piece of black taffeta wound round his neck for a cravat. At his side hung a long sword he had used at Narva, and his hand often rested on its hilt. The conversation ran entirely on his great jack-boots. Charles told King Augustus that he had not taken them off for six years except when he went to bed. These trivialities were the only topics discussed by two kings, one of whom was depriving the other of his crown. Augustus, in particular, appeared to be enjoying the small-talk; his face wore that expression of pleasure and satisfaction which princes and men accustomed to dealing with great matters are able to assume when they are being most cruelly mortified. The two kings dined together twice. Charles always insisted that King Augustus should sit in the seat of honour and pretended to defer to him; but, far from mitigating his demands, he made even harder ones. It was bad enough for a sovereign to be forced to hand over a general who was an allied sovereign's minister; it was a greater humiliation to be obliged to send the crown jewels and archives to his successor, Stanislas; but the final and worst humiliation was to be compelled to congratulate the man who was going to replace him on the throne on his accession to it. Charles demanded that Augustus should write a letter to Stanislas. The deposed king had to be asked more than once, but Charles was determined to have his letter, so he had to write it. Here is a faithful copy, which I have recently seen, of the original which King Stanislas still preserves:

Sire and brother,
We have not thought it necessary to enter into a private correspondence with your majesty; nevertheless, to please his Swedish majesty, and in order that we shall not be accused of being unwilling to satisfy his desire, we hereby congratulate you on your accession to the crown and hope that you will find more faithful subjects in your country than those we left there. Everyone will do us the justice of believing that we have been repaid for all our benefits with nothing but ingratitude, and that the majority of our subjects devoted themselves only to hastening our downfall. We hope that you may not be exposed to such misfortunes, and commit you to God's keeping.

　　　　　　　　　　　　　　　　　Your brother and neighbour,
　　　　　　　　　　　　　　　　　AUGUSTUS Rex

Dresden, 8 April 1707

Augustus had personally to order all his officials no longer to style him King of Poland, and to have the title he was renouncing expunged from public prayers. It did not distress him so much to release the Sobieskis: these princes refused to see him when they left prison; but the sacrifice of Patkul would be a far more costly one. On the one hand the tsar was clamouring for the return of his ambassador; on the other the King of Sweden was demanding, with threats, that he should be surrendered to him. Patkul was then imprisoned in Saxony, in the castle of Königstein. King Augustus thought he could satisfy Charles XII and his own honour at the same time. He sent guards to deliver up this unfortunate man to the Swedish troops; but beforehand he sent the governor of Königstein a secret order to allow his prisoner to escape. Patkul's bad luck defeated the effort that was being made to save him. The governor, knowing that Patkul was very rich, wanted to make him buy his freedom. The prisoner, when informed of King Augustus's intention, still relying on international law, refused to pay for what he thought he ought to obtain for nothing. During this interval the guards ordered to seize the prisoner arrived and immediately handed him over to four Swedish captains, who took him first to the head-quarters in Alt-Ranstadt, where he remained for three months tied to a stake by a heavy iron chain; from there he was conveyed to Casimir.

Charles XII, forgetting that Patkul was the tsar's ambassador, and remembering only that he had been born his subject, ordered the council of war to judge him with the utmost severity. He was sentenced to be broken on the wheel and quartered. A chaplain came to inform him that he must die, but without telling him the manner of his execution. Then this man, who had braved death in so many battles, finding himself alone with a priest, and his courage no longer sustained either by anger or thirst for glory, those great sources of men's intrepidity, shed bitter tears on the chaplain's breast. He was engaged to a Saxon lady named Madame d'Einsiedel, who was well-born, talented and beautiful, and whom he had hoped to marry almost on the very day he was to be executed. He asked the chaplain to visit her and comfort her, and to assure her that he died full of tender affection for her. When he had been led to the place of execution, and saw the wheels and stakes set up, he fell into convulsions of terror and flung himself into the arms of the priest, who embraced him with tears and covered him with his cloak. Then a Swedish officer read aloud a paper, whose words ran thus:

'Be it known that the express order of his majesty, our *most clement* sovereign is that this man, who is a traitor to his country, be broken on the wheel and quartered in atonement for his crimes and as an example to others. Let every man beware of treason and serve his king faithfully.' At those words *most clement sovereign*, Patkul said 'What clemency!' and at those of *traitor to his country*, he said 'Alas, I have served it too well.' He received sixteen blows and suffered the most prolonged and appalling torture imaginable. Thus perished the Emperor of Russia's ill-starred ambassador, General Johan Reinhold Patkul.

Those who saw in him only a subject who had rebelled against his king said that he had deserved his death; those who saw him as a Livonian, born in a province which had privileges to defend, and who remembered that he had left Livonia only to uphold its rights, called him a martyr for his country's liberty. Nevertheless all agreed that as the tsar's ambassador, his person should have been sacred. The King of Sweden alone, brought up on despotic principles, thought he had done no more than an act of justice, while the whole of Europe condemned his cruelty.

Patkul's quartered limbs remained exposed on stakes until 1713, when Augustus, having regained his throne, ordered these evidences of the necessity to which he had been reduced at Alt-Ranstadt to be collected together; they were brought to him in Warsaw, in a box, in the presence of Buzenval, the French envoy. The King of Poland, indicating the box to Buzenval, merely said: 'It contains the limbs of Patkul,' without adding any expression of remorse or pity for his fate, so that none of those present dared say a word on so delicate and painful a subject.

About that time a Livonian named Paykul, an officer in the Saxon troops who had been taken prisoner on the field, had just been sentenced to death by decree of the senate, but he had been condemned only to be beheaded. This difference between the penalty imposed in a similar case, made it all too evident that, in sentencing Patkul to so cruel a death, Charles had been more intent on personal revenge than on just punishment. However that may be, Paykul, after he had been condemned to death, proposed to the senate that if the king would pardon him he would reveal to him the secret of manufacturing gold. He performed his alchemical experiment in prison, in the presence of Colonel Hamilton and the town magistrate, and, whether he really had discovered some useful art, or, as is far more likely, was merely a clever fraud, the gold found in the crucible after the experiment was taken to the mint in Stockholm to be examined by experts. After judicial investigation, such an apparently impressive report of their findings was given to the senate that the queen, Charles's grandmother, ordered Patkul's execution to be postponed until the king, who had been informed of this extraordinary discovery, should send his orders to Stockholm.

The king replied that he had denied his friends' requests to pardon the criminal and that he would never grant for gain what he had refused to grant for friendship. There was something heroic in this inflexibility shown by a prince who really believed that he was being offered the secret of manufacturing gold. When King Augustus was told of it, he said: 'I am not surprised that the King of Sweden should have so little interest in acquiring the philosophers' stone; he has already found it in Saxony.'

When the tsar learnt of the extraordinary peace which King Augustus had concluded at Alt-Ranstadt, in spite of their treaties, and that Patkul, his ambassador plenipotentiary, had been handed over to the King of Sweden in defiance of international law, he bombarded all the courts of Europe with his complaints. He wrote to the Emperor of Germany, to the Queen of England, and to the States-General of the United Provinces of the Netherlands; he called the painful necessity to which Augustus had yielded cowardice and perfidy; he entreated all these powers to intervene to secure the return of his ambassador and prevent the affront which would be offered, in his person, to all crowned heads. He urged them, for the sake of their honour, not to stoop so low as to give the guarantee to the Peace of Alt-Ranstadt which Charles XII was endeavouring to extort from them by threats. The only effect of these letters was to make the power of the King of Sweden even more obvious. The emperor, England and Holland, being then involved in a disastrous war against France, did not consider it expedient to anger Charles XII by refusing the empty formality of guaranteeing a treaty. As for the unfortunate Patkul, not one single power would use its good offices on his behalf, which only shows how little a subject should rely on kings, and how much all kings at that time feared Sweden's.

The tsar's council proposed that he should retaliate on the Swedish officers who were prisoners in Moscow. The tsar refused to consent to a barbarity which might have had such fatal consequences; for there were more Russian prisoners in Sweden than Swedish ones in Russia.

He sought a more effective vengeance. His enemy's main army was in Saxony and out of action. Lewenhaupt, one of the Swedish king's generals, who had remained in Poland at the head of some twenty thousand men, could not guard the frontiers of an unfortified country rife with factions. Stanislas was at the camp of Charles XII. The tsar seized this favourable opportunity and re-entered Poland with over sixty thousand men. He divided them into several corps, and marched, with a flying column, to Leopold, where there was no Swedish garrison. All Polish towns are at the mercy of anyone who presents himself at their gates with troops. He had a diet convoked in Leopold, very similar to the one which had dethroned Augustus.

Poland at that time had two primates, as well as two kings, one nominated by Augustus, the other by Stanislas. The primate nominated by Augustus convoked the Diet of Leopold, to which came all those whom that prince had abandoned by the Peace of Alt-Ranstadt and those whom the tsar's money had won over to his side. The diet proposed to elect a new sovereign. So Poland came within an ace of having three kings, without anyone being able to say which was the real one.

During the discussions in Leopold, the tsar, whose interests were linked with those of the Emperor of Germany through their common fear of the King of Sweden, secretly persuaded him to send him a great many German officers. These arrived from day to day, bringing with them the discipline and experience which considerably increased the efficiency of his forces. He enlisted them in his service by making them handsome presents, and, for the further encouragement of his own troops, he gave the generals and colonels who had fought at the battle of Kalisz, his miniature set in diamonds; the junior officers had gold medals and the privates silver ones. These mementoes of the victory of Kalisz were all struck in his new city of

St Petersburg where the arts prospered as a result of his teaching his troops to strive for fame and glory.

The general confusion, the multiplicity of factions, and the continual ravages in Poland prevented the Diet of Leopold from making any decision. The tsar had it transferred to Lublin. The change of place in no way lessened the trouble and uncertainty in everyone's minds; the diet contented itself with recognizing neither Augustus who had abdicated, nor Stanislas, who had been elected against their will, but they were neither sufficiently bold nor sufficiently united to nominate a king. While these futile debates were going on, the party of the Princess Sapieha, Oginski's party, those who secretly supported Augustus and the new subjects of Stanislas were all fighting each other, pillaging each other's estates, and completing the ruin of their country. The Swedish troops, commanded by Lewenhaupt, one part of which was in Livonia, another in Lithuania and another in Poland, were all searching for the Russian troops. They burnt everything belonging to Stanislas's enemies. The Russians ruined friends and foes alike; nothing was to be seen but towns in ashes and wandering bands of Poles, despoiled of everything they possessed, who equally detested their two kings, Charles XII and the tsar.

King Stanislas left Alt-Ranstadt on the 15th of July 1707, with General Rehnskiöld, sixteen Swedish regiments, and a great deal of money, to appease the troubles in Poland and re-assert his authority by peaceful means. He was acknowledged wherever he went; the discipline of his troops, which made people all the more conscious of the barbarous behaviour of the Russians, won them over to him; his extreme graciousness reconciled nearly all the factions to him; his money bought him the greater part of the crown army. The tsar, fearing lack of provisions for his troops in a country they had devastated, withdrew the operational base of his army to Lithuania, where he had established supply stores. This retreat left King Stanislas to reign in peace over nearly all Poland.

The only person in his realm who then troubled him was Count Siniawski, the commander-in-chief of the crown army, who owed his appointment to King Augustus. This man, who was very able and extremely ambitious, was the head of a third party. He acknowledged neither Augustus nor Stanislas, and, having done everything he could to have himself elected, he contented himself with being a party chief since he could not be king. The crown troops, which had remained under his command, had no pay other than freedom to pillage their own country with impunity. All those who feared these ravages, or who had suffered from them, soon submitted to Stanislas whose power became more firmly established every day.

Meanwhile the King of Sweden was receiving ambassadors from nearly all the princes of Christendom at his camp at Alt-Ranstadt. Some came to beg him to leave the domains of the empire; others would have been only too glad for him to turn his arms against the emperor; there was even a widespread rumour that he intended to join France in order to overthrow the house of Austria. Among all these ambassadors came the famous John, Duke of Marlborough, representing Queen Anne of Great Britain. This man, who had never besieged a town without taking it or fought a battle without winning it, was a favourite at the court of St James's, the leader of a parliamentary party and the most skilful foreign diplomat of his century. His brilliant diplomacy had done as much harm to France as his victorious armies. Fagel, secretary of the States-General and a highly intelligent man, has been heard to say that, more than once, when the States-General had decided to oppose what Marlborough was going to suggest to them, the duke arrived, talked to them in French, a language which he spoke very badly, and persuaded them all to change their mind. Lord Bolingbroke told me this and assured me it was true.

Together with Prince Eugène, his fellow victorious commander, and Heinsius, the grand-pensionary of Holland, he was bearing the whole brunt of the allies' campaigns against France. He knew that Charles was feeling bitter resentment against the emperor and the empire, that he was being secretly solicited by the French, and that if this conqueror embraced the cause of Louis XIV, the allies would be defeated.

It is true that Charles had given his word in 1700 to take no part in Louis XIV's war against the allies, but the duke did not believe any prince would be such a slave to his word as not to break it in the interest of his own aggrandisement. He therefore left The Hague for the purpose of sounding the King of Sweden's intentions. Fabrice, who was with Charles XII at the time, told me that when the Duke of Marlborough arrived, he spoke secretly, not to Count Piper, the prime minister, but to Baron Görtz, who was beginning to share the king's confidence with Piper. He even arrived at Charles XII's quarters in this baron's carriage, and there was a marked chilliness between him and Chancellor Piper. When Piper later presented him to the king, together with the English minister, Robinson, he spoke to him in French; he told him that he would consider himself lucky to be able to learn, under his command, what he had yet to learn of the art of war. The king did not reply to this compliment with any polite remark, and seemed to forget that it was Marlborough who was speaking to him. I even surmise that he thought this great man was too elegantly dressed and looked too little like a soldier. The conversation was tedious and general, Charles speaking Swedish and Robinson acting as interpreter. Marlborough, who was never in a hurry to make his proposals and who, from long habit, had acquired the art of fathoming men and perceiving the connections between their innermost thoughts and their actions, speech and gestures, studied the king closely. Speaking to him of war in general, he thought he discerned in his majesty a natural antipathy to France; he noticed that he spoke with pleasure of the allies' victories. He noticed that whenever he mentioned the name of the tsar, the king's eyes always lit up, as if something had momentarily excited him during his otherwise perfunctory conversation. He noticed, more-over, that a map of Russia was spread out on a table. He needed no more to convince him that the King of Sweden's real intention and only ambition was to dethrone the tsar, as he had already dethroned the King of Poland. He realized that Charles was remaining in Saxony only so that he could impose some rather harsh conditions on the Emperor of Germany. He knew very well that the emperor would accept them and that matters would thus be satisfactorily settled. He left Charles to follow his natural bent, and, satisfied that he had seen through him, he made no proposition to him. These details have been confirmed to me by the Duchess of Marlborough, his widow, who is still alive.

Since few negotiations are concluded without money, and min-isters have sometimes been known to sell their master's hatred or favour, it was believed throughout Europe that the Duke of Marl-borough had succeeded with the King of Sweden only by the timely gift of a large sum to Count Piper; this belief has cast a slur on his reputation which remains to this day. I myself, having, to the best of my ability, traced this rumour to its source, have learnt that Piper had received a moderate sum as a gift from the emperor, through the medium of Count Wratislaw, with his master's permission, but nothing at all from Marlborough. It is certain that Charles was inflexible in his intention to go and dethrone the Emperor of Russia, that he took no counsel from anyone, and that he did not need Count Piper's advice to wreak his long-sought revenge on Peter Alexeiovitch.

Finally, this minister is completely vindicated by the fact that when Charles XII heard that Piper had died in Russia, he had his body transported to Stockholm and gave him a magnificent funeral at his own expense.

The king who had never yet experienced any reverse, or even any set-back in his successful career, thought that it would take him no more than a year to dethrone the tsar, and that he could then retrace his steps and set himself up as the arbiter of Europe, but he wanted first to humiliate the Emperor of Germany.

Baron Stralheim, the Swedish ambassador in Vienna, had had a quarrel, during a banquet, with Count Zobor, the emperor's chamberlain; the latter having refused to drink Charles XII's health, saying sternly that this prince was treating his master too badly. Stralheim had given him the lie and struck him, and, after this insult, had dared to demand reparation from the imperial court. The fear of offending the King of Sweden had forced the emperor to banish his subject, whom he ought to have avenged. Charles XII was not satisfied; he wished Count Zobor to be handed over to him. The Court of Vienna was forced to swallow its pride and hand him over to the king, who sent him back, after keeping him prisoner for a while in Stettin.

In addition, he demanded, contrary to all international law, that fifteen hundred wretched Russians who had escaped his sword and fled to imperial territory should be delivered up to him. Once again the Court of Vienna had to accede to this extraordinary demand, and, if the Russian ambassador in Vienna had not cleverly arranged for them to escape by different routes, they would all have been handed over to their enemies.

The third and last of his demands was the most exorbitant. He proclaimed himself the protector of the emperor's protestant subjects in Silesia, a province belonging to the house of Austria, not to the empire. He wished the emperor to grant them the liberties and privileges which had, in fact, been established by the Treaty of Westphalia, but abolished, or, at least, evaded, by that of Ryswick. The emperor, whose one desire was to get rid of so dangerous a neighbour, yielded once more and granted him all he wanted. The Lutherans in Silesia acquired more than a hundred churches which the catholics were obliged to cede to them by this treaty, but many of these concessions, which the King of Sweden secured for them when his fortunes were at their height, were wrested from them as soon as he was no longer in a position to impose laws.

The emperor who made these forced concessions and yielded to Charles XII's will in everything was named Joseph; he was the eldest son of Leopold, and the brother of Charles VI, who succeeded him. The then papal legate to the Court of Vienna severely rebuked Joseph for having sacrificed the interests of his own religion to those of heretics. 'It is very lucky for you,' replied the emperor, with a smile, 'that the King of Sweden did not propose that I should turn protestant, for, if he had wished it, I do not know what I should have done.'

Count Wratislaw, his ambassador to Charles XII, brought the treaty in favour of the Silesians, signed by his master, to Leipzig. Charles then said that he was the emperor's best friend; nevertheless he was resentful that Rome had thwarted him as much as it could. He despised the weakness of this court, which nowadays has half Europe as its irreconcilable enemy, yet still mistrusts the other half and only maintains its credit by skilful diplomacy, but all the same he wanted to take revenge on it. He told Count Wratislaw that in the past the Swedes had subjugated Rome, and that they had not degenerated as she had. He warned the pope he would one day demand him to return the property which Queen Christina had left behind in Rome. No one knows how far this young conqueror would have carried his resentment and his arms, had fortune favoured his designs. Nothing at that time seemed to him impossible; he had even secretly sent several officers into Asia and as far away as to Egypt to draw up plans of cities and inform him of the military strength of those countries. It is certain that if anyone could have overthrown the Persian and Turkish empires and then gone on to invade Italy, it was Charles XII. He was not only as young, warlike and adventurous as Alexander but also more indefatigable, robust and abstemious; perhaps, too, the Swedes were better men than the Macedonians. But such projects, which are called sublime when they succeed, are regarded as mere chimeras when they fail.

Finally, all the difficulties having been smoothed out, all his commands executed, after having humiliated the emperor, laid down the law in the empire, protected his protestant religion in the midst of catholics, dethroned one king and crowned another, and seeing himself the terror of all princes, he prepared to depart. The amenities of Saxony, where he had remained idle for a whole year, had not made him relax his austere mode of life in the slightest degree. He rode three times a day, got up at four in the morning, dressed himself unaided, never drank wine, never sat more than a quarter of an hour at table, drilled his troops every day and indulged in no other pleasure than that of making Europe tremble.

The Swedes still did not know where the king intended to lead them. The army merely suspected that Charles might be going to Moscow. A few days before his departure, he ordered his commander-in-chief to give him, in writing, the route from Leipzig to . . . He paused a moment at this word, and for fear that the field-marshal might guess something of his plans, added with a smile: 'to all the capitals of Europe.' The field-marshal brought him a list of all these routes, and purposely put at the top one headed in large letters: *Route from Leipzig to Stockholm.* The majority of the Swedes longed only to return there, but the king was very far from thinking of letting them go back home. 'I see where you would like to lead me,' he told the field-marshal, 'but we shall not be returning to Stockholm so soon.'

The army was already on the march, and passing near Dresden, when Charles, riding at its head, and as usual two or three hundred paces ahead of his guards, suddenly disappeared from their view. Some officers dashed ahead at full gallop to find out where he could possibly be; they rode in all directions but could not find him. In a moment the whole army was in a state of alarm; a halt was called, the generals assembled, and there was growing consternation until

finally they learnt from a passing Saxon peasant what had become of
the king.

As he was passing so close to Dresden, he had taken a sudden
fancy to pay a visit to King Augustus. He had entered the town on
horseback, followed by three or four generals. When they were asked
to give their names at the barrier, Charles said his was Carl and that
he was a drabant* and the others used false names too. Count
Flemming, seeing them pass through the barrier, had only just time
to go and warn his master. All the use that could be made of such
an opportunity had already occurred to the minister, but, as he was
speaking of this to Augustus, Charles strode into the room, still
booted and spurred, before Augustus even had time to recover from
his surprise. He was ill at the time and in his dressing-gown, but he
hastily got dressed. Charles breakfasted with him, like a traveller
who had come to take leave of a friend, after which he wished to see
the fortifications. During the short time he spent examining them, a
Livonian, proscribed in Sweden, thought that he would never have
a more favourable opportunity of obtaining his pardon. He begged
King Augustus to ask Charles to grant it him, quite convinced that
the King of Sweden would not refuse so slight a favour to a prince
whom he had just deprived of his crown and in whose power he had
put himself. Augustus willingly undertook to deal with the matter.
He was standing a little way away from King Charles, talking to
Hord, one of the Swedish generals. 'I think,' he said with a smile,
'that your master will not refuse me.' 'You don't know him,' retorted General Hord. 'He would rather refuse you here than anywhere else.' This did not deter Augustus from urging the king in
the most pressing terms to pardon the Livonian. Charles refused
in a manner which made it impossible to repeat the request. After
having spent some hours on this strange visit, he embraced Augustus
and departed. When he rejoined his army he found all his generals
still in great consternation; they told him that they had been considering whether they ought to besiege Dresden in case his majesty
had been kept prisoner there. 'You need not have worried,' said the
king. 'They wouldn't dare!' The next day, on receiving the news
that Augustus was holding a council extraordinary in Dresden,
Baron Stralheim exclaimed: 'You'll see, they are discussing what

*A soldier of the body-guard of the Kings of Sweden. (*Translator's note*)

they ought to have done yesterday.' A few days later, Rehnskiöld, while talking to the king, expressed his amazement at this visit to Dresden. 'I trusted to my good luck,' said Charles, 'still, at one moment things looked critical. Flemming was anything but willing for me to leave Dresden so soon.'

BOOK IV

CHARLES finally left Saxony in September 1707, followed by an army of forty-three thousand men, no longer clad in iron, as formerly, but resplendent with gold and silver and enriched with the spoils of the Poles and Saxons. Each soldier carried with him fifty crowns in ready cash, and not only were all the regiments complete but there were several supernumeraries in every company. Besides this army, Count Lewenhaupt, one of his best generals, awaited him in Poland with twenty thousand men; he had yet another army in Finland, and new recruits were coming to him from Sweden. With all these forces, no one doubted that he would dethrone the tsar.

The emperor was then in Lithuania, engaged in re-animating a party which King Augustus seemed to have deserted. His troops, split into several bodies, fled at the first rumour of the King of Sweden's approach. He himself had advised all his generals never to await this conqueror with unequal numbers, and he was well and truly obeyed.

In the midst of his victorious march the King of Sweden received an ambassador from the Turks. The ambassador had his audience in Count Piper's quarters, where official ceremonies always took place. He kept up his master's dignity by living with some outward show of splendour, and the king, who was always worse lodged, worse served, and more plainly dressed than the lowest officer in his army, said that Piper's quarters were his palace. The Turkish ambassador presented Charles with a hundred Swedish soldiers who had been captured by the Kalmucks and sold in Turkey, and whom the sultan had bought back and was sending to the king as the most acceptable gift he could make him. The proud sultan did not make this gesture with any intention of paying homage to Charles XII's glory, but because, as the natural enemy of the Emperors of Russia and Germany, he wished to strengthen himself against them by friendship with Sweden and alliance with Poland. The ambassador congratulated Stanislas on his accession, so that, in a short space of time, this king was acknowledged by Germany, France, England, Spain and Turkey. Only the pope wished to delay acknowledging him until time had settled that crown, of which misfortune might still deprive him, more firmly on his head.

Hardly had Charles given audience to the ambassador of the Sublime Porte than he hastened off in search of the Russians. The tsar's troops had left Poland and re-entered it twenty times in the course of the war; this country, open on all sides and having no strongholds to cut off the retreat of an army, left the Russians free to reappear often on the very spot where they had been beaten and even to penetrate as far into the country as the victor. During Charles's sojourn in Saxony, the tsar had advanced as far as Leopold, in the extreme south of Poland; he was now further north, at Grodno in Lithuania, a hundred leagues from Leopold.

Charles left Stanislas in Poland, to preserve his newly-acquired kingdom against enemies at home and abroad with the aid of ten thousand Swedes and his new subjects; he then put himself at the head of his cavalry and marched towards Grodno, in icy winter weather, in January 1708.

He had already crossed the Niemen, two leagues from the town, before the tsar had any idea that he was on the march. At the first news that the Swedes were coming, the tsar left by the northern gate and Charles entered by the southern one. The king had only six hundred guards with him, the rest having been unable to follow him. The tsar fled with two thousand men, under the impression that an entire army was entering Grodno. He learnt the very same day from a Polish deserter that he had left the town to a mere six hundred men and that the main body of the enemy army was still more than five leagues away. He wasted no time, but sent a detachment of fifteen hundred horse at nightfall to go and surprise the Swedish King in the town. Thanks to the darkness, the fifteen hundred Russians reached the first Swedish outpost without being recognized. This outpost was manned by thirty men, and these thirty on their own stood up to the attacks of fifteen hundred for over ten minutes. The king, who was at the other end of the town, soon galloped up with the rest of his six hundred guards and the Russians fled precipitately. It did not take long for his army to join him nor for him to pursue the Russians. All the Russian corps scattered over Lithuania hastily retreated eastward into the Palatinate of Minsk, near the frontiers of Russia, where their base was. The Swedes, whom the king also split up into different sections, pursued them relentlessly for more than thirty leagues along their escape routes. Those who were fleeing and those who were pursuing made almost daily forced marches, although it was the middle of winter. For a long while all seasons had become alike for Charles's soldiers and those of the tsar; only the terror inspired by the name of King Charles now made the difference between the Russians and the Swedes.

Between Grodno and the Dnieper, going eastwards, lie marshes, deserts and vast forests. There are no victuals to be found in the cultivated areas, for the peasants bury their grain and everything edible that will keep, so that one has to probe the earth with great iron-shod poles to discover these underground stores. The Russians and the Swedes made use of these provisions in turn, but they did not always find them, and when they did, they were insufficient.

The King of Sweden, who had foreseen these difficulties, had brought supplies of biscuit as emergency rations for his army, so that nothing hindered his march. After he had traversed the forest of Minsk, where trees had to be felled all the way to make a path for his troops and baggage, he arrived, on the 25th of June 1708, at the river Beresina, opposite Borislou.

The tsar had assembled the greater part of his forces at this spot and was well entrenched there, with the object of preventing the Swedes from crossing the river. Charles posted a few regiments on the bank of the Beresina opposite Borislou, as if he intended to attempt the crossing in full view of the enemy. At the same time, he took his main army three leagues further up the river, had a bridge thrown over it, and having overwhelmed a corps of three thousand men defending that position, marched straight on the enemy army. The Russians, who were not expecting them, decamped and retreated towards the Dnieper, spoiling all the roads and destroying everything on their way, so as at least to delay the Swedes.

Charles surmounted all the obstacles and continued to advance towards the Dnieper. On his way, he encountered twenty thousand Russians entrenched in a place called Hollosin, behind a marsh which could only be reached by crossing a river. Charles did not wait for the rest of his infantry to arrive before attacking them; he threw himself into the water at the head of his footguards, and crossed the river and the marsh, often up to his neck in water. He had ordered his cavalry, while he was thus making his way to the enemy camp, to go round the marsh in order to attack it in the flank. The Russians, amazed that no barrier could defend them, were subjected to a simultaneous onslaught from the king who was attacking them on foot and from the Swedish cavalry who were charging them from the rear.

This cavalry, having hacked its way through the enemy, joined the king in the midst of the battle. He then mounted a horse, but, soon afterwards, finding a young Swedish noble named Gyllenstiern, of whom he was very fond, wounded and unable to walk, he forced him to take his horse, and continued to command on foot, at the head of his infantry. Of all the battles he had fought, this was perhaps the most glorious; the one in which he braved the most dangers and displayed the greatest ability. It was commemorated by a medal, inscribed on one side: *Sylvae paludes aggeres hostes victi* [Woods, marshes, ramparts, the enemy, all conquered] and, on the other, this quotation from Lucan: *Victrices copias alium laturus in orbem* [The conquerors will remove their forces to another world].

The Russians, pursued everywhere, re-crossed the Dnieper which separates Poland from their country. Charles did not hesitate to follow them; he crossed this great river after them at Mohilou, the last town in Poland, which belonged now to the Poles, now to the tsars; a common fate of frontier towns.

The tsar, who now saw his empire, where he had just begun to establish commerce and the arts, involved in a war which could, in a short space of time, upset all his great plans and even totter his throne, considered negotiating for peace. He risked making some proposals through a Polish nobleman whom he sent to the Swedish army. Charles XII, not accustomed to grant peace to his enemies except in their capitals, replied: 'I will treat with the tsar in Moscow.' When this arrogant reply was reported to the tsar, he said: 'My brother Charles always sees himself as Alexander, but I flatter myself he will not find me a Darius.'

If you follow the course of the Dnieper northward along the frontiers of Poland and Russia, from Mohilou, the place where King Charles crossed that river, you will find yourself thirty leagues from the country of Smolensk, through which runs the main road from Poland to Moscow. The tsar was fleeing along this road, and the king was pursuing him by forced marches. Part of the Russian rearguard was more than once engaged in hand-to-hand fights with the Swedish vanguard. The advantage was nearly always to the Swedes, but they were weakening themselves by winning these skirmishes which decided nothing and in which they always lost some men.

Near Smolensk, on the 22nd of September in that year 1708, the king attacked a body of ten thousand cavalry and six thousand Kalmucks.

These Kalmucks are Tartars who live between the kingdom of Astrakhan, which belongs to the tsar, and that of Samarcand, the country of the Uzbek Tartars and the birthplace of Timur, famous under the name of Tamburlaine. The country of the Tartars extends to the east as far as the mountains which separate Mongolia from Western Asia. Those who live near Astrakhan are tributaries of the tsar; he claims absolute rule over them, but their nomadic life prevents him from exerting it, so that he treats them as the sultan does the Arabs, sometimes tolerating their brigandry and sometimes punishing it. There are always some of these Kalmucks in the Russian army and the tsar had even succeeded in disciplining them like the rest of his soldiers.

King Charles fell on this army, though he had with him only six cavalry regiments and four thousand foot-soldiers. His first charge, at the head of his Ostrogothian regiment, broke through the Russian lines, and the enemy retreated. The king pursued them over rough, uneven roads, where the Kalmucks lay in ambush; they then suddenly appeared and threw themselves between the regiment in which the king was fighting and the rest of the Swedish army. Immediately both Russians and Kalmucks surrounded this regiment and broke right through to the king. They killed two aides-de-camp who were fighting close beside him. The king's horse was killed under him: an equerry was just offering him another when both equerry and horse were shot dead. Charles fought on foot, surrounded by some officers who immediately rushed to form a bodyguard to protect him.

Several were captured, wounded or killed, or carried far from the king by the crowd which hurled itself on them, till only five men remained near Charles. He had killed more than a dozen enemies with his own hand, without receiving a single wound, thanks to that mysterious good luck which had hitherto accompanied him everywhere and on which he always relied. Finally a colonel named Dahldorf cut his way through the Kalmucks with only a single company of his regiment, and arrived just in time to rescue the king. The rest of the Swedes effectively disposed of the Tartars, and the army reformed its ranks. Charles mounted a horse, and, exhausted as he was, pursued the Russians for two leagues.

The conqueror was still on the high road to the capital of Russia. It is about a hundred of our French leagues from Smolensk, near which this battle took place, to Moscow, and the army had almost run out of provisions. The king was strongly advised to wait until General Lewenhaupt, who was to bring him supplies and a reinforcement of fifteen thousand men, joined him. Not only did the king, who rarely took counsel, not listen to this judicious advice, but to the amazement of the entire army, he left the Moscow road and marched south towards the Ukraine, the land of the Cossacks, situated between Little Tartary, Poland and Russia. This country is about a hundred of our leagues from north to south and almost as much from east to west. It is divided into two almost equal parts by the Dnieper which crosses it, flowing from the north-west to the south-east: the principal town is Baturin, on the little river Sem. The most northerly part of the Ukraine is well cultivated and prosperous; the most southerly, situated near the forty-eighth degree, is one of the most fertile regions in the world, yet one of the barrenest. Bad government prevented its naturally rich soil from being cultivated. The inhabitants of those districts bordering on Little Tartary neither sowed nor planted, because the Tartars of Budriak, Prokop and Moldavia, who are all marauders, would have ravaged their crops.

The Ukraine has always aspired to be free, but, being surrounded by Russia, the dominions of the sultan and Poland, it has had to seek a protector, consequently a master, in one of these three states. She first put herself under the protection of Poland, who treated her too much as a subject nation; later she appealed to the Russians, who did their utmost to reduce her to serfdom. At first the Ukrainians enjoyed the privilege of electing a prince, who was known as the general, but they were soon deprived of this right and their general was nominated by the Court of Moscow.

The man who filled this position at that time was a Polish noble named Mazeppa, who had been born in the Palatinate of Podolia; he had been a page to King John Casimir and had acquired a little learning at his court. In his youth he had had an affair with the wife of another Polish nobleman. When the husband discovered it he had him tied stark naked on the back of a wild horse and let him loose in that state. The horse, which came from the Ukraine, returned there, carrying Mazeppa, half-dead from fatigue and hunger. Some peasants succoured him, and he remained among them for a long time, distinguishing himself in several expeditions against the Tartars. His superior learning gave him great prestige among the Cossacks; finally, his daily-increasing reputation forced the tsar to make him prince of the Ukraine.

One day, when he was dining with the tsar in Moscow, the emperor proposed that he should discipline the Cossacks and make them more obedient subjects. Mazeppa replied that the situation of the Ukraine, and the character of its people, presented insurmountable obstacles. The tsar, who was beginning to get drunk and who was not always in control of his temper, called him a traitor and threatened to have him impaled.

On his return to the Ukraine Mazeppa began to plan a revolt. The appearance of the Swedish army on the frontier shortly afterwards made the project more feasible. He resolved to become independent and to create himself a powerful kingdom out of the Ukraine and the remnants of the Russian Empire. He was a courageous and enterprising man and, in spite of being very old, an indefatigable worker. He made a secret alliance with the King of Sweden, in order to hasten the downfall of the tsar and take advantage of it.

The king gave him a rendezvous near the river Desna. Mazeppa promised to meet him there with thirty thousand men, munitions of war, provisions, and all the immense amount of treasure he possessed. This was why the Swedish army changed the course of its march, to the great regret of all the officers, who knew nothing of the king's treaty with the Cossacks. Charles sent orders to Lewenhaupt to bring his troops and provisions as quickly as possible to him in the Ukraine, where he planned to spend the winter, so that, having secured the allegiance of that country, he could conquer Russia in the following spring. Meanwhile he advanced towards the river Desna which flows into the Dnieper at Kiev.

The obstacles they had hitherto encountered on the route were slight compared with those they met with on this new road. They had to traverse a forest fifty leagues wide and full of swamps. General Lagercron, who was marching ahead with five thousand men and pioneers, led the army astray, thirty leagues too far east of the real road. After four days' marching, the king realized Lagercron's mistake: with difficulty they got back on the right path, but nearly all the artillery and all the waggons remained stuck fast in the mud of the swamps.

At last, after twelve days of such laborious marching, during which the Swedes had eaten what little biscuit they had left, this exhausted and famished army reached the banks of the Desna at the spot where Mazeppa had appointed the rendezvous. But, instead of finding this prince, they found a body of Russian troops advancing towards the opposite bank of the river. The king was amazed, but he decided then and there to cross the river and attack the enemy. The banks of this river were so steep that the soldiers had to be let down on ropes. They crossed the river in their usual way, some on hastily-constructed rafts, the others swimming. The Russian corps which arrived at that very moment was only six thousand strong: it did not resist long, and this obstacle too was surmounted.

Charles advanced into this unknown country, uncertain of his way and of Mazeppa's fidelity: the Cossack appeared at last, but more like a fugitive than a powerful ally. The Russians had discovered and forestalled his plans. They had fallen on his Cossacks and cut them to pieces: thirty of his closest friends had been captured in the fray and suffered the agonizing death of being broken on the wheel; his towns had been reduced to ashes, his treasures pillaged and the provisions he had prepared for the King of Sweden seized; he had barely managed to escape with six thousand men and a few horses laden with gold and silver. Nevertheless, he brought the king the hope of maintaining his troops in this unknown country, because of his knowledge of it and because all the Cossacks were devoted to him. Enraged against the Russians, they soon began to arrive at the camp in flocks, bringing much-needed provisions with them.

Charles hoped that at least his own general, Lewenhaupt, would come and repair this ill fortune. He was to bring about fifteen thousand Swedes, who would be more useful than a hundred thousand Cossacks, as well as supplies of ammunition and food. He arrived almost in the same state as Mazeppa.

He had already crossed the Dnieper above Mohilou and had advanced twenty leagues beyond it on the road to the Ukraine, bringing the king a convoy of eight thousand waggons, together with the money he had levied in Lithuania on his way. When he had almost reached the town of Lesno, near the spot where the rivers Pronia and Sossa unite to flow, much further down, into the Dnieper, the tsar suddenly appeared at the head of nearly forty thousand men.

The Swedish general, who had less than sixteen thousand, had no intention of retreating. So many victories had given the Swedes such great self-confidence that they never required to know their enemies' numbers, but only where they were. Lewenhaupt therefore marched against them without a moment's hesitation, on the afternoon of the 7th of October 1707. In the first assault, the Swedes killed fifteen hundred Russians. The tsar's soldiers panicked and fled in all directions. The tsar saw that, in a moment, he was going to be utterly defeated. He realized that the safety of his empire depended on this day, and that he was lost if Lewenhaupt rejoined the King of Sweden with a victorious army.

As soon as he saw his troops beginning to retreat, he galloped back to the rearguard, which was composed of Cossacks and Kalmucks: 'I order you,' he told them, 'to shoot anyone who runs away and even to kill me should I be so cowardly as to retreat.' He then returned to the vanguard and rallied his troops himself, aided by Prince Menzikoff and Prince Gallitzin. Lewenhaupt, who had urgent orders to rejoin his master, preferred to continue his march, rather than renew the battle, thinking he had done enough to discourage the enemy from pursuing him.

The very next morning the tsar attacked him at the edge of a swamp and extended his lines to surround him. The Swedes faced up to the Russians everywhere and stood their ground; the battle lasted two hours, with both sides fighting equally stubbornly. The Russians lost three times as many men, but not one retreated, and victory was still undecided.

At four o'clock General Bayer brought the tsar reinforcements. The battle was then renewed for the third time, and raged even more furiously. It lasted till nightfall, when finally sheer force of numbers prevailed. The Swedish ranks were broken and the routed regiments driven back to their baggage-lines. Lewenhaupt rallied his troops behind the waggons; the Swedes were vanquished but they did not flee. Not one of the nine thousand who survived ran away; the general drew them up in battle-order as easily as if they had not been defeated. The tsar spent the night under arms and forbade the officers, under pain of being cashiered, and the privates, under pain of death, to leave the camp to pillage.

At daybreak, he ordered a fresh attack. Lewenhaupt had withdrawn a few miles to an advantageous position, after spiking some of his guns and setting fire to his waggons.

The Russians arrived in time to prevent the entire convoy from being burnt and managed to save over six thousand waggons from the flames as booty. The tsar, who wished to complete the defeat of the Swedes, sent one of his generals, named Phlug, to attack them for the fifth time. This general offered them honourable terms if they would capitulate, but Lewenhaupt refused and launched into a fifth battle, as bloody as the earlier ones. He lost about half of his remaining nine thousand soldiers; the other half closed their ranks and the enemy could not breach them. At last night came on, and Lewenhaupt, after having fought five battles against forty thousand men, crossed the Sossa with the some five thousand soldiers he had left. The tsar lost nearly ten thousand men in these five battles, in which he had the glory of conquering the Swedes and Lewenhaupt that of disputing the victory for three days and of withdrawing without having been forced from his last position. He therefore arrived at his master's camp with the honour of having defended himself so well, but bringing with him neither munitions nor an army. The King of Sweden thus found himself without provisions and cut off from communication with Poland, surrounded by enemies, in the midst of a country where he had no resources other than his courage.

In these dire straits, the memorable winter of 1709, which was even more terrible on those frontiers of Europe than it was in France, destroyed part of his army. Charles was determined to brave the seasons as he braved his enemies; he risked taking his troops on long marches in this freezing weather. It was on one of these marches that two thousand men fell dead of cold before his eyes. The cavalrymen no longer had any boots; the foot-soldiers had no shoes and hardly any clothes. They were reduced to making themselves some sort of footgear from the skins of animals. They had been forced to throw nearly all their guns into marshes and rivers, for lack of horses to draw them. This army, formerly so flourishing, was reduced to twenty-four thousand men on the verge of starvation. They could no longer get any news from Sweden or send any back there. Only one officer complained of this state of affairs. 'Why, are you worried at being so far from your wife?' the king said. 'If you are a true soldier, I will lead you so far that you will hardly be able to get news from Sweden once in three years.'

The Marquis de Brancas, who was later ambassador to Sweden, told me that a private dared, in the presence of the entire army, to show the king a piece of black mouldy bread, made of barley and oats – the only food they had, and little enough even of that – protesting it was not fit to eat. The king took the piece of bread from his hands, ate every morsel of it and then calmly said to the soldier: 'It is not good, but it is edible.' This characteristic act, trivial enough in itself – though nothing which increases respect and confidence is trivial – contributed more than anything else to make the Swedish army able to bear hardships which would have been unendurable under any other general.

In this situation, he at last received news from Stockholm; it was to tell him of the death of his sister, the Duchess of Holstein, who had died of smallpox in December 1708, in her twenty-seventh year. She was a princess as gentle and compassionate as her brother was imperious in his will and ruthless in his vengeance. He had always been very fond of her, and he was all the more afflicted by her loss, because he was beginning to experience misfortune and this made him a little more sensitive.

He also learnt that they had raised troops and money, in obedience to his orders; but nothing could reach his camp, because between him and Stockholm there were nearly five hundred leagues to traverse and enemies in superior numbers to combat on the way.

The tsar, who was as active as himself, after sending fresh troops to assist the confederates in Poland united against Stanislas, under General Siniawski, soon advanced into the Ukraine, in the depths of this bitter winter, to confront the King of Sweden. There he pursued his policy of weakening the Swedes by small engagements, convinced that in the end the Swedish army would be entirely destroyed because it could not be recruited. The cold must have indeed been excessive, for the two enemies were forced to grant each other a truce. But as early as the 1st of February they began to fight each other again in the midst of ice and snow.

In April, after several small engagements and some defeats, the king found himself with only eighteen thousand Swedes left. Mazeppa alone kept them supplied with the bare means of subsistence; without this help, the army would have perished of hunger and want. At this juncture the tsar proposed to Mazeppa that he should submit himself once more to his rule, but the Prince of the Cossacks was faithful to his new ally, whether because the appalling punishment of the wheel that his friends had suffered made him fear for himself, or whether because he wished to avenge them.

Charles, with his eighteen thousand Swedes, had abandoned neither the project nor the hope of getting to Moscow. Towards the end of May he set out to besiege Poltava, on the river Vorskla, at the eastern extremity of the Ukraine, a good thirteen leagues from the Dnieper. This is the land of the Zaporavians, the strangest people on earth; they are a motley collection of former Russians, Poles and Tartars, all professing a kind of Christianity, but devoting themselves wholly to brigandage and plunder. They elect a chief, whom they frequently depose or assassinate. They allow no women to live among them, but they kidnap all the children for twenty or thirty leagues round and bring them up in their ways. In the summer they are always out-of-doors, but in winter they sleep in vast barns which accommodate four or five hundred men. They fear nothing; they live free; they risk death to gain the smallest booty, with the same intrepidity with which Charles XII braved it in order to give away crowns. The tsar gave them sixty thousand florins in the hopes that they would take his side; they took his money, but thanks to Mazeppa, they declared for Charles XII. However, very few joined his army, as they think it ridiculous to fight for anything but booty. The great thing was that they did no harm to the Swedes, though only two thousand of them at the most enlisted as soldiers. Ten of their chiefs were introduced to Charles one morning, but it was very difficult to make them agree to be sober, as they always begin the day by getting drunk. They were taken to a trench, where they displayed their skill in shooting with long carbines; standing on its outer edge, they killed the enemies they selected as targets at a distance of six hundred paces. Charles added to these bandits some thousand Wallachians, sold to him by the Khan of Little Tartary. He besieged Poltava with all these troops of Zaporavians, Cossacks and Wallachians, which, with his eighteen thousand Swedes, made up an army of some thirty thousand men, but it was a ramshackle army, lacking everything it needed. The tsar had made Poltava a supply depot. If the king took it the way to Moscow would be open to him again, and he would at least have abundant supplies while he waited for the help he still hoped for from Sweden, Livonia, Pomerania and Poland. His one resource, therefore, was to capture Poltava, and he threw all his energy into the siege. Mazeppa, who had spies in the town, assured him that he would soon be master of it. Hope revived in the army; the soldiers saw the capture of Poltava as the end of all their miseries.

The king realized, right from the beginning of the siege, that he had taught his enemy the art of warfare. In spite of all his precautions, Prince Menzikoff managed to get reinforcements into the town, bringing the garrison up to nearly five thousand.

They made sorties, sometimes successfully, and exploded a mine; but what made their town impregnable was the approach of the tsar, who was advancing with seventy thousand soldiers. Charles XII went out to meet them on the 27th of June, his birthday, and defeated one of their detachments; but, as he was returning to his camp, a shot pierced his boot and shattered his heelbone. No one saw the slightest change in his face to make them suspect he had been wounded; he went on calmly giving orders and remained another six hours on horseback. One of his servants, noticing that the sole of his boot was dripping blood, ran to fetch surgeons. By the time they arrived the pain was becoming so agonizing that they had to help him dismount and carry him into his tent. The surgeons examined his wound and decided that the leg must be amputated. The consternation of the army was indescribable. But one of the surgeons, named Neuman, who was bolder and more skilful than the others, was convinced that by making deep incisions he could save the king's leg. 'Get to work at once then,' said the king. 'Cut boldly and don't be afraid.' He held his leg himself in both hands, watching the incisions being made as if the operation were being performed on someone else.

Even while they were putting a dressing on the wound, he ordered an assault for the next day, but hardly had he given this order than news was brought to him that the entire enemy army was advancing on him. Another decision had then to be made. Charles, wounded and incapacitated for action, realized that he was trapped between the Dnieper and the river that flows past Poltava, in a desert region without strongholds or means of supply, and confronted with an army which cut off his retreat and his one hope of obtaining provisions. In this extremity, he did not summon a council of war, as so many accounts have alleged, but during the night of the 7th-8th of July, he summoned Field-Marshal Rehnskiöld to his tent and unhesitatingly, and apparently without a qualm, ordered him to make all preparations to attack the tsar the next day. Rehnskiöld did not argue, but went off at once to obey. At the door of the king's tent he met Count Piper, with whom he had long been on bad terms, as often happens between a minister and a general. Piper asked him if there was any news. 'No,' said the general coldly, and pushed past him to go and give his orders. As soon as Count Piper entered the tent the king asked him: 'Has Rehnskiöld told you anything?' 'Nothing,' replied Piper. 'Well then,' the king went on, 'I tell you that tomorrow we go into battle.' Count Piper was alarmed by such a desperate resolve, but knowing that nothing ever made his master change his mind, he registered his surprise only by silence, and left Charles to sleep till daybreak.

It was on the 8th of July 1709 that this decisive battle of Poltava was fought between the two most remarkable monarchs then living: Charles XII, illustrious for nine years of victories: Peter Alexeiovitch for nine years of hard work undertaken in order to create troops equal to the Swedish ones; one famous for having given away kingdoms, the other for having civilized his own; Charles loving danger and fighting only for glory; Peter, not afraid to take risks, but making war only from motives of self-interest; the Swedish monarch liberal from natural generosity, the Russian never giving anything without an ulterior motive; the former outstandingly temperate and abstemious, the latter so addicted to excesses that they actually shortened his life; the Swede, magnanimous by nature, had only once been barbarous; the Russian had never thrown off the barbarity of his education and his race and was as much dreaded by his subjects as he was admired by foreigners. Charles had the title of 'Invincible' which he might lose any moment; the nations had already dubbed Peter Alexeiovitch 'the Great', a title which he could not lose through a defeat since he did not owe it to victories.

To have a clear idea of this battle and of the terrain on which it was fought, one must picture Poltava to the north, the King of Sweden's camp to the south and slightly to the east, with his baggage-lines about a mile behind him, and the Poltava river north of the town, flowing from east to west.

The tsar had crossed the river a league from Poltava, on the western side, and was beginning to set up his camp.

At daybreak the Swedes emerged from their trenches, with only four cannons for artillery; the rest were left in the camp, with about three thousand men. Four thousand remained in the baggage-lines, so that the Swedes marched against the enemy with some twenty-one thousand men, of whom about sixteen thousand were Swedish.

Generals Rehnskiöld, Roos, Lewenhaupt, Slipenbach, Hord, Sparre, Hamilton and the Prince of Würtemberg, a relative of the king's, and some others, most of whom had been at the battle of Narva, all reminded the junior officers of that day when eight thousand Swedes had destroyed an army of eighty thousand Russians in an entrenched camp. The officers told the privates of it, and they all encouraged each other as they marched.

The king led the march, carried in a litter at the head of his infantry. Part of the cavalry advanced, by his order, to attack the enemy's. The battle began with this engagement, at four o'clock in the morning. The enemy cavalry was on the west, to the right of the Russian camp: Prince Menzikoff and Count Gollovin had disposed it at intervals between redoubts fortified with cannons. General Slipenbach, at the head of the Swedes, fell on this cavalry. All those who had served in the Swedish troops knew that it was almost impossible to withstand the fury of their first charge. The Russian squadrons were broken and routed. The tsar himself rushed into the fray to rally them; his hat was pierced by a bullet; Menzikoff had three horses killed under him; the Swedes shouted 'Victory!'

Charles did not doubt that the battle was won; in the middle of the night he had sent General Creutz with five thousand dragoons to take the enemy in the rear while he was attacking their front, but as ill luck would have it, Creutz missed his way and did not appear. The tsar, who thought all was lost, had time to rally his cavalry. He counter-attacked, and the king's cavalry, not being supported by Creutz's detachment, was routed in turn; Slipenbach was even taken prisoner in this engagement. At the same time, seventy-two cannons fired from the camp on the Swedish cavalry and the Russian foot emerged from their trenches and attacked Charles's infantry.

The tsar then detailed Prince Menzikoff to station himself between Poltava and the Swedes: the prince executed his master's order so promptly and efficiently that not only did he cut the communication lines between the Swedish army and the troops who had remained in the camp before Poltava but, having encountered a reserve force of three thousand men, he surrounded it and cut it to pieces. If Menzikoff executed this manoeuvre on his own initiative, Russia owed its salvation to him; if the tsar ordered it, he was a worthy adversary of Charles XII. Meanwhile, the Russian infantry left its lines and advanced in battle-order into the open plain. On the other side the Swedish cavalry rallied itself a quarter of a league from the enemy, and the King, helped by his field-marshal, Rehn-skiöld, ordered everything to be prepared for a general engagement.

He drew up his remaining troops in two lines, with his infantry in the centre and his cavalry on both wings. The tsar disposed his army in the same manner; in addition to the advantage of numbers, he had seventy-two cannons, whereas the Swedes had only four and were beginning to run short of powder.

The Russian emperor was at the centre of his army, officially only as a major-general under the command of General Sheremetoff, but, as emperor, he rode all through the ranks, mounted on a Turkish horse, presented to him by the sultan, exhorting the officers and privates and promising each man rewards.

At nine in the morning, the battle re-commenced. One of the first volleys from the Russian artillery killed the two horses bearing Charles's litter; he had two others harnessed, but a second volley smashed the litter and the king was thrown out. Of the twenty-four soldiers who then carried him in relays, twenty-one were killed. The dismayed Swedes lost confidence and, under the constant pounding of the enemy's guns, the first line fell back on the second, and the second fled. In this last action, it was only a line of ten thousand Russian infantry that routed the Swedish army, so much had things changed!

All Swedish writers say that they would have won the battle if no mistakes had been made; but all officers claim that it was a great one to engage in it and a greater one still for Charles XII to have isolated himself, against the wisest advice, in this unknown country, where he was confronted by seasoned enemy troops, not only twice as strong in numbers but with all the resources lacking to the Swedes. The memory of Narva was the main cause of his disastrous defeat at Poltava.

The Prince of Würtemberg, General Rehnskiöld and several other principal officers were already prisoners, the camp before Poltava had been disrupted and everything was in hopeless confusion. Count Piper and some of the chancery officials had left this camp, and, not knowing what to do or what had become of the king, were wandering hither and thither about the plain. A major named Bère offered to lead them to the baggage-lines, but the clouds of dust and smoke which covered the plain made them lose all sense of direction and they were led straight to the counterscarp of the town itself, where they were all captured by the garrison.

The king was most unwilling to flee, but he was disabled and defenceless. He had with him, at that moment, General Poniatowski, a man of outstanding merit, who had been a colonel in King Stanislas's Swedish Guard and whose personal attachment to Charles had induced him to follow him to the Ukraine, without any position of command. He was a man who, in all emergencies and in all dangerous situations, where others at the most show courage, always made up his mind on the spot, and well and wisely. He beckoned two soldiers, who lifted the king by his armpits and put him on a horse, in spite of the agonizing pain of his wound.

Poniatowski, although he had no official command in the army, became a general on this occasion through sheer necessity. He rallied five hundred cavalrymen, some of them officers, some ordinary troopers, round the king's person; this band, inspired with new heart by the plight of their prince, cut a way through more than ten Russian regiments and escorted Charles, in the midst of his enemies, a league's distance to the baggage-lines of the Swedish army.

The king, fleeing and pursued, had his horse killed under him; Colonel Gieta, wounded and bleeding to death, gave him his. Thus, this conqueror who had been unable to mount a horse during the battle, was twice put on the back of one during his flight.

This amazing retreat rescued Charles from immediate danger, but it was necessary to flee further. Among the baggage they found Count Piper's carriage (the king had never had one since he left Stockholm); they put him in this and, without a moment's delay, took the road to the Dnieper. The king, who had not uttered a word from the moment when they lifted him on to a horse till he arrived at the baggage-lines, then asked what had become of Count Piper. 'He has been captured, along with all the chancery,' he was told. 'And General Rehnskiöld and the Duke of Würtemberg?' he enquired. 'They are prisoners too,' said Poniatowski. 'Prisoners of the Russians!' exclaimed Charles, with a shrug. 'Come then, let us rather be taken by the Turks!' Yet his face showed no sign of despondency, and anyone unaware of his situation who had seen him at that moment would never have suspected that he was a defeated and wounded man.

While he was escaping the Russians seized his artillery in the camp before Poltava, his baggage and his war-chest, in which they found six million in specie, the spoils of Poland and Saxony. Nearly nine thousand of the Swedes and Cossacks had been killed in the battle, and about six thousand captured. There still remained about sixteen thousand men, Swedes, Poles and Cossacks, who were fleeing towards the Dnieper, led by General Lewenhaupt. He marched by one road with his escaping troops; the king by another, with a few horsemen. The carriage he was in broke down on the way, and he was put back on a horse. To crown his misfortunes, he got lost one night in a wood. In this plight, his courage could no longer make up for his exhausted strength, and fatigue made the pain of his wound even harder to bear. Finally his horse fell, too tired to rise, and he was forced to dismount and rest it. He lay down for some hours at the foot of a tree, in danger of being surprised at any moment by the Russians who were searching for him everywhere.

At last, on the night of the 9th-10th July, he found himself on the banks of the Dnieper, where Lewenhaupt had just arrived with the remains of the army. It was with a mixture of joy and sorrow that the Swedes once more saw their king whom they believed dead. The enemy was approaching; they had neither a bridge to cross the river, nor time to make one, nor powder to defend themselves, nor provisions to prevent an army which had not eaten for two days from dying of hunger. Nevertheless, the remains of this army were Swedes, and this defeated king was Charles XII. Nearly all the officers believed that they would stand their ground and await the Russians and conquer or die on the banks of the Dnieper. No doubt this is what Charles would have decided to do, had he not been so utterly weak and exhausted. His wound was suppurating and he was feverish. Now it has been observed that the majority of the most intrepid men, when they are suffering from the fever caused by a suppurating wound, lose that instinctive courage which, like other virtues, demands a clear head. Charles was no longer himself: this is what I have been assured and what is most probable. They carried him away like a sick man who is barely conscious. Luckily they still had a wretched calash which they had brought as far as this, at great risk; they loaded it on to a little ship, and put the king in another, with General Mazeppa. The latter had rescued several coffers full of silver, but as the current was very swift and a strong wind was beginning to blow, the Cossack threw three-quarters of his treasure

overboard to lighten the ship. Muller, the king's chancellor, and
Count Poniatowski, a man more necessary to the king than ever
because of his resourcefulness in emergencies, crossed the river in
other boats, together with some officers. Three hundred cavalrymen
and a great many Poles and Cossacks, relying on the excellence of
their horses, risked swimming across the river. Their troops, keeping tight together, resisted the current and breasted the waves, but
all those who tried to cross separately a little lower down were
swept away and drowned. Of all the infantrymen who risked
swimming across not one reached the other bank.

While the remnants of the army were in this dire situation,
Prince Menzikoff was approaching with ten thousand horsemen,
each with a foot-soldier mounted behind him. The corpses of Swedes
who had died on the way of wounds, exhaustion and hunger showed
Prince Menzikoff the route the main body of the escaping army had
taken. He sent a herald to the Swedish general to offer him terms
of capitulation; four general officers were promptly despatched by
Lewenhaupt to accept them. Until that day, sixteen thousand
soldiers of King Charles XII would have attacked the entire forces
of the Russian Empire and died to the last man rather than surrender. But after losing a battle, and fleeing for two days without a
sight of their prince, who had been forced to flee himself, every
soldier's strength was exhausted, and their courage being no longer
sustained by any glimmer of hope, the love of life proved stronger
than valour. Only Colonel Troutfetre, seeing the Russians advancing, started forward with a Swedish battalion to charge them,
hoping to induce the rest of the troops to follow him, but Lewenhaupt was obliged to stop this futile charge. The capitulation was
completed, and the entire army was made prisoners of war. Some
soldiers, in despair at falling into the hands of the Russians, threw
themselves into the Dnieper; two of the brave Troutfetre's officers
killed each other; the rest were made slaves. They all defiled before
Prince Menzikoff and laid their arms at his feet, as thirty thousand
Russians had done nine years earlier before the King of Sweden at
Narva. But, instead of sending back all those Russian prisoners as
Charles had done then, the tsar kept all the Swedes captured at
Poltava.

These unfortunate men were afterwards dispersed throughout

the tsar's realms, particularly in Siberia, a vast province of Great Tartary which stretches eastward to the frontiers of the Chinese Empire. In this barbarous land, where even bread is an unknown commodity, necessity forced the Swedes to exercise their ingenuity and practise any trade or craft of which they happened to have a rudimentary knowledge. Thus all distinctions of wealth and class were abolished; the officer who had not been brought up to any trade was reduced to cutting and carrying wood for the private who had become a tailor, draper, carpenter, mason or goldsmith, and who could gain a livelihood. Some officers became painters, others architects; some taught languages or mathematics and even established schools there which, in time, became so well-known for their excellence that children were sent to them from Moscow.

Count Piper, Charles's prime minister, was imprisoned for a long while in St Petersburg. The tsar was convinced, like the rest of Europe, that Piper had sold his master to the Duke of Marlborough, and had been responsible for the military power of Sweden, which might have brought peace to Europe, being used against Russia; he therefore made the conditions of his captivity harsher. This minister died a few years later in Russia, having received little help from his family who lived in opulence in Stockholm, and none from his king, who, much as he lamented Piper, would never lower himself to offer a ransom for him which he feared the tsar would not accept, for there had never been any agreement for the exchange of prisoners between the two monarchs.

The Russian Emperor took no pains to conceal his jubilation as he received the prisoners who were brought to him in a body on the battlefield, and kept asking every moment: 'Where is my brother Charles?'

He did the Swedish generals the honour of inviting them to his table. Among other questions he put to them, he asked General Rehnskiöld how many troops the king his master had been able to muster before the battle. Rehnskiöld replied that only the king had the list of them, which he never communicated to anyone, but that he personally thought that, in all, it would be about thirty thousand men, to wit sixteen thousand Swedes and the rest Cossacks. The tsar seemed surprised and asked how they could have risked invading such a distant country and laying siege to Poltava with this small force. 'We were not always consulted,' replied the Swedish general, 'but, as loyal servants, we obeyed our master's orders without questioning them.' At this reply, the tsar turned to some of his courtiers, who had formerly been suspected of plotting against him, and exclaimed: 'Now you see how one's sovereign should be served!' Then, raising a glass of wine, he said: 'To the health of our masters in the art of war.' Rehnskiöld asked him who were those whom he honoured with so noble a title. 'You, gentlemen, the Swedish generals,' replied the tsar. 'Then your majesty is very ungrateful to have treated your masters so harshly!' retorted the count. After the meal, the tsar had the swords of all the Swedish generals returned to them and treated them like a prince who wished to give his subjects a lesson in generosity and courtesy. But this same prince, who treated the Swedish generals so well, had all the Cossacks who fell into his hands broken on the wheel.

That Swedish army, which had left Saxony so triumphant, no longer existed; half of it had perished from want and the other half had been massacred or enslaved. Charles XII had lost in one day the fruit of nine years' labours and nearly a hundred battles; he was fleeing in a wretched calash, with Major-General Hord, who had been dangerously wounded, seated beside him; the rest of his troop followed him, some on foot, others on horseback and a few in carts, across a desert where there were neither huts, tents, animals or roads, and where everything, even water, was lacking. It was early in July. This country is in the forty-seventh degree of latitude; the arid sand of the desert made the heat of the sun more intolerable; many horses fell dead and the men were nearly dying of thirst. Towards nightfall they found a muddy stream; they filled leather bottles with this water, which saved the lives of the Swedish King's little troop. After five days' march, he found himself on the bank of the river Hypanis, now called the Bug by the barbarians who have disfigured even the very names of these regions which were once flourishing Greek colonies. This river joins the Dnieper some miles from there and flows with it into the Black Sea.

On the southern side of the Bug lies the little town of Oczakou, the frontier town of the Turkish Empire. The inhabitants, seeing a band of warriors approaching them, dressed in outlandish clothes and speaking an unknown language, refused to let them cross over to Oczakou without an order from Mehemet Pasha, the governor. The king sent a messenger to the governor to ask him to allow them to cross, but this Turk, doubtful as to what he ought to do in a country where a false step often costs a man his life, dared not undertake such a responsibility without having first obtained the permission of the seraskier of the province, who lived at Bender in Bessarabia. While they were waiting for this permission, the Russians who had taken the king's army prisoner had crossed the Dnieper and were approaching to capture Charles himself; finally the Pasha of Oczakou sent word to the king that he would provide a small boat for him and two or three members of his suite. In this critical situation, the Swedes bandied no more words, but took what they wanted by force. A few of them went over to the other bank in a little skiff, seized some boats and brought them back to their own side; this was their salvation, for the owners of the Turkish boats, fearing to lose a chance of making a handsome profit, came over in a body to offer their services: at the very same time the favourable response from the seraskier arrived too. But unfortunately the Russians arrived before they could all get across and the king had the sad sight of five hundred of his followers being seized by his enemies, whose insulting boasts reached his ears on the other bank. The Pasha of Oczakou asked him, through an interpreter, to pardon these delays which had been the cause of the capture of these five hundred men and implored him not to complain about them to the sultan. Charles promised him he would not, but not without reprimanding him as if he had been one of his subjects.

The commander of Bender who was also its seraskier – a title which corresponds to that of general – and pasha of the province, which means its governor and administrator, hastily despatched an aga to present his compliments to the king and offer him a magnificent tent, together with provisions, chariots and a retinue of officers and attendants; everything, in fact, necessary to conduct him in state to Bender, for it is the custom of the Turks not only to defray all the expenses of ambassadors, even the cost of their residence, but to give lavish hospitality to princes who take refuge with them.

BOOK V

ACHMET III then ruled the Turkish Empire; he had been put on the throne in 1703, in place of his brother Mustapha, by a revolution similar to the one in England which had deposed James II and given the throne to his son-in-law William. Mustapha, who was ruled by his mufti, whom the Turks detested, roused the whole empire against him; his army on which he relied to punish the malcontents joined forces with them. He was captured and solemnly deposed, and his brother was taken from the seraglio and made sultan, with hardly a drop of blood being shed. Achmet imprisoned the deposed sultan in the seraglio of Constantinople where he lived on for some years, to the great astonishment of the Turks who are accustomed to see the dethronement of their princes invariably followed by their death.

The new sultan's only reward to those to whom he owed his crown – ministers, generals, officers of the janissaries, in short all who had taken part in the revolution – was to have them all put to death, one after the other, for fear they should attempt a second one. By the sacrifice of so many worthy people he weakened the strength of the empire, but he secured his throne, at least for a few years. After this, he devoted himself to amassing treasure. He was the first of the Ottoman Emperors who ventured to debase the coinage a little and to impose new taxes, but he was obliged to abandon these two enterprises for fear of a rebellion, for the victims of the rapacity and tyranny of the grand seignior are almost invariably the state officials. These, no matter what their rank, are the sultan's domestic slaves; but the rest of the Moslems live in complete security, with no fear for their lives, money or liberty.

Such was the Emperor of Turkey with whom the King of Sweden had come to take refuge. He wrote to him as soon as he was on his territory; his letter is dated 13th of July 1709. Several different copies of it are extant, which are all regarded nowadays as inaccurate, but of all those I have seen, there is not one which was not arrogant in tone and more audacious than befitted a man in his situation. The sultan did not reply to him till towards the end of September. The pride of the Sublime Porte demanded that Charles should be made aware of the difference between the Turkish Emperor and a king of part of Scandinavia, an infidel and a vanquished fugitive. Moreover, all such letters, which are very seldom written by the sovereigns themselves, are only empty formalities which add nothing to one's knowledge of their characters or activities.

Charles XII's situation in Turkey was, in fact, no more than that of an honourably treated prisoner. Nevertheless, he conceived the idea of persuading the Turks to take up arms against his enemies; he flattered himself that he could bring Poland back into subjection and conquer Russia. He had an ambassador in Constantinople, but the man who helped him most in his vast projects was Count Poniatowski, who went to Constantinople unofficially and soon made himself indispensable to the king, agreeable to the Porte and, finally, dangerous to the grand-viziers themselves.*

One of those who most skilfully furthered his plan was a doctor named Fonesca, a Portuguese Jew who had settled in Constantinople; a learned and highly intelligent man, perhaps the only philosopher of his race, and one expert at handling men and affairs. His profession procured him access to members of the Turkish government, and often the confidence of viziers. I knew him very well in Paris, and he confirmed all the details I am about to relate. Count Poniatowski has told me himself that he was clever enough to get letters through to the Sultana Valida, the reigning emperor's mother, who had been ill-used by her son, but who was beginning to gain influence in the seraglio. A Jewess, who often saw this princess, never ceased telling her about the exploits of the King of Sweden and enchanting her with her accounts of them. The sultana,

---

* It is from him that I received not only the *Remarques*, which have been published, and of which the chaplain Nordberg has made use, but also a great many other manuscripts concerning this history.

secretly fascinated, as nearly all women are, by extraordinary men, even if they have never seen them, openly took Charles's part in the seraglio; she always referred to him as her 'lion'. Sometimes she would say to her son, the sultan: 'When are you going to help my lion to devour this tsar?' She even went so far as to infringe the strict rules of the seraglio by writing several letters in her own hand to Count Poniatowski, in whose possession they still are at the time of writing this history.

Meanwhile the king had been conducted in state to Bender, through the desert formerly called the wilderness of the Getae. The Turks took care that nothing should be lacking on his way to make his journey pleasanter. Many Poles, Swedes and Cossacks who had escaped from the hands of the Russians came by different routes to swell his train on the way; by the time he reached Bender he was accompanied by eighteen hundred men; all this crowd of followers, including their horses, was fed and lodged at the expense of the sultan.

The king wished to camp near Bender, instead of remaining in the town. The seraskier, Yussuf-Pasha, had a magnificent tent erected for him, and others were provided for all the nobles in his retinue. Some time later, Charles built a house for himself on this site, his officers followed his example and the soldiers erected barracks, so that imperceptibly the camp became a little town. At first the king had not recovered from his wound and had to have a carious bone extracted from his foot, but as soon as he could mount a horse he resumed all his usual exertions, always getting up before sunrise, tiring out three horses a day, and making his soldiers do their drill. His only amusement was to play an occasional game of chess. Since small things reveal a man's character, it is worth recording that he always moved his king when he was playing; he used it more than any of his other pieces and, as a result, lost all his games.

At Bender he was abundantly supplied with everything, a rare situation for a vanquished and fugitive prince, for besides the more than ample provisions and the five hundred crowns a day he received from the sultan's bounty, he was still drawing money from France, and he was borrowing from the merchants of Constantinople. Part of this money was used to carry on intrigues in the seraglio, to buy the favour of viziers or bring about their downfall; the other part he distributed lavishly among his officers and the janissaries who served as his guards at Bender. Grothusen, his favourite and treasurer, was the dispenser of his bounties; he was a man who, unlike most of those in his situation, enjoyed giving as much as his master did. One day he brought him an account in two lines of how he had spent sixty thousand crowns: 'Ten thousand crowns given to the Swedes and the janissaries by the generous orders of his majesty, and the rest squandered by me.' – 'That is how I like my friends to render me their accounts,' said the king: 'Muller makes me read through whole pages for sums of ten thousand francs; I prefer Grothusen's laconic style.' One of his old officers, suspected of being somewhat miserly, complained to him that his majesty gave everything to Grothusen. 'I only give money to those who know how to make use of it,' replied the king. This generosity often reduced him to having nothing left to give. It would have been just as honourable and more advisable to have been less lavish in his gifts, but it was one of this prince's failings to carry all virtues to excess.

Many foreigners flocked from Constantinople to see him. Neighbouring Turks and Tartars came in crowds, all of whom admired and respected him. His rigid abstinence from wine and his regular attendance twice daily at public prayers made them say: 'He is a true Moslem.' They were burning with impatience to march with him to conquer Russia.

During his life of leisure at Bender, which lasted longer than he expected, he gradually acquired a taste for reading. The person responsible for this was Baron Fabrice, a courtier who had been sent to him from Holstein to look after the interests of its young duke. He was an amiable young man, with that gaiety and ease of manner which princes appreciate and which made him a successful ambassador. Having read all the good French authors himself, he induced the king to read the tragedies of Corneille, Racine, and the works of Despréaux. The king did not care at all for Despréaux's satires, which indeed are not his best works, but he greatly liked his other writings. When someone read him that passage in the *Eighth Satire* where the author calls Alexander a frenzied madman, he tore out the pages.

Of all the French tragedies the one that appealed to him most was *Mithridate*, because the situation of that king, vanquished but breathing vengeance, resembled his own. He pointed out to Fabrice, with his finger, the passages that struck him most, but he would never read any of them aloud or risk uttering a word in French. Even when, later on at Bender, he saw the French ambassador to the Porte, M. Désaleurs, a most able and distinguished man, but who knew no language but his mother-tongue, he replied to him in Latin; and when the ambassador protested that he did not understand a word of that language, rather than speak French, the king sent for an interpreter.

Such were Charles XII's occupations at Bender, where he was waiting for an army of Turks to come to his aid. His ambassador presented requests in his name to the grand-vizier and Poniatowski supported them with the considerable influence he had acquired by his shrewdness. Ingratiation is a method that succeeds everywhere; he never appeared except dressed in Turkish costume and he had access to all the highest in the land. The sultan made him a present of a purse containing ten thousand ducats, and the grand-vizier told him: 'I will take your king by one hand and a sword in the other, and I will lead him to Moscow at the head of two hundred thousand men.' This grand-vizier, Chourlourli-Ali-Pasha, was the son of a peasant from the village of Chourlou. Such an origin is no disadvantage in Turkey, where noble birth is by no means a necessary concomitant of high office; only the services the holder of it renders the state are considered important. This is the custom almost everywhere in the east, a very good and proper custom, if dignities could be conferred only on those who deserved them, but viziers are usually merely the creatures of some black eunuch or favourite concubine.

The grand-vizier soon changed his mind. Charles XII could only negotiate, while the tsar could pay; he did pay, and even used Charles's own money to do so; the war-chest captured at Poltava provided new weapons against the defeated king. There was no longer any question of making war on Russia. The tsar's influence was all-powerful with the Porte; it granted his ambassador privileges which Russian ministers had never before enjoyed in Constantinople; he was allowed to have a seraglio, which means a palace, in the Franks' quarter, and to communicate with foreign diplomats. The tsar even believed that he could demand that Mazeppa should be handed over to him, as Charles had caused the unfortunate Patkul to be handed over to himself. Chourlourli-Ali-Pasha was by now incapable of refusing anything to a prince who gave millions for compliance with his demands: thus this same grand-vizier, who had previously promised to lead the King of Sweden into Russia with two hundred thousand men, was daring enough to suggest to him that he should consent to the sacrifice of General Mazeppa. Charles was outraged by this demand. No one knows to what lengths the vizier could have gone in the matter, if Mazeppa, who was seventy, had not died at that precise moment. The king's sorrow and resentment were increased when he learnt that Tolstoy, the tsar's then ambassador to the Porte, was publicly waited on by Swedes who had been captured at Poltava and forced to become slaves, and that these brave soldiers were being sold every day in the Constantinople market. The Russian ambassador even openly proclaimed that the Turkish troops at Bender were there to make sure that the king did not escape, rather than as a guard of honour.

Charles, abandoned by the grand-vizier, after having been defeated by the tsar's money in Turkey as he had been by his arms in the Ukraine, realized that he had been deluded and slighted by the Porte, and was virtually a prisoner among the Tartars. His followers were beginning to despair; he alone stood firm and seemed not in the least dejected. He believed that the sultan was unaware of the intrigues of his grand-vizier, Chourlourli-Ali-Pasha, and he decided that the sultan should be informed of them. Poniatowski undertook this hazardous task. The sultan goes to the mosque every Friday, surrounded by his Solaks, a kind of bodyguard whose turbans are adorned with such tall plumes that they hide him from the sight of the people. When anyone has some petition to present to the sultan he tries to mingle with this guard and then holds the petition up high; sometimes the sultan deigns to take it himself, but more often he orders an aga to take charge of it, and has petitions presented again when he leaves the mosque. There is no fear that people will dare to importune him with trivial requests, for they write less in a year in Constantinople than in a single day in Paris; still less do they risk writing complaints against ministers, for the sultan usually sends them on to the minister named without reading them. This was the only way Poniatowski had of getting the King of Sweden's complaints through to the sultan; he drew up a strongly worded indictment of the grand-vizier, and M. de Fériol, who was then the French ambassador and who told me these facts, had it translated into Turkish. A Greek was given some money to present it; this Greek mingled with the sultan's guards and held up the paper so high and so persistently and made so much noise that the sultan saw him and took the petition himself.

The only answer the sultan made to Charles XII's complaints was to send him, a few days later, twenty-five Arab horses, one of which had carried His Highness and was caparisoned with a be-jewelled saddle and housings and solid gold stirrups. This present was accompanied by a polite letter, but this was couched in such general terms that it made Charles suspect that the grand-vizier had done nothing without the sultan's consent. Chourlourli, being a practised dissembler, also sent the king five rare horses. Charles said haughtily to the man who brought them: 'Go back to your master and tell him I never accept presents from my enemies.'

Poniatowski, having already dared to get a petition presented against the grand-vizier, now conceived the bold plan of getting him dismissed. Knowing that the sultan's mother disliked Chourlourli and that the kislar-aga, the chief of the black eunuchs, and the aga of the janissaries hated him, he incited all three of them to speak against him. It was an astonishing thing for a Christian, a Pole, an unaccredited agent of a Swedish king who had taken refuge among the Turks, to intrigue almost openly at the Porte against a viceroy of the Ottoman Empire who was, moreover, liked and much esteemed by his master. Poniatowski would never have succeeded, and the mere suspicion of such a project would have cost him his life, had not a power stronger than all those which were working in his interests struck the final blows which brought down Grand-Vizier Chourlourli.

The sultan had a young favourite, who later governed the Ottoman Empire and was killed in Hungary, in 1716, at the battle of Petervaradin, in which the Turks were defeated by Prince Eugène of Savoy. His name was Coumourgi-Ali-Pasha, and his birth was as humble as Chourlourli's: he was the son of a coal-heaver, as Coumourgi signifies, for *coumour* means 'coal' in Turkish. The Emperor Achmet II, the uncle of Achmet III, had met Coumourgi, then only a child, in a little wood near Adrianople, and, struck by his extraordinary beauty, had had him taken to his seraglio. Mustapha, the eldest son and successor of Mahomet, was delighted with him, and Achmet III made him favourite. At that time he only held the office of *Selictar-Aga*, or sword-bearer to the crown; his extreme youth prevented him from aspiring as yet to the rank of grand-vizier, but it was his ambition to become this one day. The Swedish faction had never been able to win over this favourite; he had never been anything but hostile to Charles and all other Christian princes and their ministers but on this occasion he was unintentionally of service to him, by joining with the Sultana Valida and the high officials of the Porte to bring about the downfall of Chourlourli, whom they all hated. This old minister, who had served his master long and well, was the victim of the caprice of a boy and the intrigues of a foreigner. He was deprived of his office and his wealth; his wife, who was the daughter of the former sultan, Mustapha, was taken away from him, and he was banished to Caffa, formerly Theodosia, in Crimean Tartary. The *bul*, that is to say the imperial seal, was given to Numan Couprougli, grandson of the great Couprougli who took Candia. This new vizier was what ill-informed Christians find it hard to imagine a Turk: a man of inflexible virtue and a scrupulous observer of the law, who frequently stood out for justice against the arbitrary will of the sultan. He refused to hear of war against Russia, which he regarded as unjust and futile, but the same respect for law which prevented him from making war on the tsar in defiance of treaties, made him respect the duties of hospitality to the King of Sweden. He told his master: 'The law forbids you to attack the tsar who has committed no offence against you, but it orders you to help the King of Sweden who is an unhappy exile in your land.' He sent the king eight hundred purses (a purse is worth five hundred crowns), and advised him to return peacefully to his own country, either through the German Emperor's domains or by French ships, then in the port of Constantinople, which M. de Fériol, the French ambassador to the Porte, offered Charles to transport him to Marseilles. Count Poniatowski negotiated far more successfully with this new vizier who was too incorruptible to be influenced against him by Russian gold. The Russian faction thought its best plan was to poison so dangerous a negotiator. It bribed one of his servants to put poison in his coffee. The crime was discovered in time to prevent it: the little phial of poison was found in the servant's hands and taken to the sultan. The would-be poisoner was judged in a full session of the divan and sentenced to the galleys, for Turkish law never awards the death penalty for criminal attempts which have failed.

Charles XII, still convinced that sooner or later he would succeed in making Turkey declare war on Russia, refused to accept any of the proposals for his returning peacefully to his own dominions; he persisted in representing the tsar, whom he had so long despised, as a formidable menace to the Turks. His emissaries never ceased trying to persuade them that Peter Alexeiovitch intended to achieve naval supremacy in the Black Sea, and that, after having defeated the Cossacks, he had designs on Crimean Tartary. At times their protestations had some effect on the Porte; at others the Russian ministers rendered them futile.

While Charles was thus letting his fate depend on the caprices of viziers, receiving benefits and slights from a foreign power, and presenting petitions to the sultan on whose bounty he subsisted in a desert, all his sleeping enemies were rousing themselves and attacking his dominions.

The battle of Poltava was the immediate signal for a revolution in Poland. King Augustus returned there, protesting against his abdication and the Peace of Alt-Ranstadt and openly accusing Charles XII, whom he no longer feared, of robbery and barbarism. He imprisoned Fingsten and Imhof, his plenipotentiaries who had signed his abdication, as if in doing so they had exceeded their orders and betrayed their master. His Saxon troops, who had been the pretext for his dethronement, brought him back to Warsaw, accompanied by most of the Polish Palatines, who, having first sworn fidelity to him, then taken the same oaths to Stanislas, were now returning to swear allegiance once more to Augustus. Even Siniawski ranged himself again on his side, and, renouncing the idea of making himself king, was content to remain commander-in-chief of Augustus's army. Flemming, his prime minister, who had been obliged to leave Saxony for fear of being handed over to Charles XII along with Patkul, had then done much, by his diplomacy, to induce the majority of Polish nobles to return to his master.

The pope released his subjects from the oath of allegiance they had sworn to Stanislas. This step of the holy father's was well-timed and, supported by Augustus's forces, had considerable importance; it strengthened the influence of the Roman Curia in Poland where, at that time, people had no wish to dispute the chimerical right of the sovereign pontiffs to interfere in the temporal affairs of monarchs. Everyone was willing to be ruled by Augustus again and no one averse to receiving a meaningless absolution which the papal legate did not fail to represent as necessary.

Charles's power and Sweden's greatness were now on the verge of their final decline. More than ten crowned heads had long watched, with fear and envy, Sweden extending her domination far beyond her natural boundaries, across the Baltic Sea, and from the Dvina to the Elbe. Charles's fall and his absence reawakened all the ambitions and jealousies of these princes which had long been stifled by treaties they were not powerful enough to break.

The tsar, more powerful than all the rest of them put together, exploited his victory to the utmost; he took Viborg and all Karelia, inundated Finland with troops, laid siege to Riga and sent an army into Poland to help Augustus regain his throne. This emperor had now replaced Charles as the arbiter of Poland and the north, but he consulted only his own interests whereas Charles had never sought anything but glory and vengeance. The Swedish monarch had helped his allies and crushed his enemies without demanding the smallest reward for his victories; the tsar, behaving more like a prince and less like a hero, was willing to help the King of Poland only on condition that he ceded Livonia to him and that this province, for which Augustus had started the war, should belong permanently to the Russians.

The King of Denmark, forgetting the treaty of Travendal as Augustus had done that of Alt-Ranstadt, now began to think of making himself master of the Duchies of Holstein and Bremen and renewed his claims to them. The King of Prussia had ancient rights over Swedish Pomerania which he wished to revive. The Duke of Mecklenburg resented seeing Sweden still in possession of Wismar, the most beautiful city of the duchy. This prince was betrothed to one of the Russian Emperor's nieces and the tsar needed only an excuse to establish himself in Germany, in the way the Swedes had done. George, the Elector of Hanover, also sought to enrich himself with Charles's spoils. The Bishop of Munster, too, would have gladly made some claims, had he been powerful enough to do so.

Twelve to thirteen thousand Swedes were defending Pomerania and the other districts Charles held in Germany, which was about to become a theatre of war. This storm alarmed the emperor and his allies. It is a law of the empire that anyone who attacks one of its possessions is regarded as the enemy of the whole German Empire.

What made the situation even more difficult was that all these princes, with the exception of the tsar, were then leagued together against Louis XIV, whose power had for some time been as much of a menace to the empire as that of Charles XII.

At the beginning of the century Germany had found herself caught in a vice between two armies, hard pressed on the south by the French and on the north by the Swedes. The French had crossed the Danube and the Swedes the Oder: if their then victorious forces had combined the empire would have been lost. But the same fatality which overwhelmed Sweden had also humbled France; nevertheless Sweden still had some resources and Louis XIV was still engaged in active though unsuccessful warfare. If Pomerania and the Duchy of Bremen became the theatre of war, it was feared that the empire would suffer and, being weakened on that side, would not be strong enough to withstand Louis XIV. To prevent this danger the German princes, Queen Anne of England and the States-General of the United Provinces concluded at the end of 1709, at The Hague, one of the most extraordinary treaties ever signed.

It was stipulated by these powers that the war against the Swedes should not be waged in Pomerania or in any other German province, but that the enemies of Charles XII might attack him anywhere else. The King of Poland and the tsar themselves acceded to this treaty and had a clause inserted in it which was as extraordinary as the treaty itself; this was that twelve thousand Swedes who were in Pomerania could not leave it to defend the other provinces.

To guarantee the implementation of this treaty it was proposed to raise an army to preserve this imaginary neutrality. It was to encamp on the banks of the Oder. The idea of levying an army to prevent a war was certainly a strange one, since even those who were to pay it had, for the most part, considerable interest in waging this war which they claimed to wish to avoid. The treaty stated that this army would be composed of the troops of the emperor, the King of Prussia, the Elector of Hanover, the Landgrave of Hesse and the Bishop of Munster.

This project was, as one would naturally have expected, never carried out. The princes who were supposed to contribute their contingents to this army provided none; not even two regiments were mustered. There was much talk of neutrality, but no one maintained it, and all the princes of the north who had bones to pick with Charles XII remained completely free to quarrel among themselves over the spoils of the Swedish King.

At this point, the tsar, after leaving his troops stationed in Lithuania and ordering the siege of Riga to be continued, returned to Moscow to regale his people with a spectacle unlike anything he had ever provided for them before: a triumph which vied in splendour with those of the ancient Romans. He made his entry into Moscow (1 January 1710) under seven triumphal arches erected in the streets and adorned with everything the region could provide and all that the flourishing trade he had established could supply to decorate them. A regiment of guards headed the procession, followed by pieces of artillery captured from the Swedes at Lesno and Poltava, each one drawn by eight horses draped in scarlet housings that hung to the ground: next came the standards, kettle-drums and colours taken in these two battles, carried by the officers and privates who had captured them; all these spoils were followed by the tsar's finest troops. When they had filed past, there appeared, displayed on a chariot specially built for that purpose,* Charles XII's litter which had been found on the battlefield, shattered by two cannon-balls. Behind this litter marched all the prisoners, two by two; their ranks included Count Piper, the Prime Minister of Sweden, the famous Field-Marshal Rehnskiöld and Generals Slipenbach, Stackelberg and Hamilton, as well as all the officers and privates who were later dispersed all over Russia. The tsar appeared immediately after them,

---

* M. Nordberg, Charles XII's confessor, reproves the author here and asserts that this litter was carried by hand. On these vital matters we rely on those who actually witnessed the event.

mounted on the horse he had ridden at the battle of Poltava. Close behind him were the generals who had had a share in the success of that day; another regiment of guards followed them and the Swedes' ammunition-waggons brought up the rear.

This splendid procession filed past to the pealing of all the bells of Moscow and the sound of drums, kettle-drums and trumpets, and of innumerable musical instruments which echoed their strains. Salvoes were fired from two hundred cannon and the streets were lined with a cheering crowd of five hundred thousand, who shouted: 'Long live our father, the emperor!' every time the tsar paused for a moment during this triumphal entry.

This imposing spectacle increased his subjects' veneration for him and perhaps impressed them more with his greatness than all the reforms he had introduced.

In the meantime the siege of Riga continued as he had ordered, and the generals took possession of the rest of Livonia and part of Finland; at the same time the King of Denmark came with all his fleet to invade Sweden and landed seventeen thousand men there whom he left under the command of Count Reventlau.

Sweden was then governed by a regency composed of a few senators which the king had set up when he left Stockholm. The body of the senate, which thought the prerogative of governing belonged to it by right, was jealous of the regency. The country suffered from these divisions, but when the first news that arrived in Stockholm after the battle of Poltava was that the king was at Bender at the mercy of the Tartars and Turks and that the Danes had invaded Scania and had taken the town of Hälsingborg, all jealousies were forgotten and the one thought was to save Sweden. It had been drained almost dry of regular troops, for, though Charles had always made his great campaigns with small armies, the innumerable battles he had fought in nine years, the continual need to recruit his troops and to supply the garrisons and army corps he had to maintain in Livonia, Pomerania, Bremen and Verden had cost Sweden over two hundred and fifty thousand soldiers in the course of the war. Less than eight thousand veterans remained, and these, together with raw recruits, constituted Sweden's entire forces.

The Swedes are born warriors, and every nation is unconsciously influenced by the character of its king. From one end of the country to the other people talked of nothing but the amazing exploits of Charles and his generals, and of those old regiments which had fought under them at Narva, the Dvina, Clissau, Pultusk and Hollosin. They inspired the humblest Swedes with a spirit of emulation and thirst for glory. Moreover they loved and pitied their king and hated the Danes with an implacable hatred. In many other countries the peasants are slaves or treated as such: in Sweden, being a politically represented body, they regard themselves as citizens and all their patriotism was aroused by this national crisis. So nobly did they respond that, in a short space of time, these peasant volunteers became the best troops in the north.

By order of the regency General Stenbock set out at the head of eight thousand seasoned veterans and about twelve thousand of these raw recruits to go and repel the Danes who were ravaging all the coast of Hälsingborg and already making raids far inland in search of plunder.

There had been neither time nor money to provide uniforms for the peasant recruits; most of these farm-labourers came dressed in their linen smocks, with pistols tied to their belts. Stenbock, at the head of this extraordinary army, was confronted with the Danes, three leagues from Hälsingborg, on March 10th 1710. He wished to let his troops have a few days' rest, to entrench his position and give his raw soldiers time to become accustomed to the enemy; but all these peasants clamoured to go into battle the very day they arrived.

Some officers who were there told me that nearly all of them were foaming with rage, so intense is the national hatred of the Swedes for the Danes! Stenbock took advantage of this state of mind, which counts as much on the battlefield as military discipline, and attacked the Danes. That day witnessed the most unprecedented sight of raw recruits going into battle for the first time with the same intrepidity as seasoned veterans. Two regiments of these hastily-armed peasants cut the Danish King's regiment of guards to pieces, leaving only two survivors.

The utterly routed Danes retreated under cover of cannon-fire from Hälsingborg. The crossing from Sweden to Zealand is so short that the news of his army's defeat reached the King of Denmark the same day in Copenhagen, and he sent his fleet to bring back what remained of his troops. The Danes left Sweden in great haste five days after the battle; as they could not take their horses with them, they killed them all rather than leave them to the enemy. They also set fire to their stores and burnt all their grain and provisions, so that most of the four thousand wounded they left behind in Hälsingborg died from the infection spread by all these dead horses and from the lack of provisions, of which their own compatriots had deprived them in order to prevent the Swedes from benefiting by them.

During this same period, the peasants of Dalecarlia, having heard, in the depths of their forests, that their king was a prisoner among the Turks, sent a deputation to the regency in Stockholm offering to raise a force of twenty thousand to go and rescue their master from the hands of his enemies. This proposition, although the regents had to reject it as impracticable, delighted them as a proof of his subjects' courage and loyalty and they did not fail to let the king know of it when they sent him the report of the battle of Hälsingborg.

Charles received this consoling news in his camp near Bender in July 1710. Shortly afterwards, another event confirmed him in his hopes.

The Grand-Vizier Couprougli, who opposed his plans, was dismissed after being only two months in office. Charles XII's little court and those who still supported him in Poland boasted that Charles made and unmade viziers, and that he ruled the Turkish Empire from the depths of his retreat at Bender. But he played no part in the disgrace of its favourite; Couprougli's fall was said to be due entirely to his rigid probity. His predecessor had never paid the janissaries from the imperial treasury, but with the money he got by his extortions: Couprougli, on the other hand, paid them out of the treasury funds. Achmet rebuked him for setting the interest of subjects above that of the emperor. 'Your predecessor Chourlourli,' he told him, 'knew how to find other means of paying my troops.' The grand-vizier replied: 'If he had the art of enriching your highness by fleecing your subjects, it is an art of which I am proud to be ignorant.'

The profound secrecy of the seraglio rarely allows such conversations to leak out to the public; but this one was known before Couprougli's dismissal. This vizier did not pay for his foolhardiness with his head, for true virtue is occasionally respected, even when it displeases; he was allowed to retire to the island of Negropont. I learnt these particulars from the letters of my relative, M. Bru, the head interpreter to the Turkish Porte, and I record them to give an idea of the mentality of that government.

The sultan then recalled Alep Baltagi Mehemet, the Pasha of Syria, who had been grand-vizier before Chourlourli. The baltagis of the seraglio, so called from *balta* which means axe, are the slaves employed to chop wood for the princes of the blood and the sultanas. This vizier had been a baltagi in his youth and had always retained the name, according to the custom of the Turks, who are not ashamed to take the name of their own first profession or their father's or of their birthplace.

In the days when Baltagi Mehemet was a slave in the seraglio, he was lucky enough to render some small services to Achmet, then a prisoner of state under the rule of his brother Mustapha. The Turkish princes of the blood were allowed, for their pleasures, some women past childbearing age (this comes early in Turkey) but still beautiful enough to be attractive. When Achmet became sultan, he gave one of his concubines, of whom he had been very fond, to Baltagi Mehemet for his wife. This woman made her husband grand-vizier by her intrigues; another intrigue displaced him, and a third made him once more grand-vizier.

When Baltagi Mehemet came to receive the imperial seal, he found the King of Sweden's faction dominant in the seraglio. The Sultana Valida, Ali Coumourgi, the sultan's favourite, the chief of the black eunuchs and the aga of the janissaries were all in favour of war against the tsar, and the sultan was determined on it. The first order he gave the grand-vizier was to go and fight the Russians with two hundred thousand men. Baltagi Mehemet had never been to war, but he was by no means an imbecile, as the Swedes who were dissatisfied with him have claimed. He said to the sultan, on being presented by him with a jewelled sabre: 'Your Highness knows that I was brought up to use an axe to chop wood, not a sword to command your armies: I will try to serve you well, but if I do not succeed, remember that I have begged you not to hold it against me.' The sultan assured him of his friendship and the vizier prepared himself to obey.

The first act of the Sublime Porte was to imprison the Russian ambassador in the castle of the Seven Towers. It is the custom of the Turks to begin by arresting the ministers of princes against whom they have declared war; observers of hospitality in all else, in this they violate the most sacred of international laws They commit this injustice on the pretext of equity, imagining, or wishing it to be believed, that they never undertake other than just wars, since they are consecrated by the approval of their mufti On this principle, they believe they have taken up arms to punish the violators of treaties, which they frequently break themselves, and are justified in punishing the ambassadors of their enemies' kings as accomplices in their masters' treachery. An additional reason is the absurd contempt they feel for Christian princes, and for ambassadors, whom they usually regard as mere consuls or merchants.

The Han of the Tartars of Crimea, whom we call the khan, received the order to hold himself ready, with forty thousand Tartars. This prince rules over Nagaï, Badziak, part of Circassia and the whole of the Crimea, the province known in antiquity as the Tauric Chersonese, where the Greeks brought their trade and their armies and founded important cities, and where the Genoese later penetrated when they were masters of Europe's commerce. Ruins of Greek towns and some monuments of the Genoese still survive in this region in the midst of desolation and barbarism.

The khan is called emperor by his subjects, but in spite of this grand title he is nonetheless the slave of the Porte. The Turkish lineage of the khans and the right they claim to the Turkish Empire, should the sultan's line become extinct, make their family respected by the sultan himself and their persons redoubtable; this is why the sultan dares not destroy the race of the Tartar Khans, though he hardly ever allows these princes to survive long on the throne. Their conduct is always closely scrutinized by neighbouring pashas, their states surrounded by janissaries, their wishes thwarted by grand-viziers and their designs always suspect. If the Tartars complain of the khan, the Porte deposes him on that pretext; if he is too well liked by them, this is a greater crime for which he is more promptly punished: thus nearly all khans go from sovereignty into exile and end their days in Rhodes, which is usually their prison and their grave.

The Tartars, their subjects, are the most notorious brigands in the world, yet, at the same time, which seems inconceivable, the most hospitable of people. They will travel fifty leagues from their country to attack a caravan or destroy a village, but when any foreigner, no matter who, enters their country, he is not only received everywhere and given free board and lodging, but, wherever he goes, the inhabitants vie for the honour of being his host; the master of the house, his wife and his daughters compete with each other to minister to his wants. Their ancestors, the Scythians, have handed down to them this inviolable respect for hospitality, which they have retained because the scarcity of foreign travellers and the cheapness of all provisions in those parts do not make this virtue at all difficult for them to practise.

When the Tartars go to war with the Turkish army they are fed by the sultan, but their booty is their only pay; hence they are more interested in pillaging than in regular fighting.

The khan, won over by the bribes and intrigues of the King of Sweden, had originally obtained permission for the general rendezvous of the troops to take place at Bender itself, under the eyes of Charles XII, so as to make it more evident that the war was being fought for him.

The new vizier, Baltagi Mehemet, not being bound by the same commitments, did not wish to flatter a foreign prince to such an extent; he revoked the permit and ordered this great army to assemble at Adrianople. When the Turks make war on Christians, their armies always assemble in the vast, fertile plains of Adrianople; the troops arrived from Asia and Africa normally rest and refresh themselves there for a few weeks, but the vizier, in order to forestall the tsar, only allowed the army three days' rest, and marched to the Danube and from thence to Bessarabia.

The Turkish troops are no longer as formidable today as they were when they conquered so many kingdoms in Asia, Africa and Europe. At that time, the physical strength, courage and sheer numbers of the Turks triumphed over enemies weaker and less disciplined than themselves. But now that the Christians have a better understanding of the art of war, they nearly always beat the Turks in pitched battle, even when the latter are superior in numbers. If the Turkish Empire has won a few victories since then, it is only against the Republic of Venice, whose citizens are reputed more wise than warlike, and which is defended by foreigners and ill-supported by Christian princes, who are always divided among themselves.

The janissaries and spahis attack in disorder, incapable of obeying words of command or rallying; their cavalry, which ought to be excellent, given their light, swift horses, cannot sustain the shock of German cavalry, and the infantry has not yet learnt to make good use of the fixed bayonet. Moreover the Turks have not had a great general since Couprougli, who conquered the island of Candia. A slave brought up in the idleness and seclusion of the seraglio, made a vizier through favouritism and a general against his will, was leading a hastily-levied, inexperienced, undisciplined army against Russian troops, seasoned by twelve years of war, and proud of having beaten the Swedes.

In the circumstances, the tsar seemed bound to defeat Baltagi Mehemet. But he made the same mistake with the Turks that the King of Sweden had made with him; he underrated his enemy. When he learnt that the Turks were arming, he left Moscow, and, having ordered the siege of Riga to be changed to a blockade, assembled eighty thousand men of his troops* on the frontiers of Poland. With this army, he marched through Moldavia and Wallachia, formerly the land of the Dacians, but now inhabited by Greek Christians who are tributaries of the sultan.

Moldavia was governed at that time by Prince Cantemir, a Greek by origin, who combined the literacy of the ancient Greeks with their skill in warfare. He was alleged to be descended from the famous Timur, known as Tamburlaine, since this ancestry seemed more illustrious than a Greek one. People proved it from the name of that conqueror: *Timur*, they argued, is very like *Temir*; the title of khan, which Timur had before he conquered Asia, reappears in the name of Cantemir; hence Prince Cantemir was descended from Tamburlaine. Such is the kind of reasoning on which most genealogies are based.

Whatever family he came from, Cantemir owed all his fortune to the Turkish Porte. Hardly had he been invested with his principality, than he deserted his benefactor the sultan for the tsar, from whom he hoped to gain still more. He was convinced that the conqueror of Charles XII would easily defeat an obscure vizier who had never been to war and who had appointed the chief customs

---

* The chaplain Nordberg claims that the tsar forced every fourth man of his subjects capable of bearing arms to follow him to this war. Had this been true, the army would have consisted of at least two million soldiers.

officer of Turkey as his *kiaia*, that is his second in command. Cantemir reckoned that all his people would rally to his side, for the Greek priests had encouraged him in this treachery. The tsar, therefore, having made a secret treaty with this prince and taken him into his army, advanced into his country, and in June 1711 reached the northern bank of the river Prut, near Yassi, the capital of Moldavia.

As soon as the grand-vizier learnt that Peter Alexeiovitch was marching from that side he promptly left his camp and, following the course of the Danube, crossed that river on a pontoon, near a town called Saccia, at the same point where Darius had long ago built the bridge which bore his name. The Turkish army marched so rapidly that it soon came in sight of the Russians on the opposite bank of the Prut.

The tsar, sure of the prince of Moldavia, did not expect that the Moldavians would fail him, but the interests of a prince and his subjects are often very different. The latter liked being under Turkish rule which is never harsh except to those in power and treats tributary peoples leniently; they feared the Christians, and above all the Russians, who had always treated them cruelly. They brought all their provisions to the Turkish army; the contractors who had promised to furnish the Russians with victuals made the same bargain with the grand-vizier as they had made with the tsar. The Moldavians' neighbours, the Wallachians, showed the same preference for the Turks: so much had the remembrance of Russian barbarisms alienated all hearts!

The tsar, thus disappointed in his hopes, which he had perhaps been somewhat rash to cherish, suddenly found his army without food or forage. The soldiers deserted in crowds and soon this army was reduced to less than thirty thousand men nearly dying of starvation. The tsar experienced on the Prut, through having relied on Cantemir, what Charles XII had experienced at Poltava through having relied too much on Mazeppa. It is surprising that the tsar did not try to prevent the Turks from crossing that river or that he did not at least repair this error by joining battle with them as soon as they had crossed it instead of giving them time to let his army perish of hunger and exhaustion. That prince seems to have done everything in this campaign to ensure that it should end in disaster.

He found himself destitute of provisions, with the river Prut behind him, a hundred and fifty thousand Turks confronting him, and forty thousand Tartars harassing him continually on the right and left. In this extremity, he said openly: 'I am in as desperate a plight as my brother Charles was at Poltava.'

Count Poniatowski, the King of Sweden's indefatigable agent, was in the grand-vizier's army, together with some Poles and Swedes who all believed the defeat of the tsar to be inevitable.

As soon as Poniatowski realized that the armies were bound to meet, he sent word to the King of Sweden, who promptly left Bender, accompanied by forty officers, rejoicing in advance at the prospect of fighting the Russian Emperor. After many losses and disastrous marches, the tsar, driven back on the Prut, had no cover for his troops but some *chevaux-de-frise* and some waggons. Some troops of spahis and janissaries made assaults on his ill-entrenched army, but they attacked in disorder and the Russians defended themselves with an energy inspired by the presence of their prince and the courage of despair.

The Turks were twice repulsed. The next day Poniatowski advised the grand-vizier to starve out the Russian army, which, lacking everything, would be obliged to surrender unconditionally, along with the emperor, within the next twenty-four hours.

The tsar has admitted more than once since then that never in his life had he suffered such tortures of anxiety as he endured that night; he went over in his mind all he had done for so many years for the glory and happiness of his people. Now so many great tasks, constantly interrupted by wars, might perhaps be going to remain unachieved and his work perish along with himself; he had either to die of hunger or attack nearly a hundred and eighty thousand men with worn-out troops reduced to less than half their number; a cavalry which had lost almost all its horses, and an infantry exhausted by hunger and fatigue.

At nightfall he summoned General Sheremetoff and, without discussing the matter or asking his advice, peremptorily ordered him to have everything ready at daybreak for an attack on the Turks with fixed bayonets.

He also gave an express order that all baggage should be burnt and that each officer should keep only a single waggon, so that, if they were defeated the enemy should at least not gain the booty they hoped for.

After arranging everything with the general for the battle, he retired to his tent, overwhelmed with sorrow and racked with spasmodic convulsions, a malady which frequently attacked him and always with redoubled violence when he was oppressed by some great anxiety. He forbade anyone to come and remonstrate with him about a desperate but necessary decision, still less that they should see him in such a state of distress.

Meanwhile the greater part of his baggage was burnt, as he had ordered. The whole army followed this example, though with regret: several buried their most precious possessions. The commanding officers were already ordering the army to march and trying to inspire the men with a confidence they did not feel themselves. Every private, exhausted by hunger and weariness, marched without enthusiasm or hope. The women, of whom there were far too many in the army, shrieked and wailed, thus demoralizing the men still further; everyone expected that the morning would bring them death or slavery. This is no exaggeration, it is literally what officers who served in that army have been heard to say.

There was at that time in the Russian camp a woman perhaps as remarkable as the tsar himself. She was still known only by the name of Catherine. Her mother was an unfortunate peasant, named Erb-Magden, from the village of Ringen, in Estonia, where the people are serfs and which was then under Swedish rule; she never knew who her father was. She was christened Martha and brought up, out of charity, by the vicar of the parish until she was fourteen. At that age she became a servant in Marienburg, in the house of a Lutheran minister named Gluck.

In 1702, at the age of eighteen, she married a Swedish dragoon. The day after the wedding a body of Swedish troops was beaten by the Russians, and this dragoon, who had been in the battle, never reappeared. His wife had no means of knowing whether he had been taken prisoner, and ever since then she had been unable to find out what had become of him.

Some days later she herself was taken prisoner by General Bauer; she became a servant in his household and afterwards in that of Marshal Sheremetoff; the latter gave her to Menzikoff, a man who experienced the most extreme vicissitudes of fortune. After having risen from a pastry-cook's boy to be a general and a prince, he had subsequently been deprived of everything and banished to Siberia, where he died in poverty and despair.

It was at a supper in Prince Menzikoff's house that the emperor saw her and fell in love with her. He married her secretly in 1707, not because he was ensnared by a woman's wiles, but because he recognized in her a strength of character capable of supporting him in his enterprises and even of carrying them on after him. He had long ago put away his first wife Ottokefa, the daughter of a boyar, who had been accused of being opposed to his political reforms. This was the greatest of all crimes in the eyes of the tsar, who did not want anyone in his family who did not think as he did. He thought he saw in this foreign slave all the qualities of a sovereign although she had none of the virtues of her sex; for her sake, he cast aside all the prejudices which would have hindered an ordinary man and had her crowned empress. The same capability which caused Peter Alexeiovitch to marry her enabled her to rule Russia very efficiently after his death. Europe was amazed to see this woman, who could neither read nor write,* make up for her lack of education and other deficiencies by her courage and prove herself a worthy successor to her husband's throne.

When she married the tsar, she renounced the Lutheran faith in which she had been brought up and adopted the Russian Orthodox religion; she was re-baptized according to the Russian rite and, instead of Martha, took the name of Catherine, by which she has been known ever since. This woman was in the camp on the Prut, and while the tsar was in his tent she held a council with the generals and the vice-chancellor, Schaffirof.

They decided they ought to sue for peace and that the tsar must be persuaded to take this course. The vice-chancellor wrote a letter to the grand-vizier in his master's name and the tsarina took this

* M. de La Motraye claims that she had been given an excellent education and that she read and wrote very well. Everyone knows the opposite; peasants in Livonia are not allowed to learn to read and write, on account of the ancient privilege called *benefit of clergy*, established in former days among barbarian Christians, and still existing in that country. The memoirs on which we base this fact say, moreover, that the Princess Elizabeth, later empress, always signed for her mother, from her childhood onwards.

letter into the tsar's tent, in spite of the prohibition to enter it, and, after much entreating and arguing and many tears, induced him to sign it. Having done so, she immediately collected together all her most precious jewels and all her money, even borrowing some from the generals, and amassed a very handsome present which she sent to Osman Aga, the grand-vizier's lieutenant, together with the letter signed by the tsar. Mehemet Baltagi at first adopted the haughty attitude of a vizier and a conqueror and replied: 'Let the tsar send his prime minister to me and I will see what I can do.' The vice-chancellor, Schaffirof, came at once, bearing some gifts which he himself openly presented to the grand-vizier; these were handsome enough to make it plain that they needed his help, but too few to be seen as an attempt to bribe him.

The vizier's first demand was that the tsar and his whole army should surrender unconditionally. The vice-chancellor replied that his master was going to attack in a quarter-of-an-hour and that the Russians would die to the last man rather than submit to such shameful conditions. Osman confirmed Schaffirof's words.

Mehemet Baltagi was no warrior: he knew that the janissaries had been repulsed the day before. Osman easily persuaded him not to risk losing definite advantages by a battle. He therefore granted a six-hour truce, during which the terms of the treaty could be agreed.

While they were parleying there occurred one of those little accidents which make one realize that the Turks keep their word more scrupulously than we think. Two Italian noblemen, relatives of Lieutenant-Colonel Brillo, an officer in one of the tsar's regiments, who had lost their way while out searching for forage, were captured by some Tartars who carried them off to their camp and offered to sell them to an aga of the janissaries. The Turk, indignant at their daring to break the truce, had the Tartars arrested and personally brought them before the grand-vizier, along with the two prisoners.

The vizier sent these two noblemen back to the tsar's camp and ordered the Tartars who had taken the most part in their kidnapping to be beheaded.

Nevertheless, the Khan of the Tartars was opposed to the conclusion of a treaty which deprived him of all hope of plunder. Poniatowski supported the khan with the most pressing arguments, but Osman triumphed over the Tartar's impatience and Poniatowski's insinuations.

The vizier thought he was doing enough for the sultan by concluding an advantageous peace. He demanded that the Russians should surrender Azov; that they should burn the galleys in that port; that they should demolish the important strongholds they had built on the shore of the Sea of Azov, and that all the artillery and munitions of these fortresses should be left in possession of the sultan; that the tsar should withdraw his troops from Poland; that he should no longer harass the few Cossacks who were under Polish protection, nor those who were dependent on Turkey, and that he should henceforth pay the Tartars a subsidy of forty thousand sequins a year, an odious tax which had been imposed long ago, but from which the tsar had exempted his subjects.

Finally, the treaty was going to be signed without so much as a mention of the King of Sweden. All that Poniatowski was able to obtain from the vizier was that a clause should be inserted whereby the Russians promised not to impede the return of Charles XII; and, what is rather strange, it was stipulated in this clause that the tsar and the King of Sweden should make peace, if they wished to and if they could agree on the terms.

On these conditions the tsar was free to retire with his army, his artillery, his standards and his baggage. The Turks furnished him with provisions and there were plentiful supplies of everything in his camp two hours after the signature of the treaty, which was inaugurated on the 21st of July 1711 and signed on the 1st of August.

Just as the tsar, having escaped from this tight corner, was withdrawing with drums beating and colours flying, the King of Sweden arrived, all impatience to come to grips with his enemy and defeat him. He had galloped more than fifty leagues from Bender to Yassy and arrived just as the Russians were beginning to make their peaceful retreat. In order to get into the Turkish camp, it was necessary to cross the Prut. There was a bridge three leagues farther up, but Charles, who never did anything like other men, swam across the river at the risk of being captured, reached the Turkish army and dismounted at the tent of Count Poniatowski, who has given me a written account of what happened. The Count went up to him sadly and told him how he had just lost an opportunity which might never occur again.

The king, beside himself with rage, went straight to the grand-vizier's tent and hotly rebuked him for the treaty he had just concluded. The grand-vizier said calmly: 'I have the right to make war and to make peace.' 'But you had the entire Russian army in your power!' exclaimed the king. 'Our law orders us to grant our enemies peace when they implore our mercy,' the vizier retorted gravely. 'And does it order you to make a bad treaty when you can impose what terms you please?' asked the king in a fury. 'What was there to prevent you from bringing the tsar to Constantinople as a prisoner?'

The Turk, at the end of his patience, replied tartly: 'And who, pray, would govern his kingdom in his absence? It would not do to have every king away from his own country.' Charles merely gave an offensive smile. Then he flung himself down on a divan, and glaring at the vizier with an expression of anger and contempt, stretched his leg out towards him and, deliberately entangling his spur in the Turk's robe, tore a great rent in it. The next moment he sprang to his feet, leapt on his horse, and rode back to Bender with despair in his heart.

Poniatowski remained a little while longer with the grand-vizier, trying to persuade him, by gentler means, to impose harder conditions on the tsar; but the call to prayer having sounded, the Turk departed, without replying a single word, to perform his ablutions and pray to Allah.

BOOK VI

THE King of Sweden, whose good luck had once been proverbial, was now fated to be unlucky even in the most trifling things. On his return he found that his little camp at Bender and all the living quarters had been flooded by the waters of the Dniester. He moved a few miles away, near a village named Varnitza, and, as if he had had a secret premonition of what was going to happen to him, had a large stone house built, which could withstand an assault for a few hours, should the need arise. He even furnished it magnificently, contrary to his usual habit, in order to impress the Turks.

He also built two others, one for his chancery and the other for his favourite, Grothusen, who kept one of his tables. While the king was thus building near Bender as if he intended to remain permanently in Turkey, Baltagi Mehemet, fearing this prince's intrigues against him in the Porte more than ever, had sent the Emperor of Germany's resident envoy to Vienna to ask in person that the King of Sweden should be allowed passage through the hereditary dominions of the house of Austria. Within three weeks this envoy had brought back a promise from the regency government to render Charles XII the honours due to him and to conduct him in all safety to Pomerania.

The request had been addressed to the regency government in Vienna because the Emperor of Germany, Charles, the successor of Joseph I, was at that time in Spain, where he was disputing the crown with Philip V. While the German envoy was executing this commission in Vienna, the grand-vizier sent three pashas to the King of Sweden to inform him that he must leave Turkish territory.

The king, who knew the order they had been given, began by

telling them that if they dared to propose anything dishonourable to him or show him any lack of respect he would have all three of them instantly hanged. The Pasha of Salonica, who was the spokesman, disguised the harshness of the message in the most respectful terms. Charles ended the audience without even deigning to reply; his chancellor, Muller, who remained behind with these three pashas, briefly explained his master's refusal, which had been quite obvious to them from his silence.

The grand-vizier was not discouraged; he ordered Ismaël Pasha, the new seraskier of Bender, to threaten the king with the sultan's wrath if he did not make up his mind without delay. This seraskier had a mild and conciliatory nature which had won him Charles's good-will and the affection of all the Swedes. The king held a conference with him but only to inform him that he would not leave unless Achmet would grant him two things; to punish his grand-vizier and to give him an escort of a hundred thousand men with which to return to Poland.

Baltagi Mehemet was well aware that Charles was remaining in Turkey in order to ruin him, so he took the precaution of having guards put on all the roads from Bender to Constantinople to intercept the king's letters. He did more; he cut off his *thaim*, that is the subsistence allowance the Porte gives to princes to whom it grants asylum. The King of Sweden's was enormous, consisting of five hundred crowns a day in money and an abundance of everything which could contribute to the maintenance of a court in splendour and luxury.

As soon as the king knew that the vizier had dared to cut off his allowance, he turned to his chief steward and said: 'Up to now you have had only two tables, as from tomorrow I order you to keep four.'

Charles XII's officials were accustomed to find nothing impossible if he ordered it; however they had neither provisions nor money and were obliged to borrow at twenty, thirty and forty per cent from the officers, servants and janissaries who had grown rich through the king's lavishness. Baron Fabrice, the envoy from Holstein, Mr Jeffreys, the English minister, and their secretaries and friends gave what they had. The king, with his usual pride, and with no care for the morrow, lived on these gifts which would not have sufficed for long. It was necessary to elude the vigilance of the guards and send

secretly to Constantinople to borrow money from European merchants. All refused to lend to a king who seemed to have put himself
past any possibility of repaying them. A single English merchant,
named Cook, finally risked lending the King of Sweden forty thous-
and crowns, prepared to lose them if Charles happened to die. This
money was brought to the king's little camp at the moment when
they were beginning to run out of everything and to lose hope of any
more supplies.

During this interval, Poniatowski wrote, from the grand-vizier's
own camp, an account of the campaign of the Prut in which he
accused Baltagi Mehemet of cowardice and treachery. An old janissary, angered by the grand-vizier, and furthermore bribed by
Poniatowski, took charge of this account, and, having been given
some leave, personally presented the letter to the sultan.

Poniatowski left the camp a few days later and went to the
Turkish Porte to plot intrigues against the grand-vizier in his usual
way.

The circumstances were favourable. The tsar, left at liberty, was
in no hurry to fulfil his promises; the keys of Azov did not arrive,
and the grand-vizier, rightly fearing his master's wrath, did not dare
to go and face him.

The seraglio was now more rife with intrigues and factions than
ever. In Constantinople, these cabals, which one sees in all courts
and which in ours normally end in some minister being dismissed,
or at the very worst banished, always result in the fall of more than
one head. They cost the life of the former Vizier Chourlourli, and of
Osman, Baltagi Mehemet's lieutenant, who was the principal author
of the peace of the Prut and who, since that peace, had been given a
high post at the Porte. They found, among Osman's treasures, the
tsarina's ring and twenty thousand gold coins minted in Saxony and
Russia; this was a proof that money alone had extricated the tsar
from his perilous situation and ruined the prospects of Charles XII.
The Vizier Baltagi Mehemet was banished to the isle of Lemnos,
where he died three years later. The sultan did not confiscate his
possessions either during his exile or at his death; he was not rich,
and his poverty vindicated his memory.

This grand-vizier was succeeded by Jussuf, that is to say Joseph,
whose fortune was as singular as that of his predecessors. Born on

the frontiers of Russia, and taken prisoner by the Turks at the age of six, along with his family, he had been sold to a janissary. For a long while he was a lackey in the seraglio, and finally became Grand-Vizier of the Empire in which he had been a slave; but he was only a shadow minister. The young selictar, Ali Coumourgi, raised him to this slippery eminence while waiting to be able to take over the position himself; and his creature, Jussuf, had no function other than to append the imperial seal to whatever the favourite wished. The policy of the Turkish court appeared to change from the very outset of this viziership; the plenipotentiaries of the tsar, who remained in Constantinople both as hostages and as ministers, were treated better than ever; the grand-vizier confirmed the peace of the Prut with them; but what mortified the King of Sweden most was to learn that the secret liaisons which were being made in Constantinople with the tsar were the result of the mediation of the ambassadors of England and Holland.

Constantinople, since Charles's retreat to Bender, had become what Rome has so often been; the centre of the diplomatic negotiations of Christendom. Désaleurs, the French ambassador, supported the interests of Charles and Stanislas; the German Emperor's minister opposed them; the Swedish and Russian factions were at loggerheads, as the French and Spanish ones have long been at the court of Rome.

England and Holland, who appeared neutral, were not; the new trade which the tsar had opened up in St Petersburg attracted the interest of these two trading nations.

The English and Dutch will always be on the side of the prince who will most encourage their trade. There was much to be gained from the tsar, so it is not surprising that the English and Dutch ambassadors secretly worked on his behalf in the Porte. One of the conditions of this new friendship was that Charles should be made to leave Turkish territory immediately, either because the tsar hoped to capture him on the way, or because he thought Charles would be less of a menace in his own dominions than in Turkey, where he was always trying to induce the Turks to take up arms against Russia.

The King of Sweden was still soliciting the Porte to send him back through Poland with a large army. The divan did indeed decide to send him back, but only with an escort of seven or eight thousand men; no longer as a king whom they wished to help but as a guest whom they wished to be rid of. With this object, the sultan wrote to him in the following terms:

Most mighty of the kings who worship Jesus, redresser of wrongs and injuries, and protector of justice in the ports and republics of the North and South; resplendent in majesty, lover of honour and glory and friend of our Sublime Porte, Charles, King of Sweden, whose enterprises God crowns with success.

As soon as the most illustrious Achmet, former *Chiaoux-Pash,*★ has the honour to present to you this letter, adorned with our imperial seal, be persuaded and convinced of the truth of our intentions expressed therein, to wit that, although we had proposed to march our ever victorious troops once more against the tsar, this prince having meanwhile, in order to avoid our just resentment at his delay in implementing the treaty concluded on the banks of the Prut, and since renewed in our Sublime Porte, surrendered to us the castle and town of Azov, and sought, through the mediation of the ambassadors of England and Holland, our ancient allies, to establish a permanent peace with us, we have granted him this and given his plenipotentiaries, who remain with us as hostages, our imperial ratification, after having received his from their hands.

We have given the most honourable and valiant Delvet Gherai, Khan of Budziack, Crimea, Nagaï and Circassia, and our most wise and generous counsellor, Ismaël, Seraskier of Bender (may God preserve them and increase their magnificence and wisdom) our inviolable and salutary orders for your return through Poland according to your first plan, which you have again put before us. You must therefore prepare to leave, under the auspices of providence and with an honourable escort, before next winter, to return to your own territories, taking care to pass through those of Poland in a friendly and peaceful manner.

Everything necessary for your journey will be provided by my Sublime Porte; money as well as men, horses and chariots. We exhort you and recommend you, above all, to give the clearest and most definite orders to the Swedes and all the other people with you,

---

★ Marshal of the royal household. (*Translator's note*)

not to commit any act of disorder or do anything which could tend directly or indirectly to the breach of this peace and friendship.

By doing this you will retain our goodwill, of which we seek to give you as great and frequent proofs as opportunities present. Our troops destined to accompany you will receive orders in conformity with our imperial intentions.

Given at our Sublime Porte of Constantinople, the 14th of the months *rebryul eurech* 1214. (This corresponds to the 19th of April, 1712.)

This letter did not make the King of Sweden lose hope yet. He wrote to the sultan that he would be grateful all his life for the favours which his highness had heaped on him, but that he thought the sultan too just to send him back, with only the escort of a flying column, into a country still overrun with the troops of the tsar. In fact the Russian Emperor, in spite of the first article of the peace of the Prut by which he had promised to withdraw all his troops from Poland, had sent in fresh ones; and, what seems amazing, the sultan knew nothing of this.

The Porte's bad policy of always having ambassadors of Christian princes in Constantinople, out of vanity, but of not maintaining a single agent in Christian courts, means that these ambassadors are aware of, and sometimes influence, the sultan's most secret decisions, while the divan is always totally ignorant of what goes on openly among the Christians.

The sultan, shut up in his seraglio among his women and his eunuchs, sees only through the eyes of his grand-vizier; this minister, as inaccessible as his master, occupied with the intrigues of the seraglio and with no communication with the outside world, is usually deceived by, or deceives the sultan, who dismisses him or has him strangled for his first mistake, in order to choose another as ignorant or as treacherous, who behaves like his predecessors and soon suffers their fate.

Such, normally, is the inertia and profound sense of security of this court that if the Christian princes leagued together against it, their fleets would be in the Dardanelles and their land armies at the gates of Adrianople before the Turks had thought of defending themselves: but the divergent interests which will always divide

Christendom will save the Turks from a fate which their lack of policy and their ignorance of military and naval warfare seem to be preparing them for today.

Achmet was so ill-informed as to what was going on in Poland that he sent an aga to see if it was true that the tsar's armies were still there: two of the King of Sweden's secretaries, who knew Turkish, accompanied the aga so as to act as witnesses if he made a false report.

This aga saw the truth with his own eyes and came to report it to the sultan himself. The enraged Achmet was about to have the grand-vizier strangled, but the favourite, who protected him and thought he still needed him, obtained his pardon, and kept him still in the ministry for a while.

The Russians were openly protected by the vizier, and secretly by Ali Coumourgi, who had changed sides; but the sultan was so angry, the breach of the treaty so patent, and the janissaries, who often make ministers, favourites and sultans tremble, were clamouring so loudly for war that no one in the seraglio dared counsel moderation.

The sultan promptly had the Russian ambassadors, already as accustomed to going to prison as to an audience, incarcerated in the Seven Towers. War was once again declared against the tsar, the horse-tails hoisted, and all the pashas given orders to assemble an army of two hundred thousand fighting men. The sultan himself left Constantinople and established his court in Adrianople to be nearer the theatre of war.

Meanwhile, a solemn embassy from Augustus and the Republic of Poland to the sultan was proceeding along the road to Adrianople; the Palatine of Mazovia was at the head of the embassy, with a retinue of more than three hundred.

Everyone who formed part of this embassy was arrested and held prisoner in one of the suburbs of the town. Never had the hopes of the King of Sweden's party risen higher than they did at that moment; nevertheless this great display of force turned out to be meaningless, and all his hopes were dashed.

If one can believe a public minister, a wise and clear-sighted man who was then living in Constantinople, young Coumourgi already had ideas in his head other than quarrelling over deserts with the tsar in a war the Turks might well lose. He was planning to wrest the Peloponnese, now called Morea, from the Venetians, and to make himself master of Hungary.

All he was waiting for to carry out his great plans was the post of grand-vizier, from which his youth still precluded him. With this in mind, he had more need of the tsar as an ally than an enemy; it was contrary both to his interests and his wishes that the King of Sweden should stay any longer in Turkey, and even more undesirable that the Turks should go to war on his behalf. Not only did he wish to send this prince away but he said openly that no Christian minister ought henceforth to be allowed in Constantinople; that all these resident ambassadors were nothing but respectable spies who corrupted or betrayed viziers and had for too long instigated intrigues in the seraglio; that the Franks settled in Pera and the commercial ports of the Levant were merchants who needed only a consul, not an ambassador. The grand-vizier, who owed his position and his very life to the favourite, and who moreover feared him, fell in with his wishes all the more readily since he had sold himself to the Russians and hoped to revenge himself on the King of Sweden, who had tried to ruin him. The mufti was also Ali Coumourgi's creature and the slave of his caprices; he had counselled war against the tsar when the favourite wanted this, and discovered that it was unjust as soon as that young man changed his mind; thus the army had hardly been assembled before proposals for a peaceful settlement were being considered. Vice-Chancellor Schaffirof and young Shere-metoff, the tsar's plenipotentiaries and hostages at the Porte, promised, after much bargaining, that the tsar would withdraw his troops from Poland. The grand-vizier, who was well aware that the tsar would not carry out this treaty, signed it all the same; and the sultan, satisfied at having given the impression of laying down the law to the tsar, still remained in Adrianople. Thus, in less than six months, the peace sworn with the tsar was followed by a declaration of a war and followed again by a renewal of the peace.

The principal article of all these treaties remained the same, viz that the King of Sweden must be made to leave Turkey. The sultan did not want to imperil his own or his country's honour by exposing the king to the risk of being captured by his enemies *en route*. It was stipulated that he should leave, but that the ambassadors of Poland

and Russia should answer for the safety of his person: these ambassadors swore, in the name of their masters, that neither the tsar nor King Augustus would molest him on his journey, and that Charles, on his side, would not attempt to stir up any trouble in Poland. Charles's fate having been thus settled by the divan, Ismaël, the Seraskier of Bender, went to Varnitza where the king was encamped and informed him of the Porte's decisions, tactfully explaining that no further delay was possible and that he must depart.

Charles replied nothing except that the grand-vizier had promised him an army, not an escort, and that kings ought to keep their word.

In the meantime, General Flemming, King Augustus's minister and favourite, was maintaining a secret correspondence with the Khan of Tartary and the Seraskier of Bender. La Mare, a French gentleman who was a colonel in the Saxon army, had made more than one journey from Bender to Dresden and all these journeys were suspect.

Just at that very time, the King of Sweden had a courier whom Flemming was sending to the Prince of Tartary arrested on the borders of Wallachia. The letters were brought to him and deciphered; it was obvious from them that there was a definite understanding between the Tartars and the Court of Dresden, but they were couched in such ambiguous and general terms that it was difficult to make out whether the end Augustus had in view was merely to detach the Turks from the Swedish party or whether he wanted the khan to hand Charles over to his Saxons while he was escorting him back to Poland.

It seemed difficult to imagine that so generous a prince as Augustus would have wanted to seize the person of the King of Sweden at the risk of the lives of his ambassadors and of the three hundred Polish nobles who were detained in Adrianople as hostages for Charles's safety. But, on the other hand, Flemming, Augustus's autocratic minister, was known to be very shrewd and none too scrupulous. The outrages committed against the Elector-King by the King of Sweden seemed to make any vengeance justifiable; and it might be thought that, if the Court of Dresden bought Charles from the Khan of Tartary it could easily buy the liberty of the Polish hostages from the Turkish court.

The motives were discussed between the king, his private chancellor, Muller, and his favourite, Grothusen. They read and reread the letters and, because their unfortunate situation made them more suspicious, they decided to believe the worst.

A few days later the king's suspicions were confirmed by the hurried departure of one Count Sapieha, who had taken refuge with him, who suddenly left him to return to Poland and throw himself into the arms of Augustus. On any other occasion Sapieha would have seemed to him merely a malcontent, but at this critical juncture he had no hesitation in believing him a traitor. The repeated demands which were now being made to him to leave changed his suspicions into certainty. All these probabilities, combined with his natural obstinacy, left him firmly convinced that there was a plot to betray him and deliver him up to his enemies, although this plot has never been proved.

He may have been mistaken in his idea that King Augustus had bargained with the Tartars for his person, but he was even more mistaken in counting on the help of the Turkish court. In any case, he resolved to gain time.

He told the Pasha of Bender that he could not leave without first having something with which to pay his debts; for, although his *thaïm* had long been restored to him, his liberal gifts had always forced him to borrow. The pasha asked him how much he wanted: the king replied at random 'a thousand purses', which is fifteen hundred thousand francs in our money. The pasha wrote to the Porte about it; the sultan, instead of the thousand purses he was asked for, granted twelve hundred and wrote the following letter to the pasha:

Letter from the Grand-Seignior to the Pasha of Bender.
The object of this imperial letter is to inform you that, at your recommendation and request and that of the most noble Delvet Gherai, Khan to our Sublime Porte, our imperial magnificence has granted a thousand purses to the King of Sweden, which will be sent to Bender under the conduct and charge of the most illustrious Mehemet-Pasha, formerly *Chiaoux-Pash*, to remain in your custody until the time of the departure of the King of Sweden – may God guide his steps! – and then to be given to him with two hundred

purses more, as an additional gift of our imperial bounty which exceeds his demand.

As to the route through Poland which he is determined to take, you and the khan, who must accompany him, must be careful to take such wise and prudent measures as will ensure that, throughout the journey, the troops under your command and the King of Sweden's cause no damage, and commit no act which might be deemed contrary to the peace which still exists between our Sublime Porte and the kingdom and republic of Poland: so that the king may pass through as a friend under our protection.

By doing this, as you will most expressly enjoin him to do, he will receive all the honour and respect due to his majesty from the Poles, as the ambassadors of King Augustus and the republic have assured us, by offering themselves and some other nobles, should we require it, as hostages for the safety of his journey.

When the time you and the most noble Delvet Gherai have agreed upon for the march arrives, you will place yourself at the head of your gallant soldiers, among whom will be the Tartars, led by the khan, and you will escort the King of Sweden and his men.

May it so please the one almighty God to guide your steps and theirs! The Pasha of Aulos will remain at Bender to guard it in your absence with a corps of spahis and another of janissaries. By following our imperial orders and wishes in all these particulars, you will render yourself worthy of our continued imperial favour, as well as of the praise and recompenses due to all those who observe them.

Given at our Imperial Residence of Constantinople, the 2nd of the month of Schewal, 1214 of the Hegira.

While they were awaiting this reply from the sultan the king wrote to the Porte complaining of the supposed treachery of the Khan of Tartary; but the routes were well guarded and, moreover, the vizier was hostile to him. The letters never reached the sultan and the vizier even prevented M. Désaleurs from coming to Adrianople, where the Porte was, for fear this minister, who was acting for the King of Sweden, might try to upset the plan they had made for his departure.

Charles, indignant at seeing himself virtually driven out of the sultan's territory, decided not to leave at all.

He could have asked to return through Germany, or to board a ship in the Black Sea and sail to Marseilles via the Mediterranean, but he preferred to ask nothing and await events.

When the twelve hundred purses had arrived, his treasurer, Grothusen, who had learnt Turkish during this long stay, went to see the pasha without an interpreter, hoping to extract the twelve hundred purses from him and start some new intrigue in the Porte, still on the false supposition that the Swedish faction would finally induce the Turkish Empire to take up arms against the tsar.

Grothusen told the pasha that the king's equipage could not be got ready without money. 'But,' said the pasha, 'it is we who will defray all the expenses of your departure. Your master has nothing to pay as long as he is under the protection of mine.'

Grothusen retorted that there was so much difference between a Turkish equipage and those used by the Franks that they would have to employ the Swedish and Polish craftsmen in Varnitza to do the work.

He assured him that his master was willing to leave and that this money would facilitate and hasten his departure. The too trustful pasha gave him the twelve hundred purses, and a few days later came to ask the king, in the most respectful manner, for his orders for the departure.

He was astounded when the king told him that he was not ready to leave and that he must have another thousand purses. The pasha was so shattered by this reply that for some moments he was unable to speak. He went over to a window where he was seen to shed some tears. Finally he said to the king: 'It will cost me my head for having obliged your majesty. I gave the twelve hundred purses against the express order of my sovereign.' Having spoken these words, he turned away and was about to depart, overcome with grief.

The king stopped him and told him he would make excuses for him to the sultan. 'Ah!' retorted the Turk as he left. 'My master never excuses faults, he only punishes them.'

Ismaël Pasha went to give this news to the Khan of Tartary, who, having received the same order as the pasha, on no account to allow the twelve hundred purses to be given to the king before his departure, and having consented to this money being handed over, was equally apprehensive of the sultan's wrath. They both wrote to the Porte to justify themselves; they protested that they had only given the twelve hundred purses on the positive assurance of one of the king's ministers that the departure would take place at once; and they implored his highness that the king's refusal should not be attributed to their disobedience.

Charles, still persisting in his conviction that the khan and the pasha wished to hand him over to his enemies, ordered M. Funk, then his envoy at the Turkish Court, to lodge complaints against them and to demand another thousand purses. His extreme generosity and the little store he set by money prevented him from seeing anything degrading in this proposal. He made it only in order to provoke a refusal and to have another pretext for not leaving; but a man must be reduced to dire straits to need to resort to such tricks. Savari, his interpreter, a clever and enterprising man, carried his letter to Adrianople, in spite of the strict guard the grand-vizier ordered to be kept on the roads.

Funk was obliged to go and make this dangerous request. The only reply was to have him put in prison. The enraged sultan called an extraordinary session of the divan and appeared at it himself, which he rarely did. His speech, according to the translation made of it at the time, ran as follows:

'I might well have known nothing of the King of Sweden but for his defeat at Poltava and the request he made to me to grant him asylum in my empire: I have no need of him and no reason either to love him or to fear him: nevertheless, influenced by no motives other than the hospitality of a Moslem and my own generosity which sheds the dew of its bounties on high and low alike, I have received him into my country and have succoured him, his officials and his soldiers in every possible way, and have not ceased, for three and a half years, to load him with presents.

'I have granted him a considerable escort to conduct him to his own domains. He asked me for a thousand purses to pay some expenses, although I defray them all; instead of a thousand, I granted him twelve hundred. After having extracted them from the Seraskier of Bender, he demands still another thousand, on the pretext that the escort is too small, whereas it is only too large for a journey through a friendly country.

'I ask therefore whether it is a breach of the laws of hospitality to send this prince away and whether foreign powers could accuse me of violence and injustice, in case we were reduced to compelling him to leave by force.'

The whole divan replied that the sultan was acting justly. The mufti declared that Moslems are not bound to offer hospitality to infidels, still less to the ungrateful, and he gave his *fetfa*, a kind of mandate which nearly always accompanies the important orders of the sultan. These fetfas are revered like oracles, although those from whom they emanate are slaves of the sultan like the others.

The order and the fetfa were brought to Bender by the *Bouyouk Imraour*, the Master of the Horse, and the *Chiaoux Pasha*, the Marshal of the Household. The Pasha of Bender received the order at the home of the Khan of Tartary; he promptly went to Varnitza to ask if the king were willing to leave amicably, or he would have to force him to carry out the sultan's orders.

Threatened like this, Charles XII lost his temper. 'Obey your master if you dare,' he told him, 'and get out of my sight!'. The outraged pasha departed at full gallop, an unusual thing for a Turk: on his way back he met Fabrice and shouted to him, without slowing down: 'The king will not listen to reason. You are going to see some very strange things.' That very day he cut off the king's supply of provisions and removed his guard of janissaries. He sent word to the Poles and Cossacks at Varnitza that if they wanted to have food, they must leave the King of Sweden's camp, move into the city of Bender and put themselves under the protection of the Porte. All obeyed, and left the king with only the officers of his household and three hundred Swedish soldiers as his sole defence against twenty thousand Tartars and six thousand Turks.

There were no longer any provisions in the camp, either for men or horses. The king ordered twenty of those splendid Arab horses the sultan had sent him to be shot outside the camp, saying: 'I want neither their provisions nor their horses.' This was a banquet for the Tartar troops, who, as is well known, regard horseflesh as a delicacy. Meanwhile the Turks and the Tartars besieged the king's little camp on all sides.

This prince, quite unperturbed, had regular fortifications constructed by his three hundred Swedes: he worked at them himself; his chancellor, his treasurer, his secretaries, the valet and all his servants helped with the task. Some barricaded the windows, others pushed beams against the doors to act as buttresses.

When the house had been well barricaded and the king had made a tour of his so-called fortifications, he proceeded to play chess with his favourite, Grothusen, as calmly as if everything were completely safe and secure. Luckily, Fabrice, the envoy from Holstein, did not live in Varnitza, but in a little village between Varnitza and Bender where Mr Jeffreys, the English envoy to the King of Sweden, lived too. These two ministers, seeing the storm about to burst, took it upon themselves to act as mediators between the Turks and the king. The khan, and especially the Pasha of Bender, who had no desire to do violence to that monarch, eagerly welcomed the offer of these two ministers; they had two conferences with them in Bender, at which the master of the horse and the marshal of the household who had brought the sultan's order and the mufti's fetfa were present.

Baron Fabrice* admitted to them that His Swedish Majesty had good reason to believe that they wished to deliver him up to his enemies in Poland. The khan, the pasha and the others swore on their heads, calling God to witness, that they abhorred the very idea of such a horrible piece of treachery and that they would shed their blood rather than permit even the slightest disrespect to be shown to the king in Poland; they said that they had the Russian and Polish ambassadors in their power, and that these would answer with their lives for the least affront offered to the King of Sweden; finally, they complained bitterly of the outrageous suspicions the king was harbouring against persons who had received him so cordially and treated him so well. Although oaths are often the language of treachery, Fabrice allowed himself to be persuaded by the Turks; he thought their protestations had that ring of truth which lying never wholly succeeds in counterfeiting. He well knew that there had been a secret correspondence between the khan and King Augustus, but he remained convinced that the only purpose of their negotiations had been to make Charles XII leave Turkish territory. Whether Fabrice was mistaken or not, he assured them that he would represent to the king the injustice of his suspicions. 'But do you intend to force him to go?' he added. – 'Yes,' said the

* All this is recorded by Baron Fabrice in his letters.

pasha. 'Such is our master's order.' Then he implored them once again to consider carefully whether this order extended to shedding the blood of a crowned head. 'Yes,' retorted the khan angrily, 'if that crowned head disobeys the sultan in his own dominions.'

In the meantime, everything now being ready for the assault, the death of Charles XII seemed inevitable. But, as the sultan's order did not positively say they were to kill him if he resisted, the pasha persuaded the khan to agree that a message should be sent post-haste to Adrianople, where the sultan then was, to get his highness's final orders.

Mr Jeffreys and Baron Fabrice, having obtained this brief respite, galloped off to tell the king of it. They arrived with the eager excitement of people bringing good news, but they were received very coldly. He called them impudent meddlers and persisted in maintaining that the sultan's order and the mufti's fetfa were forgeries, since the pasha and the khan had just asked for fresh orders from the Porte.

The English minister withdrew, firmly determined not to involve himself any more in the affairs of so stubborn a prince. Fabrice, of whom the king was fond, and who was more used to his ill-temper than the English minister, remained with him to implore him not to risk so precious a life in so hopeless a cause.

The king's only reply was to show him his fortifications, and to beg him to use his intervention only to procure him some victuals. The Turks were easily persuaded to let provisions go through to the king's camp while waiting for the courier to return from Adrianople. The khan himself had forbidden his Tartars, who were impatient for loot, to make any attack on the Swedes till further orders, so that Charles XII sometimes went out of his camp with forty horse, and galloped through the midst of the Tartar troops, who respectfully made way for him; he even marched right up to their lines, and they opened their ranks to let him through instead of resisting.

Finally, the sultan's order arrived: all Swedes who offered the least resistance to be put to the sword and the king's life not spared. The pasha was kind enough to show this order to Baron Fabrice so that he might make a last effort to persuade the king to change his mind. Fabrice went straight to him with this bad news. 'Have you seen this order you speak of?' said the king. 'Yes,' replied Fabrice.

'Well then, tell them from me that this is the second order they have forged, and that I have no intention of going.' Fabrice threw himself at his feet, lost his temper and soundly rated him for his obstinacy, but all in vain. 'Go back to your Turks,' said the king, with a smile. 'If they attack me I can defend myself.'

The king's chaplains also implored him on their knees not to expose the wretched survivors of Poltava and above all his sacred person to certain massacre; assuring him moreover that he was violating the laws of hospitality by insisting on remaining by force among strangers who had helped him so long and so generously. The king, who had not been at all angry with Fabrice, was furious with these priests and told them that he had employed them to offer prayers, not to offer him their advice.

General Hord and General Dahldorf, who had always been against attempting a fight whose result could only be disastrous, showed the king their breasts covered with wounds received in his service, and, while assuring him that they were ready to die for him, begged him that it might at least be on a more necessary occasion. 'I know by your wounds and mine,' Charles told them, 'that we have fought bravely together. You have done your duty hitherto; do it again now.' There was nothing left but to obey; each of them was ashamed of not seeming eager to die with the king. This prince, having prepared for the attack, was secretly revelling in the gratification and honour of withstanding an entire army with a band of three hundred Swedes. He assigned each one to his post; his chancellor, Muller, the secretary, Ehrenpreus, and the clerks were to defend the chancery house; Baron Fief, the head of the household, was at another post; the grooms and cooks had another place to guard; for, to him, everyone was a soldier. He galloped to and fro from his trenches to his house, promising everyone rewards, creating officers and promising to make the least lackey who would fight bravely a captain.

It was not long before they saw the army of the Turks and Tartars advancing to attack the little stronghold with ten cannons and two mortars. The horse-tails streamed out in the breeze, the clarions brayed and shouts of *Allah! Allah!* were heard on all sides. Baron Grothusen noticed that the Turks were not hurling insults at the king in their war-cries, but merely calling him *Demirbash* – 'Ironhead', so he decided to go out alone and unarmed from the trenches and parley with them. He advanced into the lines of the janissaries, almost all of whom had received money from him. 'What, my friends,' he said to them in their own language, 'have you come to massacre three hundred defenceless Swedes? You, brave janissaries, who pardoned fifty thousand Russians when they cried *amman* (pardon), have you forgotten the benefits you have received from us? And do you wish to assassinate this great King of Sweden, whom you love so much and who has been so generous to you? My friends, he asks only three days, and the sultan's orders are not so strict as you have been made to believe.'

These words had an effect which Grothusen himself had not expected. The janissaries swore on their beards that they would not attack the king, and that they would give him the three days he asked for. The signal to attack was given in vain; the janissaries, far from obeying, threatened to turn on their leaders if they did not grant the King of Sweden three days' grace. They came in a mob to the Pasha of Bender's tent, shouting that the sultan's orders were forged. The only weapon the pasha could use against this unforeseen mutiny was patience.

He pretended to be pleased with the janissaries' generous decision, and ordered them to withdraw to Bender. The Khan of Tartary, a violent man, wished to make an immediate attack with his troops, but the pasha, who did not want the Tartars to have the sole honour of capturing the king, whereas he might perhaps be punished for the disobedience of his janissaries, persuaded the khan to wait till the next day.

On his return to Bender, the pasha called together all the officers of the janissaries and the oldest privates; he read and showed to them the sultan's definite order and the mufti's fetfa. Sixty of the oldest, who had venerable white beards and who had received innumerable presents from the king, offered to go in person to implore him to put himself in their hands and let them serve him as guards.

The pasha gave them permission to go; there was no expedient he would not have tried rather than be forced to have Charles killed. These sixty old men therefore went the next morning to Varnitza, carrying only long white staves, the only weapons janissaries carry when they are not going into battle, for the Turks regard the Christian custom of wearing swords in peacetime, and of entering armed into their friends' houses and their churches, as barbarous.

They addressed themselves to Baron Grothusen and Chancellor Muller and told them that they had come with the object of serving as faithful guards to the king and that, if he wished, they would escort him to Adrianople, where he could speak in person to the sultan. While they were making their proposal, the king was reading some letters which had come from Constantinople and which Fabrice, who had not been able to see him again, had had secretly sent to him by a janissary. They were from Count Poniatowski, who could serve him neither in Bender nor in Adrianople, having been detained in Constantinople by order of the Porte ever since the imprudent demand for the thousand purses. He told the king that the sultan's orders to seize his royal person, or to assassinate him in case of resistance, were only too authentic; that the sultan had, in fact, been deceived by his ministers, but the more he was deceived in this matter, the more he was determined to be obeyed; that the king must yield to circumstances and bow to necessity; that he took the liberty of advising him to attempt everything that could be done by way of negotiation with the ministers, not to be inflexible when it was essential to be persuasive, and to wait for diplomacy and time to remedy an evil which violence would only aggravate.

But neither the proposals of these old janissaries nor Poniatowski's letters could make the king conceive even the possibility of giving in without dishonour. He preferred to die at the hand of the Turks rather than be, in some sense, their prisoner. He sent the janissaries away without seeing them, and sent a message to tell them that if they did not go at once he would have their beards cut off, which, in the East, is the most outrageous of all insults.

The old men returned home furious with indignation, crying: 'Down with the Ironhead! Since he is determined to die let him do so!' They gave the pasha an account of their mission and told their comrades in Bender of the extraordinary manner in which they had been received. All then swore to obey the pasha's orders without more delay and were as eager to attack the Swedes as they had been reluctant the day before. The order was given instantly; the Turks marched to the fortified camp where the Tartars were already awaiting them, and the cannons opened fire.

The janissaries attacking from one side and the Tartars from the other stormed this little camp in a matter of moments; hardly twenty Swedes had time to draw their swords and the three hundred soldiers were surrounded and taken prisoner without resistance. The king was then on horseback, riding between his house and his camp, along with Generals Hord, Dahlesdorf and Sparre: seeing that all the soldiers had let themselves be captured before his very eyes, he said calmly to these three officers: 'Let us go and defend the house,' adding, with a smile, 'We will fight *pro aris et focis* [for hearth and home].'

He promptly galloped with them up to the house, where he had placed about forty servants as sentinels, and which had been fortified as best they could.

These generals, well accustomed as they were to their master's headstrong courage, could not but be amazed that he should calmly and cheerfully propose to defend himself against ten cannons and an entire army; they followed him with a few guards and servants, making in all twenty men.

But when they reached the door, they found it besieged by janissaries; two hundred Turks and Tartars had already got in through a window and taken possession of all the rooms, except for a large hall to which the king's servants had retreated. This hall was luckily near the door through which the king wanted to enter with his little band of twenty; he leapt down from his horse, pistol and sword in hand, and his followers did likewise.

The janissaries fell on him from all sides, excited by the pasha's promise to give eight gold ducats to each man who so much as touched his coat, if they were able to capture him. He wounded and killed all those who came near him. A janissary whom he had wounded, thrust his musket in his face; if the Turk's arm had not been jostled by the surging crowd, the king would have been dead. The bullet glanced off his nose, carried off the lobe of one ear and ended by breaking the arm of General Hord, who was fated always to be wounded at his master's side.

The king plunged his sword in the janissary's breast at the very moment the servants who were shut up in the great hall opened its door: the king entered in a flash, followed by his little troop; the door was instantly shut again and they barricaded it with everything they could find. So Charles was now imprisoned in this hall with his entire retinue, which consisted of nearly sixty men – officers, guards, secretaries, valets and servants of all kinds.

The janissaries and Tartars were pillaging the rest of the house and every room was full of them. 'Come and help me drive these barbarians out of my house,' said the king, and, placing himself at the head of his men, he opened the door of the hall, which led into his bedroom and fired on the Turks who were looting it.

The Turks, loaded with booty, were so terrified by the sudden appearance of this king whom they were accustomed to revere, that they threw down their arms and jumped out of the window or retreated to the cellars. The king, taking advantage of their confusion, and his followers, excited by success, pursued the Turks from room to room, killing or wounding those who did not flee, and in a quarter-of-an-hour cleared the house of enemies.

In the heat of the combat the king noticed two janissaries hiding under his bed. He killed one of them with a blow of his sword; the other begged for mercy, crying *amman*. 'I will spare your life,' the king told him, 'on condition that you go and give the pasha a true account of what you have seen.' The Turk readily promised to do as he wished, and he was allowed to jump out of the window like the others.

When the Swedes were finally masters of the house they shut all the windows again and barricaded them. They had no lack of weapons, for a room on the ground floor full of muskets and powder had escaped the tumultuous search of the janissaries, and the Swedes made good use of them. They fired through the windows, almost at point blank range, on this mob of Turks and killed two hundred of them in less than ten minutes.

The cannon bombarded the house, but, as it was built of very soft stone, the shells only made holes in the walls and did not knock them down.

The Khan of Tartary and the pasha, who wished to take the king alive and were ashamed of losing men and employing a whole army against sixty people, decided to set the house on fire in order to force the king to surrender. They ordered arrows with lighted wicks twisted round them to be shot on to the roof and against the windows and doors; in a moment the house was in flames. The blazing roof was on the verge of falling in on the Swedes. The king calmly gave orders to extinguish the fire. Finding a little barrel full of liquid he seized it, and, helped by two Swedes, he flung it at the place where the fire was fiercest. This barrel happened to be filled with brandy, but in the inevitable haste of such a crisis no one remembered this. The flames shot up and raged more furiously than ever; the king's bedroom was burnt out, and the great hall, where the Swedes were assembled, was filled with suffocating smoke, mingled with tongues of flame that darted in through the doors of the neighbouring rooms; half the roof collapsed into the house itself, and the other fell outside in a shower of blazing timbers.

In these dire straits a guard named Walberg dared to cry that they ought to surrender. 'What an extraordinary man!' exclaimed the king. 'Fancy not thinking it better to be burned than taken prisoner!' Another guard, named Rosen, took it upon himself to say that the chancery house, which was only fifty paces away, had a stone roof which was fireproof and that they ought to make a sally, get to this house and defend themselves there. 'Ah, now there is a true Swede!' cried the king: he embraced this guard and made him a colonel on the spot. 'Come, my friends,' he said, 'bring as much powder and shot as you can, and we will fight our way to the chancery.'

The Turks, who were all this while surrounding the blazing house, were both amazed and horrified to see that the Swedes were not leaving it, but they were even more astonished when they saw the doors open and the king and his followers rush out and fall on them like desperate men. Charles and his principal officers were armed with swords and pistols; each fired two shots simultaneously as the door opened; then, in the twinkling of an eye, they threw away their pistols, drew their swords, fell on the Turks and drove them back more than fifty paces. But the next moment this little troop was surrounded: the king who, as usual, was wearing high boots, got his spurs entangled and fell: twenty-one janissaries promptly flung themselves on him. He threw his sword away to spare himself the humiliation of surrendering it, and the Turks carried him off to the pasha's quarters; some supporting his legs and others holding him under the arms, as people carry a sick man whom they are afraid of hurting.

The moment the king realized that he was captured, the fury into which a man of his violent nature must have worked himself up during so long and terrible a fight suddenly gave way to gentleness and calm. Not one sign of anger did he betray, not so much as an impatient word or an irate frown. He smiled at the janissaries, who bore him away, crying *Allah!* with a mixture of indignation and respect. His officers were captured at the same time and stripped almost bare by the Turks and Tartars.

This strange event, which occurred on the 12th of February 1713, was to have even stranger consequences.*

* In his history, M. Nordberg, who was not present at this event, has here done no more than copy M. de Voltaire's account of it, but he has curtailed it; he has omitted the peculiar circumstances of it, and has not been able to justify Charles XII's rashness. Everything he has been able to say against M. de Voltaire on the subject of this affair at Bender is reduced to the fate which befell Frederick, the King of Sweden's valet, whom some assert to have been burnt to death in the king's house and others to have been cut in half by the Turks. La Motraye also claims that the King of Sweden never said those words: 'We will fight *pro aris et focis* [for hearth and home].' But Baron Fabrice, who was present, affirms that the king uttered those words and that La Motraye was no more within earshot of them than he was capable of understanding them, not knowing a word of Latin.

BOOK VII

THE Pasha of Bender was ceremoniously awaiting Charles in his tent, with Marco present as interpreter. He received him with profound respect and begged him to rest on a divan, but the king took no notice of the Turk's civilities and remained standing. 'The Almighty be blessed that your majesty is alive!' said the Turk. 'I am deeply grieved that your majesty has forced me to carry out his highness's orders.' The king, whose only vexation was that his three hundred soldiers had let themselves be captured in their trenches, said to the pasha: 'Ah! if they had defended themselves as they should, we could have held out for at least ten days.' 'Alas,' said the Turk, 'such courage would only have been wasted.' He had the king conducted back to Bender on a richly caparisoned horse. His Swedes had all been killed or captured, and his possessions, furniture, papers and even his most necessary personal belongings looted or burnt. The roads presented the sorry sight of Swedish officers, stripped almost naked, chained together in pairs, following Tartars or janissaries on foot. The chancellor and the generals had fared no better; they were slaves of the soldiers to whom they had fallen by lot.

Ismaël Pasha, having brought Charles to his seraglio in Bender, gave up his own apartment to him and had him waited on as befitted a king, though not without taking the precaution of posting janissaries as sentinels outside the door. A bed was made up for him, but he flung himself down, still in his boots, on a divan and fell fast asleep. An officer, who was standing beside him, covered his head with a nightcap, which the king threw off when he woke from this first sleep; the Turk was amazed at the sight of a sovereign who slept in his boots and bareheaded. The next day Ismaël brought Fabrice into the king's bedroom. Fabrice found him with his clothes torn, his boots, hands and his entire person covered with blood and powder, and his eyebrows scorched, but looking perfectly serene in spite of his appalling state. He threw himself on his knees before him, unable to utter a word, but, soon reassured by the free and easy way the king spoke to him, he resumed his usual familiarity with him, and the two of them talked and laughed over the 'Battle of Bender'. 'They say,' said Fabrice, 'that your majesty killed twenty janissaries with his own hand.' 'Well, well!' said the king, 'people always exaggerate things by half.' In the middle of this conversation, the pasha brought in the king's favourite, Grothusen, and Colonel Ribbing, whom he had been generous enough to ransom at his own expense. Fabrice undertook to ransom some of the other prisoners.

Jeffreys, the English ambassador, helped him to provide the ransom money. A Frenchman, whose curiosity had brought him to Bender and who has written an account of some of the events recorded here, also gave what he had. These foreigners, assisted by the pasha's good offices and even his money, bought back not only the officers, but their clothes as well from the Turks and Tartars.

The next day the captive king was put in to a chariot draped with scarlet and taken on his way to Adrianople. His treasurer Grothusen was with him, Chancellor Muller and some officers followed in another carriage, and several more on horseback. When these saw the chariot which they knew must be the king's, they could not restrain their tears. Fabrice told the pasha, who was at the head of the escort, that it was shameful to leave the king without a sword, and begged him to give him one. 'Heaven forbid!' exclaimed the pasha. 'He would want to cut off my beard.' However he gave him one a few hours later.

While this king who, a few years previously, had laid down the law to so many states and been the arbiter of the north and the terror of Europe, was being led away, an unarmed prisoner, another example of the frailty of human greatness was to be seen in the place he had just left.

King Stanislas had been arrested on Turkish territory and was being taken, as a prisoner, to Bender at the very time Charles XII was being transferred from it.

Stanislas, no longer supported by the hand that had made him king, found himself without money and hence without a party in Poland. He first withdrew to Pomerania, and, being unable to conserve his own kingdom any longer, he had defended his benefactor's to the best of his ability. He had even gone to Sweden to hasten the help needed in Pomerania and Livonia; in fact, he had done everything that could be expected of a friend of Charles XII. At that time, the first King of Prussia, a very wise prince, rightly uneasy at the near neighbourhood of the Russians, planned to ally himself with Augustus and the Republic of Poland in order to send the Russians back to their own country, and to include Charles XII himself in the project, from which three great things were to result: the peace of the north, the return of Charles to his dominions, and a barrier set up against the Russians who had become a menace to Europe. The preliminary condition of this treaty, on which public peace depended, was the abdication of Stanislas. Not only did Stanislas accept it, but he undertook to be the negotiator of a peace which would deprive him of his crown. The motives which determined him were necessity, the public good, the glory of self-sacrifice and the interests of Charles, to whom he owed everything and whom he loved. He wrote to Bender; he explained the unhappy state of affairs to the King of Sweden and proposed the remedy; he implored him not to oppose an abdication which circumstances had rendered necessary and honourable; he urged him not to sacrifice the interests of Sweden to those of an unlucky friend who would cheerfully sacrifice himself for the public good. Charles XII received these letters at Varnitza; he flew into a rage and told the courier in the presence of several witnesses: 'If my friend does not want to be king I can easily make another.'

Stanislas was determined on the sacrifice which Charles refused. Those times were destined to produce extraordinary emotions and actions. Stanislas wished to go himself to persuade Charles to change his mind, and he risked more to abdicate a throne than he had done to gain it. One night, at ten o'clock, he slipped away from the Swedish army he was commanding in Pomerania, and set off with Baron Sparre, who has since been ambassador to England and to France, and another colonel. He took the name of a Frenchman named Haran, then a major in the Swedish army, who later died

Governor of Danzig. He came in contact with the entire enemy army and was arrested several times, but was released by producing a passport he had acquired in the name of Haran. Finally, after perils, he reached the Turkish frontier.

When he arrived in Moldavia, he sent Baron Sparre back to his army, and went into Yassi, the capital of Moldavia, thinking himself safe in a country where the King of Sweden had been so much respected; he was far from suspecting what was then going on.

He was asked who he was, and said he was a major in one of Charles XII's regiments. He was arrested at the very mention of this name, and brought before the hospodar of Moldavia who, knowing already from the newspapers that Stanislas had disappeared from his army, had some suspicion of the truth. The king's appearance had been described to him, so it was very easy to recognize him from his plump, kindly face and unusually sweet expression.

The hospodar interrogated him, asked him a number of leading questions, and finally what his position was in the Swedish army. Stanislas and the hospodar were speaking Latin. *Major sum* [I am a major], Stanislas told him; *Imo maximus es* [No, you are *maximus*], the Moldavian replied, and promptly offering him an armchair he treated him as a king. But he also treated him as a captive king, and he was obliged to remain in a Greek monastery, under strict guard, until orders were received from the sultan. The orders came that he was to be taken to Bender, which Charles had just left.

The news of this reached the pasha as he was accompanying the King of Sweden on his way to Adrianople. He told it to Fabrice, who rode up to Charles's chariot and informed him that he was not the only king who was a prisoner in the hands of the Turks, and that Stanislas was a few miles away being conducted to Bender under military escort. 'Go to him at once, my dear Fabrice,' said Charles, not in the least perturbed by this news: 'Tell him that he must never make peace with King Augustus, and assure him that our luck will very soon change.' So inflexible was Charles in his opinions that, although he was abandoned in Poland, being attacked in his own dominions, and at that moment a prisoner being conveyed in a Turkish litter to an unknown destination, he still relied on his luck and still hoped to make the Turkish Porte give him a hundred thousand men to support his cause. Fabrice galloped off, with the pasha's permission and accompanied by a janissary, to fulfil his commission. A few miles away he met the body of soldiers that was escorting Stanislas; he accosted a man dressed like a Frenchman who was riding in the midst of them on a rather sorry horse and asked him in German where the King of Poland was. The man he spoke to was Stanislas himself whom he had not recognized in this disguise. 'Why, do you no longer remember me then?' said the king. Then Fabrice told him of the King of Sweden's sad situation, and his unshakeable determination to persist with his impossible plans.

When Stanislas was near Bender, the pasha, who returned there after accompanying Charles XII a few miles, sent the Polish King a splendidly caparisoned Arab horse.

He was received in Bender with a salute of guns, and, apart from being a prisoner at first, he had nothing to complain of in the treatment he was given.* Meanwhile, Charles was being escorted along the road to Adrianople. The town was already filled with the rumours of his great fight. The Turks condemned yet admired him, but the exasperated divan was already threatening to banish him to an island in the archipelago.

The King of Poland, Stanislas, who did me the honour of telling me most of these particulars, also assured me that it was proposed in the divan that he himself should be confined on a Greek island, but a few months later the sultan relented and allowed him to leave.

M. Désaleurs, who might have taken Charles's part and prevented this affront to Christian kings, was in Constantinople, as was also Count Poniatowski, whose fertile and resourceful mind was still feared. And, as most of the Swedes who remained in Adrianople were in prison, the sultan's throne seemed completely inaccessible to the King of Sweden's complaints.

The Marquis de Fierville, who had been sent as a secret envoy from France to Charles at Bender, was at that time in Adrianople. He was bold enough to seek some way of doing a service to this prince when everyone was abandoning or oppressing him. Luckily he was seconded in this plan by a young French nobleman, named

---

* The good chaplain Nordberg asserts that we contradict ourselves here by saying that King Stanislas was kept a prisoner and waited on like a king in Bender. How could the poor man not see that one can be a prisoner and at the same time treated with honour?

Villelongue, the scion of an old Champagne family, an intrepid man, whose courage was much greater than his fortune. Fascinated by the King of Sweden's reputation, he had come to Turkey intending to put himself at his service.

With the help of this young man M. de Fierville wrote a petition in the name of the King of Sweden, in which this monarch demanded vengeance from the sultan for the insult offered to his person and to all crowned heads, and for the treachery – real or imaginary – of the khan and the Pasha of Bender.

In it the vizier and the other ministers were accused of having been bribed by the Russians, of having deceived the sultan, of having induced the sultan, by their wiles, to issue that order, so contrary to Moslem hospitality and which violated international law in a manner so unworthy of a great emperor, to send twenty thousand soldiers to attack a king who had only his servants to defend him and who relied on the sultan's sacred word.

When this petition had been composed, it had to be translated into Turkish and written in a special script on specially made paper which had to be used for everything presented to the sultan.

They applied to several French interpreters who were in the city, but the King of Sweden's affairs were in such a parlous state and the vizier so openly opposed to him that no interpreter dared even to translate M. de Fierville's document. Finally they found another foreigner, whose handwriting was not known to the Porte, who, for a certain sum of money and on condition of complete secrecy, translated the petition into Turkish and wrote it out on the correct paper. Baron d'Arvidson, an officer in the Swedish army, forged the king's signature; Fierville, who had the royal seal, stamped it on the document, and the whole was sealed with the arms of Sweden. Villelongue undertook to deliver the packet himself to the sultan when he went to the mosque, as was the custom. They had already used the same means to present petitions to the sultan, but this actually made the success of this enterprise more dubious and the danger much greater.

The vizier, who foresaw that the Swedes would demand justice for their master and who was only too well aware of the unhappy fate of his predecessors, had expressly forbidden that anyone should be allowed to approach the sultan, and above all had ordered that all those who came anywhere near the mosque with petitions were to be arrested.

Villelongue knew of this order and was well aware that he risked his life by going there. He discarded his Frankish dress, arrayed himself like a Greek, and having hidden the letter in his bosom, went in good time to the neighbourhood of the mosque which the sultan was due to attend. He pretended to be a lunatic, and went dancing along between the two files of janissaries who were lining the route which the sultan would take, purposely letting some silver coins drop out of his pockets to distract the guards.

As soon as the sultan was seen arriving they tried to push Villelongue out of the way; he flung himself on his knees and struggled in the grip of the janissaries. In the struggle, his Greek cap fell off and, realizing from his long hair that he was a Frank, they set upon him and severely manhandled him. The sultan, who by then was very near, heard the tumult and demanded to know the cause of it. Villelongue, drawing the letter from his bosom, shouted to him with all his might: *amman! amman!* (mercy!). The sultan ordered that he should be allowed to approach; Villelongue immediately rushed to him, kissed his stirrup, and presented the document to him, saying: *Sued crall dan* ('It is the King of Sweden who presents it to thee'). The sultan put the letter in his bosom and proceeded on his way to the mosque. Nevertheless, Villelongue was arrested and imprisoned in the outbuildings of the seraglio.

The sultan, when he emerged from the mosque after having read the letter, wished to interrogate the prisoner himself. What I am about to recount may perhaps seem incredible; but, after all, I state nothing except on the strength of M. Villelongue's own letters; when so brave an officer certifies a fact on his honour, he deserves some credence. He assures me that the sultan discarded his imperial robes and also the special turban he wore, and disguised himself as an officer of janissaries, which was something he frequently did. He brought with him an old Maltese, who acted as his interpreter. Thanks to this disguise Villelongue enjoyed an honour which no Christian ambassador has ever had; a quarter-of-an-hour's tête-à-tête conversation with the Turkish Emperor. He did not fail to explain the King of Sweden's grievances, to accuse the ministers and to demand vengeance all the more freely, because, though he was talking to the Sultan himself, he was supposed only to be talking to an equal. He had easily recognized the Grand Seignior, in spite of the darkness of the prison, and this made him all the bolder in his speech. The pretended officer of janissaries said to Villelongue: 'Christian, be assured that the sultan my master has the soul of an emperor and that, if your King of Sweden is in the right, he will do him justice.' Villelongue was soon released, and a few weeks later a sudden change took place in the seraglio, which the Swedes attributed entirely to this conversation. The mufti was deposed, the Khan of Tartary exiled to Rhodes and the Seraskier of Bender banished to an island in the archipelago.

The Turkish Porte is so subject to such storms that it is very difficult to decide whether the sultan really meant to appease the King of Sweden by these sacrifices. The manner in which this prince was treated does not prove that the Porte was over-zealous to please him.

The favourite, Ali Coumourgi, was suspected of having made all these changes for his own private ends. It was said that he had had the Khan of Tartary and the Seraskier of Bender banished on the pretext that they had given the King the twelve hundred purses in spite of the sultan's order. He put the deposed khan's brother, a young man of his own age, who had little love for his brother and on whom Ali Coumourgi relied for military support in the wars he was contemplating, on the throne of Tartary. As for the grand-vizier, Jussuf, he was not dismissed till some weeks later, and Soliman Pasha was given the post.

I am bound to say that M. de Villelongue and several Swedes have assured me that the letter presented to the sultan in the name of the king was the sole cause of all these changes in the Porte, but M. de Fierville has assured me of quite the opposite. I have sometimes found similar contradictions in the memoirs which have been entrusted to me. In that case, all that a historian should do is simply to record the facts without trying to assess motives, and to limit himself to saying exactly what he knows, instead of guessing what he does not.

Meanwhile Charles XII had been taken to the little castle of Demirtash, near Adrianople. A vast crowd of Turks had flocked to the spot to see this prince arrive; he was carried from his chariot into the castle on a divan but, in order not to be seen by this crowd, he covered his head with a cloth.

The Porte took some days to consent to his living in Demotica, a little town six leagues from Adrianople, near the famous river Hebrus, now known as the Maritza. Coumourgi told the Grand-Vizier Soliman: 'Go and tell the King of Sweden that he can stay in Demotica all his life. I promise you that within a year he will ask to leave of his own accord. But, above all, do not let him have any money.'

So the king was transferred to the little town of Demotica where the Porte granted him a considerable *thaïm* of provisions for himself and his retinue, and allowed him twenty-five crowns a day in cash to buy pork and wine, two victuals the Turks do not provide, but the allowance of five hundred crowns a day he had received at Bender was cut off.

Hardly had he installed himself in Demotica with his little court than the Grand-Vizier Soliman was deposed and his place given to Ibrahim Molla, who was extremely arrogant, bold, and boorish. It is not irrelevant to know his history, so that one can form a clearer picture of all these viceroys of the Turkish Empire on whom Charles's fortunes so long depended.

He had been an ordinary sailor at the accession of Sultan Achmet III. This emperor often disguised himself as a private citizen, an imam or a dervish, and went secretly at night into the coffee-houses of Constantinople to hear what was being said about him and gather for himself how the people felt. One day he heard this Molla complaining that the Turkish ships never returned with prizes and swearing that if he were the captain of a ship he would never return to the port of Constantinople without bringing some vessel captured from the infidels back with him. The very next day the sultan ordered that he should be given a ship to command and sent out privateering. The new captain returned a few days later with a Maltese barque and a Genoese galley. In two years' time he was made an admiral, and finally grand-vizier. As soon as he reached this position, he thought he could dispense with the favourite, and to make himself indispensable he planned to make war on the Russians. With this purpose in mind, he set up a tent near the place where the King of Sweden was living.

He invited this prince to come and meet him there, together with the new Khan of Tartary and the French ambassador. The king, whose misfortunes had made him all the more haughty, regarded it as the most outrageous insult that a subject should dare to send for him. He ordered his chancellor, Muller, to go in his stead; and, for fear that the Turks should show any lack of respect for him and force him to compromise his dignity, he took to his bed and decided not to get up as long as he was in Demotica. He stayed in bed ten months, pretending to be ill, with Chancellor Muller, Grothusen and Colonel Duben as his only table companions. As all their silver and tableware had been looted in the battle of Bender, their meals were far from being stately or elegantly served. They waited on themselves and during the whole of this time Chancellor Muller did the cooking.

While Charles XII was spending his life in bed, he learnt of the devastation of all his overseas dominions.

General Stenbock, famous for having driven the Danes out of Scania and for having conquered their best troops with peasants, maintained the reputation of Swedish arms for a while. He defended Pomerania and Bremen and what the king still possessed in Germany, as best he could, but he could not prevent the combined Saxons and Danes from besieging Stade, an important fortified town near the Elbe, in the Duchy of Bremen. The town was bombarded and reduced to ashes and the garrison forced to surrender unconditionally before Stenbock could bring aid to it.

The general, who had about twelve thousand men, of whom half were cavalry, pursued the enemy, who were twice that strength, and finally caught up with them in the Duchy of Mecklenburg, near a place called Gadebesk and a little river of that name. He came face to face with the Danes and Saxons, separated from them by a marsh, on the 20th of December 1712. The enemies, encamped behind this marsh, were backed by a wood; they had the advantage of numbers and terrain, and they could only be reached by crossing the marsh under their artillery fire.

Stenbock crossed it at the head of his troops, arrived in battle order, and engaged in one of the fiercest and bloodiest battles which had yet been fought between these two rival nations. After three hours of this strenuous fighting, the Danes and Saxons were routed and left the battlefield.

A son of King Augustus and the Countess of Köenigsmark, known under the name of Count de Saxe, served his apprenticeship to the art of war in this battle. Later, as the Maréchal de Saxe, he won glory for himself by saving France at the battle of Fontenoy and earned the reputation of being the greatest general of our times. He commanded a regiment at Gadebesk, and had a horse killed under him. I have heard him say that the Swedes always kept their ranks and that, even after the victory had been won and the front lines of these brave troops had their dead enemies at their feet, not one Swedish soldier would dare so much as bend down to strip the corpses before prayers had been offered on the battlefield, so firmly did they maintain the strict discipline to which their king had accustomed them.

After this victory, Stenbock, remembering that the Danes had reduced Stade to ashes, proceeded to take vengeance for this on Altona, which belonged to the King of Denmark. Altona lies above Hamburg, on the river Elbe, which can carry quite large ships into its port. The King of Denmark granted this town many privileges with the intention of establishing a flourishing trade there. The industry of the Altonese, encouraged by the King's foresight, had already begun to establish their town as one of the rich commercial cities. Hamburg was jealous of it and wished for nothing so much as its destruction. As soon as Stenbock came in sight of Altona, he sent a herald to announce to the inhabitants that they must evacuate it, with such belongings as they could carry away, for he was going to raze their town to the ground.

The magistrates came and threw themselves at his feet, and offered a hundred thousand crowns as ransom. Stenbock demanded two hundred thousand. The Altonese implored that they might be allowed to send to Hamburg, where their correspondents were, and promised to bring him that sum the next day. The Swedish general replied that they must give it at once, or he would set fire to Altona then and there.

His troops were on the outskirts, torch in hand, and the city's only defence was a wooden gate and a dried-up moat. These poor wretches were forced to leave their houses, with the utmost haste, in the middle of the night. It was the 9th of January 1713, and the bitter cold was increased by a violent north wind which made the fire spread through the town all the faster and made the sufferings of the people driven out in the open country all the more intolerable. Men and women, bent under the load of household goods they were carrying, took refuge, weeping and wailing, in the neighbouring hills which were covered with ice. One saw many young people carrying paralysed old ones on their shoulders. Some newly-delivered women carried their babies, and died of cold with them on the hills, watching from afar the flames that were devouring their homes. All the inhabitants had not yet left the town when the Swedes set fire to it. Altona burnt from midnight till ten o'clock in the morning. Nearly all the houses were built of wood; everything was burnt to ashes, and the next day one might never have known there had been a town there.

The aged, the sick and women in the most delicate health who had taken refuge in the icy hills while their homes were burning, dragged themselves to the gates of Hamburg and beseeched the citizens to open them to them and save their lives. But they refused to let them in because there had been some cases of contagious diseases in Altona and the Hamburgers were not sufficiently fond of the Altonese to risk infecting their own city by admitting them. So the majority of these poor wretches died under the walls of Hamburg, calling heaven to witness the cruelty of the Swedes and that of the Hamburgers which seemed no less inhuman.

The whole of Germany was scandalized by this violence. The ministers and generals of Poland and Denmark wrote to Count Stenbock to rebuke him for such a wanton and unpardonable piece of cruelty, which revolted both God and man.

Stenbock replied 'that he had only gone to these lengths to teach the enemies of the king, his master, to stop waging war like barbarians and to respect international law; that they had filled Pomerania with their atrocities, devastated this beautiful province, and sold nearly a hundred thousand of its inhabitants to the Turks; that the torches which had reduced Altona to ashes were reprisals for the red-hot bullets which had destroyed Stade.'

If Charles had appeared in Pomerania at that time, when the Swedes and their enemies were engaged in such furious warfare, it is possible that he might have retrieved his fortunes. His armies, though far away from him, were still animated by his spirit, but the absence of his leadership prevented them from gaining any advantage from their victories. Stenbock gradually lost what he had won in battles that at any other time would have been decisive.

Victorious as he was, he could not prevent the Russians, Saxons and Danes from uniting. They seized his headquarters, and he lost men in a number of skirmishes. Two thousand of his troops were drowned as they were crossing the Oder on their way to winter quarters in Holstein. All these losses were irreparable in a country where he was surrounded on all sides by powerful enemies.

He tried to defend Holstein against Denmark, but in spite of his efforts the country was lost. The entire army was destroyed and Stenbock was taken prisoner.

Pomerania, left defenceless, became, apart from Stralsund and the island of Rügen, the spoil of the allies. It was sequestrated into the hands of the King of Prussia. Bremen was occupied by a Danish garrison. At the same time, the Russians poured into Finland, where they defeated the Swedes, who were losing confidence and, besides being inferior in numbers, were beginning to lose their superiority in courage over their seasoned enemies.

To crown the misfortunes of Sweden, its king obstinately persisted in remaining in Demotica, still indulging in his vain hopes of Turkish aid.

Ibrahim Molla, that arrogant vizier who was determined on war against Russia in spite of the favourite's wishes, was pressed to death between two doors. The position of vizier had become so dangerous that no one dared occupy it. It remained vacant for six months, when, at last, the favourite, Coumourgi, assumed the title of grand-vizier. Then all Charles's hopes collapsed. He knew Coumourgi, all the better for having been supported by him when the favourite's interests had coincided with his own.

He had been in Demotica eleven months, sunk in inertia and oblivion. This total lack of exercise, following suddenly on the most violent physical exertions, finally made him really ill instead of pretending to be. The whole of Europe believed that he was dead. The council of regency, which he had set up in Stockholm when he left his capital, no longer heard him mentioned. The senate came in a body to ask Princess Ulrica-Eleonora, the king's sister, to assume the regency during her brother's long absences. She consented, but when she realized that the senate wanted to force her to make peace with the tsar and the King of Denmark who were attacking Sweden on all sides, she was sure that her brother would never ratify the peace, so she abdicated as Regent, and sent a long account of the affair to Turkey.

The king received his sister's dispatch in Demotica. The despotism he had imbibed from birth made him forget that Sweden had once been free and that the senate had formerly governed the country conjointly with the king. He regarded this body merely as a troop of servants who wanted to usurp the position of the master of the house in his absence. He wrote to them that, if they wanted to govern, he would send them one of his boots and they must take their orders from that.

To forestall these supposed attempts to over-ride his authority in Sweden and realizing at last that there was no more to be hoped from the Turkish Porte and that he must rely on himself to defend his country, he sent word to the grand-vizier that he wished to leave, and to return home by way of Germany.

M. Désaleurs, the French ambassador, who had undertaken to deal with the diplomatic affairs of Sweden, made the request on Charles's behalf. 'Well, didn't I say that, before the year was over, the King of Sweden would ask to leave?' the vizier said to Désaleurs. 'Tell him that he can go or stay as he chooses, but he must definitely make up his mind and fix the day of his departure, so that we have no repetition of all the trouble he caused us at Bender.'

Désaleurs toned down the harshness of these words when he reported the answer to the king. The day was chosen, but Charles, before he left Turkey, wished to display the pomp of a great king, in spite of being a penniless refugee. He gave Grothusen the title of ambassador extraordinary and sent him to Constantinople, accompanied by a retinue of eighty men, all superbly arrayed, to take ceremonial leave of the Porte. The pomp and splendour of this embassy gratified his pride, but the secret devices he had to employ to provide the money to pay for it could not have been more humiliating.

M. Désaleurs lent the king forty thousand crowns; Grothusen borrowed in his name, through agents he had in Constantinople, a thousand crowns from a Jew, two hundred pistoles from an English merchant and a thousand francs from a Turk, all at fifty per cent interest.

By such means they raised enough to play the brilliant comedy of the Swedish embassy in the presence of the divan. Grothusen was received in Constantinople with all the honours the Porte bestows on the ambassadors extraordinary of kings on the day of their audience. The object of all this ostentation was to extort money from the grand-vizier, but that minister was inexorable.

Grothusen proposed to borrow a million from the Porte. The vizier replied coldly that his master gave generously when he wished but that it was beneath his dignity to lend; that the king would be amply provided with everything necessary for his journey; that the Porte might perhaps make him some present of uncoined gold, but that he must not count on it.

Finally, on the 1st of October 1714, the King of Sweden set out to leave Turkey. A capigi-pasha, accompanied by six chiaoux, came to fetch him from the castle of Demirtash where Charles had been living for the past few days. He presented him, on behalf of the sultan, with a large scarlet tent embroidered with gold, a sabre with a jewelled hilt and eight superb Arab horses, with magnificent saddles and solid silver stirrups. It is not beneath the dignity of a historian to record that the groom in charge of these horses gave the King their pedigree; this is a long-established custom among the Turks who seemed to attribute far more importance to the noble ancestry of horses than that of men. Perhaps this is not so unreasonable, since in the animal world, those whose breeding is carefully supervised to keep the strain absolutely pure never degenerate.

Sixty waggons, laden with all kinds of provisions, and three hundred horses made up the convoy. The capigi-pasha, knowing that several Turks had lent money to the king's suite at huge interest, told him that, as usury was forbidden by Mohammedan law, he begged his majesty not to pay the interest on his debts and to order the resident he was leaving in Constantinople to repay only the capital. 'No,' said the king, 'if my servants have given bills for a hundred crowns I wish to pay them, even if they have only received ten.'

He suggested that the creditors should follow him, promising that their expenses would be paid and their claims fully met. Several undertook the journey to Sweden, and Grothusen took care to see that they were paid.

To show more deference to their guest, the Turks made him

travel by very short stages, but this respectful slowness exasperated the king who was impatient to get on with the journey. On the road he got up as usual at three in the morning, and as soon as he was dressed he himself roused the capigi-pasha and the chiaoux and ordered the march to proceed in pitch darkness. The Turks' ceremonial arrangements were completely upset by this novel way of travelling, but the king revelled in the trouble he was causing them and said he was revenging himself a little for Bender.

While Charles was on his way to the Turkish frontier Stanislas was leaving Turkey by another road, intending to retire to the Duchy of Zweibrücken, a province bordering on the Palatinate of the Rhine and Alsace, which had belonged to the Kings of Sweden ever since Charles X, Queen Christina's successor, had joined this inheritance to the crown. Charles assigned the revenues of this duchy, then estimated at about seventy thousand crowns, to Stanislas. Such was the end to which so many wars, so many plans and so many hopes had led. Stanislas could and would have made an advantageous treaty with King Augustus, but Charles XII's indomitable obstinacy forced him to lose his estates and possessions in Poland in order to keep the title of king.

Stanislas remained in the Duchy of Zweibrücken until Charles's death. As this province then reverted to a palatine prince, he retired to Weissenbourg in French Alsace. M. Sum, King Augustus's ambassador, complained of this to the Duke of Orleans, the Regent of France. The duke gave M. Sum this emphatic reply: 'Sir, tell the king your master that France has always been the refuge of kings in misfortune.'

The King of Sweden, having arrived at the German frontier, learnt that the emperor had ordered that he was to be received with proper state throughout his dominions. The towns and villages through which it had been arranged beforehand he would pass made preparations for his reception. All their inhabitants waited impatiently to see this extraordinary man, whose victories and misfortunes had caused such a stir in Europe and Asia that his slightest activities and even his quiescence were matters of public interest. But Charles had no desire to be received with all this pomp or to be exhibited to the public as the prisoner of Bender; he had even decided never to re-enter Stockholm until he had retrieved his misfortunes.

When he arrived at Tergowitz, on the frontier of Transylvania, he dismissed his Turkish escort, and, having assembled his own retinue in a barn, he told them not to trouble about his person, but to make their way as quickly as they could to Stralsund, in Pomerania, on the shores of the Baltic, about three hundred leagues from where they were.

He took no one with him but a young man named During, and parted cheerfully from all his followers, leaving them astounded, sad and fearful for his safety. He disguised himself by putting on a black wig (for he always wore his own hair), a gold-laced hat, grey coat and breeches and a blue cloak, and, passing himself off as a German officer, galloped from post-house to post-house with his travelling companion, stopping only to change horses

He took a route which avoided as far as possible the dominions of his avowed or secret enemies and travelled via Hungary, Moravia, Austria, Bavaria, the Palatinate, Westphalia and Mecklenburg. Thus he went almost the whole way round Germany and lengthened his journey by half. At the end of the first day, after galloping for hours on end without a break, young During, who was not so inured to extreme hardship as his king, fainted when he dismounted. The king, who did not want to stop a moment on the road, asked During, when he came to, how much money he had. During replied that he had about a thousand crowns. 'Give me half,' said the king. 'I see you are in no state to follow me, so I will finish the journey on my own.' During implored him to deign at least to wait three hours, assuring him that by then he would be fit to ride again and accompany his majesty; he begged him to think of all the risks he was going to run, but the king was inexorable. He made him give him the money and demanded a horse. During, frightened by the king's resolve, then thought of an innocent ruse; he drew the post-master aside and said to him, pointing to the King of Sweden: 'That man is my cousin, and we are travelling on the same business. He sees I am ill, but will not wait even three hours for me. Please give him the worst horse in your stable and find me some kind of vehicle.'

He slipped two ducats into the post-master's hand and the man did exactly what he wanted. The king was given a lame and stubborn horse and departed alone on this sorry mount at ten o'clock at night, riding in the pitch dark through wind, rain and snow. His travelling companion, after a few hours' sleep, set off in a cart drawn by strong horses. At daybreak he caught up with the king who, unable to make his horse go a step further, was proceeding on foot to the next post-house.

He was compelled to get into During's cart, where he fell asleep on the straw. After this, they proceeded on their way, riding on horseback by day and sleeping in the little cart at night, without stopping anywhere.

After sixteen days' hard riding, and more than one narrow escape from being arrested, they finally arrived at the gates of Stralsund at one o'clock in the morning on 21st November 1714.

The king called out to the sentinel that he was a courier despatched from Turkey by the King of Sweden, and that he must speak at once to General Ducker, the governor of the city. The sentinel replied that it was late, the governor had gone to bed and they must wait till daybreak.

Charles replied that he had come on important business and swore if the guard did not go and wake the governor at once, they would all be hanged the next day. A sergeant finally went and awakened the governor. Ducker supposed it might be one of the Swedish King's generals, so the gates were opened and this courier was brought into his bedroom.

Ducker, still half asleep, asked for news of the King of Sweden; the king took him by the arm and exclaimed: 'What, Ducker, have all my most faithful subjects forgotten me?' Hardly able to believe his eyes, the general recognized the king; he leapt out of bed and embraced his master's knees, shedding tears of joy. The news immediately spread through the town; everybody got up, and the governor's house was soon surrounded by soldiers. The streets were thronged with citizens asking each other: 'Is it true the king is here?' All the windows were illuminated, the streets ran with wine in the glare of a thousand torches, while the cannons thundered a salute.

Meanwhile, the king was put to bed. He had not gone to bed for sixteen days, and his legs were so swollen from extreme fatigue that they had to cut his boots off. He had neither clothes nor linen, so they hastily assembled a wardrobe for him from the most suitable things they could find in the town. When he had slept a few hours, he got up only to go and review his troops and inspect the fortifications. The very same day he sent out orders to all parts to start waging war again, more fiercely than ever, against all his enemies. All these details, so typical of Charles XII's character, which I first learnt from Baron Fabrice, have been confirmed to me by the Comte de Croissi who was an ambassador at this prince's court.

Christian Europe was then in a very different state from what it had been when Charles left it in 1709.

The war, which for so long had rent the southern part, that is to say Germany, England, the Netherlands, France, Spain, Portugal and Italy, was over. This general peace had been the result of party strife at the English court. Lord Oxford, an able minister, and Lord Bolingbroke, a man of brilliant genius and the greatest orator of his age, prevailed against the famous Duke of Marlborough and persuaded Queen Anne to make peace with France. France, no longer having England as an enemy, soon forced the other powers to come to terms.

Philip V, Louis XIV's grandson, was beginning to reign peacefully over what remained of the Spanish empire. The Emperor of Germany, having become master of Naples and Flanders, was consolidating his vast dominions. Louis XIV no longer had any ambition other than to finish his long career in peace.

Anne, Queen of England, had died on the 10th of August 1714, hated by half her subjects for having granted peace to so many nations. As her brother, James Stuart, that ill-starred prince, who had been excluded from the throne almost from birth, did not appear in England to claim the succession, to which new laws would have entitled him had his party prevailed, George I, Elector of Hanover, was unanimously acknowledged as King of Great Britain. The throne passed to this elector, not because he was a blood descendant, although his mother was the daughter of James I, but because he had been appointed as Anne's successor by an Act of Parliament.

George, called late in life to rule a people whose language he did not understand and a country where everything was strange to him, thought of himself as the Elector of Hanover rather than the King of England. His whole ambition was to increase the prosperity of his German dominions, and every year he crossed the sea to revisit his subjects, who worshipped him. Moreover he much preferred to live on equal terms with other men, rather than as their master. The pomp of royalty was a heavy burden to him, and he lived surrounded by a few old courtiers with whom he was on intimate terms. He was not the most brilliant king in Europe, but he was one of the wisest, and the only reigning one who enjoyed the pleasures of private life and friendship. Such were the principal monarchs of central Europe and such was its political situation.

The changes which had occurred in the north were of another kind. Its kings were at war and united against the King of Sweden.

Augustus had long ago remounted the throne of Poland, with the help of the tsar and the consent of the Emperor of Germany, Anne of England and the States-General. All of them had been guarantors of the treaty of Alt-Ranstadt when Charles XII had had Europe under his thumb, but they had withdrawn their guarantee when he was no longer to be feared.

But Augustus was not enjoying a peaceful reign. The return of its king to the republic of Poland had soon revived its fears of absolute monarchy. It took up arms to force him to comply with the *pacta conventa* [covenanted agreement], the sacred contract between subjects and kings, and seemed to have recalled its sovereign only to declare war on him. At the beginning of these disturbances the name of Stanislas was never mentioned; his party seemed to have been annihilated. As for the King of Sweden, the Poles remembered him only as they might have remembered a torrent which had once swept through the land and for a while altered everything in its course.

Poltava and the absence of Charles XII had resulted not only in the downfall of Stanislas but also of the Duke of Holstein, Charles's nephew, who had been deprived of his dominions by the King of Denmark. The King of Sweden had been extremely fond of the father, and he was distressed and humiliated by the misfortunes of the son. Moreover, as he had never done anything in his life except for glory, the fall of sovereigns he had created or reinstated galled him as much as the loss of so many provinces.

His enemies vied with each other in enriching themselves by his losses. Frederick William, the new King of Prussia, whose disposition seemed to be as warlike as his father's had been peaceable, began by acquiring rights over Stettin and part of Pomerania by paying four hundred thousand crowns to the King of Denmark and the tsar.

The King of Denmark had also pawned the Duchies of Bremen and Verden to George, the Elector of Hanover who had become King of England, for sixty thousand pistoles. Thus the spoils of Charles XII had been divided up and the vested interests of those who held them in pledge made them as dangerous enemies as those who had captured them.

As to the tsar, he was undoubtedly the most to be feared. His former defeats, his victories and even his mistakes, combined with his persistence in teaching himself and in teaching his subjects what he had learnt and his incessant labours, had made him outstanding in every field. Riga was already captured; Livonia, Ingria, Karelia, half Finland and so many of the territories which Charles's ancestors had conquered were now under Russian rule.

Peter Alexeiovitch, who twenty years earlier had not had one craft in the Baltic, was now in command of that sea, with a fleet of thirty great ships of the line.

He had built one of these ships with his own hands and was the best carpenter, the best admiral and the best pilot in the North. There was not a single difficult channel, from the Gulf of Bothnia to the Arctic Ocean, that he had not personally sounded. He had become an admiral by degrees and by dint of victories, in the same way that he had wished to rise to the rank of general on land.

While Prince Galitzin, a general whom he had trained and one of those who helped him most in his campaigns, was completing the conquest of Finland, taking the city of Vasa and beating the Swedes, the tsar put to sea to go and conquer Aland, an island in the Baltic about twelve leagues from Stockholm.

He set off on this expedition at the beginning of July 1714, while his rival Charles XII was keeping to his bed in Demotica. He embarked at the port of Cronslot, which he had built, some years earlier, four miles from St Petersburg. This new harbour and the well-manned and equipped fleet anchored in it were all the result of his initiative and wherever he cast his gaze he saw nothing that he had not in some sense created.

On the fifteenth of July the Russian fleet was off Aland. It consisted of thirty ships of the line, eighty galleys and a hundred galliots, and carried twenty thousand soldiers. It was commanded by Admiral Apraxin, with the tsar serving as rear-admiral. The Swedish

fleet, commanded by Vice-Admiral Ehrenskiöld, came to meet it on
the 16th. It was a third the strength, but nevertheless fought for
three hours. The tsar engaged Ehrenskiöld's flagship and captured
it after a stubborn fight.

On the day of the victory, he landed sixteen thousand men on
Aland and, having captured several Swedish soldiers who had not
had time to get aboard Ehrenskiöld's ships, he carried them off as
prisoners on his own. He returned to Cronslot with Ehrenskiöld's
flagship, three smaller ships, a frigate and six galleys which he had
taken in this battle.

From Cronslot he proceeded to the harbour of St Petersburg,
followed by all his victorious fleet and the ships captured from the
enemy. He was greeted with a triple salute of a hundred and fifty
guns, after which he made a triumphal entry into the city. This
gratified him even more than that triumphal entry into Moscow,
because he was receiving these honours in his favourite city, in a
place where there were now thirty-four thousand five hundred
houses, and finally because he was now in command, not only of a
victorious navy, but of the only Russian fleet that had ever been
seen in the Baltic and which had been created in a country which
had not even known what a fleet was before him.

The ceremonies which accompanied the triumphal entry into St
Petersburg were very similar to the ones in Moscow. The Swedish
vice-admiral was the principal trophy exhibited in this new triumph;
Peter Alexeiovitch appeared in his capacity as rear-admiral. A
Russian nobleman named Romanodowski, who represented the
tsar on state occasions, was seated on a throne, attended by twelve
senators. The rear-admiral presented him with an account of his
victory, and was appointed vice-admiral in consideration of his
services. This was an odd ceremony, but it had its significance in a
country where military rank and discipline were some of the novelties
the tsar had introduced.

The Russian Emperor, besides defeating the Swedes on land and
sea, had helped to drive them out of Poland. As a result he now
wielded as much power in that country as Charles XII had done. He
had set himself up as mediator between the republic and Augustus,
which perhaps gave him as much satisfaction as setting up a king.
All the power and success Charles had once enjoyed had passed to

the tsar, who made better use of them than his rival had done, for he turned all his victories to the advantage of his country. If he captured a town he made its principal artisans go to St Petersburg and set up their industries there. The manufactures, arts and sciences of the provinces he had conquered from Sweden were transported to Russia. Since his dominions were enriched by his conquests he had a better excuse for them than any other conqueror.

Sweden, on the contrary, deprived of nearly all her overseas dominions, no longer had any trade, money or credit. Her veteran troops, once so redoubtable, had died on the battlefields or perished of want. More than a hundred thousand Swedes were slaves in the tsar's vast dominions, and nearly as many had been sold to the Turks and the Tartars. The male population had visibly dwindled, but hope revived as soon as it was known that the king was in Stralsund.

The feelings of respect and admiration for him were still so strong in the minds of his subjects that the young men in the rural areas flocked to enlist in the army, although there were not enough hands to till the fields.

BOOK VIII

IN the midst of these preparations the king gave his remaining sister, Ulrica-Eleonora, in marriage to the Prince of Hesse. The dowager queen, their eighty-year-old grandmother, did the honours at the wedding feast, which was held in the palace of Stockholm on the 4th of April 1715, and died not long after.

This wedding was not honoured by the presence of the king. He remained in Stralsund, busy completing the fortification of this important town, which was menaced by the Kings of Denmark and Prussia. Nevertheless he appointed his brother-in-law generalissimo of his armies in Sweden. This prince had served the Dutch government in the wars against France; he was regarded as a good general, a qualification which had contributed not a little to Charles's choice of him as a husband for his sister.

Reverses were now following as fast on each other as victories had once done. In the month of June of that year 1715, the German troops of the King of England and the forces of the King of Denmark besieged the fortified city of Wismar; at the same time a combined force of Danes and Saxons, thirty-six thousand strong, marched to Stralsund to lay siege to it. The Kings of Denmark and Prussia sank five Swedish ships near Stralsund. The tsar was then in the Baltic Sea with five great warships and a hundred and fifty transports with thirty thousand men aboard. He was threatening an invasion of Sweden; now advancing as far as the coast of Hälsingborg, now appearing off Stockholm. All Sweden was in arms, expecting this invasion at any moment. At the same time his land forces were driving the Swedes out of every place they still possessed in Finland towards the Gulf of Bothnia; but the tsar proceeded no further in his campaigns.

At the mouth of the Oder, the river which divides Pomerania in two and which flows past Stettin on its way to the Baltic Sea, lies the little island of Usedom. This island in the Gulf of Pomerania is very important on account of its situation, which commands two entrances to the Oder; whoever holds it controls the navigation of the river. The King of Prussia had dislodged the Swedes from this island and taken possession of it, as well as Stettin, which he kept in sequestration, 'entirely', as he said, 'for the sake of peace'. The Swedes had recaptured Usedom in May 1715. There were two forts on it; one was the fort of the Swinemünde, on one arm of the Oder; the other and more important one was Peenemünde, on the opposite arm of the river. All the King of Sweden had to hold these two forts and the whole island were two hundred and fifty Pomeranian soldiers, commanded by an old Swedish officer named Kuse-Slerp, whose name deserves to be remembered.

On the 4th of August the King of Prussia sent fifteen hundred infantry and eight hundred dragoons to land on the island: they landed, without opposition, on the side of the fort of Swinemünde. The Swedish commander abandoned this fort to them as the less important; and, being unable to divide his small force, he withdrew it to the fort of Peenemünde, determined to defend himself to the last.

It was therefore necessary to subject it to a regular siege. In preparation for this, artillery was shipped from Stettin and the Prussian troops reinforced by a thousand infantry and four hundred cavalry. On the 18th August the trench was breached in two places and the place fiercely bombarded by cannons and mortars. During the siege a Swedish soldier, secretly charged with a letter from Charles XII, managed to land on the island and get into Peenemünde. He delivered the letter to the commander, which ran as follows: 'Do not fire until the enemies are on the edge of the trench; defend yourself to the last drop of your blood: I wish you good fortune. Charles.'

Having read this note, Slerp resolved to obey and to die, as he had been bid, in his master's service. At daybreak on the 22nd the enemy launched the assault; the besieged, firing only when they saw the besiegers on the edge of the trench, killed a great many of them: but the assailants, far superior to them in numbers, poured into the trench, and entered the fortress in two places simultaneously, through the wide breaches made by the artillery. The commandant's one idea then was to sell his life dear and to obey Charles's letter. He abandoned the breaches through which the enemy were swarming and entrenched his little troop, which had the courage and loyalty to follow him, near a bastion, in a position where it could not be surrounded. The enemy, amazed that he had not asked for quarter, rushed to attack him in this last stand. He fought for a whole hour, but, after losing half his soldiers, he was finally killed, along with his lieutenant and his major. Then the hundred privates and the one officer who were left, asked that their lives should be spared and were taken prisoner. In the commander's pocket they found Charles's letter, which was handed over to the King of Prussia.

All this while, when Charles was losing the island of Usedom and the neighbouring islands which were captured soon after; when Wismar was on the point of surrender, when he no longer had a fleet and Sweden was being threatened, he himself was in Stralsund, a place that was already being besieged by thirty-six thousand men.

Stralsund, a town that has become famous in Europe through the siege Charles XII sustained there, is the most important stronghold in Pomerania. It is built between the Baltic Sea and Lake Franken, on the Straits of Galla. It can only be reached by land by a narrow causeway defended by a citadel and by trenches which were thought to be impregnable. It had a garrison of nearly nine thousand, and moreover, the King of Sweden himself was in command of the town. The Kings of Denmark and Prussia set out to besiege it with an army of thirty-six thousand men, composed of Prussians, Danes and Saxons.

The honour of besieging Charles XII was such a powerful incentive that they easily overcame all the obstacles, and breached the trench on the night of the 19th–20th of the October of that year, 1715. At the beginning of the siege the King of Sweden said that he could not understand how a well-fortified city, manned with a sufficient garrison, could be taken. True, in the course of his past conquests he had taken many cities, but hardly ever by a regular siege, for in those days the terror of his arms had carried all before it; moreover he did not judge others by himself, and underrated his enemies. The besiegers pressed on assiduously with their task, and their efforts were helped by a very odd stroke of chance.

It is well known that there are no tides in the Baltic. The trench which protected the town, and which was backed on the west side by an impassable marsh and on the east by the sea, seemed safe against any assault. No one had noticed that when a strong west wind was blowing it forced the waves of the Baltic to recede, leaving the water only three feet deep in the vicinity of the trench which they thought was bounded by impassable sea. A soldier who accidently fell into it from the parapet of the trench, was surprised to find bottom. Promptly struck by the idea that this discovery might make his fortune, he deserted and went to the quarters of the general of the Saxon troops, Count Wackerbarth, to inform him that the Swedes' trenches could easily be reached and breached by wading through the sea. The King of Prussia lost no time in making good use of this information.

Accordingly, at midnight the next day, as the west wind was still blowing hard, Lieutenant-Colonel Koppen waded into the sea, followed by eighteen hundred men: at the same time two thousand advanced along the causeway which led to this trench: the whole of the Prussian artillery opened fire, and the Prussians and Danes sounded the alarm on the other side.

The Swedes were sure they could overcome these two thousand men whom they saw advancing, apparently so rashly, along the causeway, but suddenly Koppen, with his eighteen hundred men, came upon them from behind, having made their way into the trench from the side of the sea. The Swedes, surrounded and taken by surprise, were unable to resist, and the position was captured, after much slaughter on both sides. Some Swedes fled to the town; the besiegers pursued them and entered it pell-mell along with the fugitives: two officers and four Saxon privates were already on the drawbridge, but it was raised just in time; they were captured, and, for the moment, the city was saved.

The enemy found twenty-four cannons in the trenches they had taken, and turned them on Stralsund. Inspired with confidence by this first success they pressed on stubbornly with the siege, shelling and bombarding the town with relentless persistence.

Opposite Stralsund, in the Baltic Sea, is the island of Rügen, which serves as a rampart to this city, and to which the garrison and the citizens could have retired, if they had had boats to transport them. This island was of extreme importance to Charles; he was well aware that if the enemy gained control of it he would find himself besieged by land and sea, and in all probability would end up either buried under the ruins of Stralsund or a prisoner in the hands of those very enemies he had so long despised and on whom he had imposed such harsh terms. Nevertheless, his precarious situation had not permitted him to provide Rügen with an adequate garrison; there were not more than two thousand of his troops on it.

For three months his enemies had been making all the necessary preparations to invade this island, for landing troops on it presented considerable difficulties. Finally their boats were built and manned, and helped by good weather the Prince of Anhalt landed on Rügen on the 15th of November, with twelve thousand men. The king, who was everywhere, was on the island; he had joined his two thousand men who were entrenched near a little harbour, three leagues from the spot where the enemy had landed. He placed himself at their head, and marched in the middle of the night, in complete silence. The Prince of Anhalt had already entrenched his troops, with what seemed to be unnecessary precaution. The officers under his command did not expect to be attacked that very night, and they believed Charles to be in Stralsund. But the Prince of Anhalt, who knew that, with Charles, one had to be prepared for anything, had ordered a deep ditch to be dug and fenced with *chevaux-de-frise* and taken all the defensive precautions he would have taken had he had to contend with an army superior in numbers to his own.

At two o'clock in the morning Charles reached the enemy's camp, without making the slightest noise. Then some of his soldiers said to each other: 'Pull up the *chevaux-de-frise*.' These words were overheard by the sentries; the alarm was raised in the camp and the call to arms sounded. The king, having removed the *chevaux-de-frise*, saw a great ditch gaping in front of him. He was so totally unprepared for this that he could hardly believe his eyes. Surprised as he was, he was not in the least discouraged; he did not know how many troops had landed; on the other hand, his enemies did not know how few they had to deal with. The darkness of the night seemed to be in his favour; so he made up his mind on the spot to continue with his attack. He flung himself into the trench, accompanied by his boldest men, and, in a moment, by all the rest. They filled up the ditch with the wrenched-up *chevaux-de-frise*, all the tree-trunks and branches they could find, crumbling clods of earth and even the corpses of their comrades killed by random shots, to give them a foothold. The king, the generals he had with him, and the bravest of the officers and privates climbed on each other's shoulders as if mounting to the assault in a siege. A fierce fight was waged in the enemy's camp. At first the vehemence of the Swedish attack threw the Danes and Prussians into confusion; but the numbers were too unequal, and after a quarter-of-an-hour's fighting, the Swedes were repulsed and retreated back across the trench. The Prince of Anhalt then pursued them into the plain, not knowing that it was Charles XII himself who was fleeing before him. This unlucky king rallied his troops in open country, and the battle recommenced with equal stubbornness on both sides. His favourite, Grothusen, and General Dahldorf fell dead close beside him. While fighting, Charles trod on the body of Dahldorf, who was still breathing. During, his sole companion on his journey from Turkey to Stralsund, was killed before his eyes.

In the midst of this fray a Danish lieutenant, whose name I have never been able to discover, recognized Charles and wrenching his sword from him with one hand and grabbing him fast by the hair with the other, cried: 'Surrender, sire, or I kill you!' Charles had a pistol in his belt; he drew it with his left hand and shot this officer, who died of the wound the next day. The name of King Charles, which this Dane had cried out, immediately attracted a crowd of enemy soldiers. The king was surrounded. A bullet struck him below the left breast; the wound, which he called a scratch, was two fingers deep. The king was on foot, on the verge of being killed or captured. Count Poniatowski was fighting near him at that moment. He had saved his life at Poltava and he had the good fortune to save it again in this battle of Rügen and put him back on his horse.

The Swedes retreated to a place called Alteferre, where there was a fort they still held. From there the king crossed over again to Stralsund, obliged to abandon the brave troops who had supported him so well in this enterprise: they were all taken prisoners of war two days later.

Among these prisoners was that unlucky French regiment, composed of the survivors of the battle of Hochstedt, which had passed into the service of King Augustus, and from thence into that of the King of Sweden. The majority of the soldiers were incorporated into a new regiment of one of the Prince of Anhalt's sons, who was their fourth commander. The man who at that time commanded this wandering regiment in Rügen was none other than that Comte de Villelongue who had so generously risked his life in Adrianople to do a service to Charles XII. He was captured with his troops, and was subsequently very ill-recompensed for so many services, hardships and misfortunes.

The king, after all these prodigies of valour which had served only to weaken his forces, and pent up once more in Stralsund, which might be captured any moment by his besiegers, behaved exactly as he had done at Bender. Nothing disturbed him; by day he supervised the building of barricades and trenches behind the walls; by night he made sorties against the enemy. Meanwhile Stralsund was being battered for breaching. Bombs rained on the houses, and half the town was in ashes. The citizens, far from complaining, were so full of admiration for their master whose strenuous exertions, self-control and courage amazed them, that they had all become soldiers under him. They accompanied him on his sorties, and acted as a second garrison.

One day, when the king was dictating letters for Sweden to a secretary, a bomb fell on the house, went through the roof, and exploded near the very room he was in, bringing down half the floor. The study in which he was dictating was partly cut into a thick wall and was not damaged by the blast and, by astonishing luck, none of the flying splinters blew into it though the door was open. The noise of the bomb and the crash of falling timbers, which sounded as if the whole house was coming down, made the secretary drop his pen. 'What's the matter?' asked the king calmly. 'Why have you stopped writing?' The secretary could only stammer: 'But – sire – the bomb!' – 'Well, what has the bomb got to do with the letter I am dictating to you?' retorted the king. 'Get on with your work.'

Pent up with the King of Sweden in Stralsund at that time was a French ambassador, the Comte de Croissi, a lieutenant-general in the French army and the brother of the Marquis de Torci, a famous minister. He was a member of the Colbert family and a relative of that famous Colbert whose name is immortal in France. To send a man on an embassy to Charles XII was tantamount to sending him into the trenches. The king conversed with Croissi in the most exposed spots, while cannon-balls and bombs were killing people all round them, without the king paying the slightest heed to the danger or the ambassador liking so much as to hint that there were more suitable places for discussing diplomatic affairs. Before the siege this minister had done his utmost to arrange a settlement between the Kings of Sweden and Prussia, but the latter demanded too much and Charles XII refused to concede anything. Thus the only satisfaction the Comte de Croissi derived from his embassy was that of enjoying the familiar intimacy of this extraordinary man. He often slept beside him on the same cloak, and by sharing his dangers and hardships he acquired the right to talk to him freely. Charles encouraged this boldness in people he liked. Because he was talking to a Frenchman, he insisted, as always, on speaking Latin: sometimes he would say to the Comte de Croissi: *Veni, maledicamus de rege* [Now, let us speak ill of the king], the king, whom he proposed they should denigrate, being himself. It was from this ambassador's own lips that I heard this.

Croissi remained in the town until the 13th of November; but at last, having obtained permission from the enemy to pass through their lines with his baggage, he took leave of the King of Sweden, whom he left in the midst of the ruins of Stralsund, with a garrison depleted by two thirds, still determined to sustain an assault.

In fact, one was made two days later on the horn-work. The enemy captured it twice, and were twice driven out of it. The king fought the whole time among the grenadiers; finally numbers prevailed and the besiegers remained in possession of it. Charles stayed another two days in the town, expecting a general assault any moment. On the 19th he remained till midnight on a little ravelin, almost totally wrecked by shells and bombs: the next day, the principal officers begged him to leave a place which there was no longer any hope of defending; but retreat had become as dangerous as the place itself. The Baltic Sea was swarming with Danish and Russian ships. There was nothing in the harbour of Stralsund but a little sloop with sails and oars. Since so many perils made this retreat glorious, Charles decided to leave. He embarked on the night of the 20th of November 1715, with only ten men. They had to break the ice with which the sea in the harbour was covered; this laborious task took several hours before the ship could sail freely. The enemy admirals had strict orders not to let Charles escape from Stralsund and to capture him dead or alive. Luckily they were to leeward, and could not approach him. He ran a still greater risk when sailing past the island of Rügen, near a gun emplacement where the Danes had mounted a battery of twelve cannons. They opened fire on the king. The crew hoisted more sail and took to the oars as well as to get out of range; but a cannon-ball killed two men at Charles's side and another shattered the mast. In the midst of these dangers the king reached two of his ships which were cruising in the Baltic. The next day Stralsund surrendered, and the garrison were made prisoners of war. Charles landed at Ystad in Scania, and from there returned to Karlskrona, in a very different state from when he had left it fifteen years earlier, in a ship of a hundred and twenty guns, to become the master of the north.

Being so near his capital it was expected tha the would revisit it after so long an absence; but he did not intend to return to it until he had gained some victories. Moreover, he could not bring himself yet to see his people, who loved him and whom he was forced to oppress in order to defend himself against his enemies. The only person he wanted to see was his sister, so he arranged a rendezvous with her on the shore of Lake Vättern in Ostrogothia. He travelled post to the meeting-place, accompanied by a single servant, and returned after spending one day with her.

From Karlskrona, where he spent the winter, he issued orders for fresh troops to be levied throughout his kingdom. He believed that all his subjects were born for the sole purpose of following him to war, and he had accustomed them to believe so too. Lads of fifteen enlisted and in several villages only old men, women and children were left; in many places only women were to be seen ploughing the fields.

It was still more difficult to provide a fleet. To meet this deficiency, privateers were given excessive privileges which were disastrous for the country, in return for which they supplied some ships: these efforts were Sweden's last resource. To meet so many heavy expenses, the people had to be squeezed dry. There was no form of extortion which was not practised under the name of taxes and dues. All the houses were searched and half the provisions in them commandeered to put in the king's warehouses; all the iron in the kingdom was bought up on his behalf by the government which paid for it in paper money and sold it for solid cash. All those who wore anything made of silk or had wigs or gilded swords were taxed, and every householder had to pay a heavy hearth-tax. This crushing load of taxation would have caused the people to rebel against any other king, but the poorest peasant in Sweden knew that his sovereign led a harder and more frugal life than he did, so everyone put up uncomplainingly with the hardships which the king was the first to endure.

The public danger even made them forget their private troubles. They expected Sweden to be invaded any moment by the Russians, Danes, Prussians, Saxons and even the English. This fear was so strong and so well-founded, that those who had money or valuables buried them.

In fact, an English fleet had already appeared in the Baltic without anyone knowing what its orders were; and the King of Denmark had the tsar's promise that the Russians would combine with the Danes to invade Sweden in the spring of 1716.

The whole of Europe, which followed the fortunes of Charles XII with an attentive eye, was amazed when, instead of defending his country against the many princes who menaced it, he invaded Norway in the month of March 1716, with twenty thousand men.

Since Hannibal, there had been no instance of a general who, unable to hold his own against his enemies at home, had gone to attack them in their own dominions. His brother-in-law accompanied Charles in this expedition.

The only way he could enter Norway from Sweden was by quite dangerous mountain passes, and when his army had marched through these, it was confronted at intervals with sheets of water formed between the rocks by the sea, which meant that bridges had to be built every day. A handful of Danes could have halted the Swedish army, but they had not foreseen this sudden invasion. Europe was still more amazed that the tsar remained quiet in the midst of these events and did not invade Sweden as he had promised his allies.

The reason for this inactivity was that he was involved in one of the greatest plans, and at the same time one of the most difficult to execute, ever conceived by the human mind.

Baron Henry de Görtz, a Franconian by birth and a hereditary baron of the empire, having rendered important services to the King of Sweden during his sojourn in Bender, had since become his favourite and prime minister.

Never was a man at once so versatile and so audacious, so full of resources when things were at their worst, so vast in his aims or so active in furthering them. No project dismayed him, and there was no length to which he would not go to achieve it; gifts, promises, oaths, truth and falsehood were all means he used lavishly to serve his end.

He went from Sweden to France, England and Holland to test for himself the feasibility of the means he intended to employ in the great design he had conceived and which he was quite capable of executing. Had he succeeded in doing so the whole face of Europe would have been changed. What his master was at the head of an army, Görtz was in the cabinet: thus he gained an influence over Charles which no minister had ever had before him.

This king, who, at the age of twenty, had never given anything but orders to Count Piper, now took lessons from Baron Görtz; he was all the more submissive to this minister because misfortune had made it necessary for him to listen to advice, and because Görtz only gave him advice which suited his courageous nature. He noticed that, of the many princes leagued against Sweden, George, Elector of Hanover and King of England, was the one against whom Charles felt most resentment, because he was the only one whom Charles had never offended, and because George had entered into the quarrel on the pretext of pacifying it, but in reality only to keep Bremen and Verden, to which he seemed to have no right other than having bought them at a bargain price from the King of Denmark, to whom they did not belong.

He also perceived very early that the tsar was secretly displeased with his allies, who had all prevented him from gaining a foothold in the German Empire, considering this monarch too dangerous to do so, much as he longed to. Wismar, the only town on the German coast which still remained to the Swedes, had just surrendered at last to the Prussians and Danes on the 14th of February 1716. These had not allowed the Russian troops, who were in Mecklenburg, to take any part in the siege. Similar instances of mistrust, repeated over a period of two years, had alienated the tsar and perhaps saved Sweden. There are many examples of allied nations being conquered by a single power; there are very few of a great empire being conquered by several allies. If their combined forces overthrow it, their divisions soon raise it up again.

The tsar could have invaded Sweden as long ago as 1714. But whether because he did not agree with the kings of Poland, England, Denmark and Prussia, his justifiably jealous allies, or because he did not think his troops sufficiently seasoned yet to attack a nation whose mere peasants had defeated the pick of the Danish troops, on its native soil, he always postponed this enterprise.

Another thing which had prevented him was lack of money. The tsar was one of the most powerful monarchs in the world, but one of the poorest; his revenues at that time amounted to no more than twenty-four million of our francs. He had discovered gold, silver, iron and copper mines, but the profit from them was uncertain and the working of them ruinously expensive. He was establishing a great trade, but in its early stages it brought him no more than hopes: his newly-conquered provinces increased his power and glory, but not his revenues. Time was needed to heal the war wounds of Livonia, a fertile country, but one which had been so devastated for fifteen years by fire, sword and pestilence, that it was almost depopulated, and was now a liability to its conqueror. The fleets he maintained and the new enterprises he launched every day drained his finances. He was reduced to the bad expedient of devaluing the currency, a remedy which never cures a nation's ills and which is particularly injurious to a country which imports more goods than it exports.

Such were some of the foundations on which Görtz based his revolutionary plan. He dared to propose to the King of Sweden that he should make peace with the Russian Emperor at any price, pointing out to him that the tsar was angry with the Kings of Poland and England and suggesting that if Charles and Peter united they could make the rest of Europe tremble.

There was no way of making peace with the tsar except by ceding the greater part of the provinces to the east and north of the Baltic, but he drew Charles's attention to the fact that, by ceding these provinces, which the tsar already possessed and which could not be recaptured from him, he might have the glory of replacing Stanislas on the throne of Poland, setting the son of James II on that of England, as well as re-establishing the Duke of Holstein in his dominions.

Charles, flattered by these grand notions, though without putting too much faith in them, gave his minister a free hand. Görtz left Sweden, furnished with a mandate which authorized him to do whatever he wished, and gave him plenipotentiary status in the courts of all the princes with whom he thought it expedient to negotiate. He first sounded out the Court of Moscow by means of the tsar's chief physician, who was a Scot, and like nearly all the Scots who did not depend on the favours of the English court, devoted to the cause of the pretender.

With the enthusiasm of a man who had a keen personal interest in it, this doctor persuaded Prince Menzikoff of the greatness and importance of the plan. Prince Menzikoff was convinced by his arguments, and the tsar approved of the project. Instead of invading Sweden, as had been agreed with his allies, he sent his troops to winter in Mecklenburg, and went there himself on the pretext of settling some quarrels which were arising between the Duke of Mecklenburg and the nobility of that country, but in fact in pursuance of his favourite plan of acquiring a principality in Germany, and hoping to make the Duke of Mecklenburg sell him his.

The allies were angered at this step: they did not want so formidable a neighbour, who, once he had a territory in Germany, might get himself elected emperor and oppress the German princes. The angrier they became the more successfully Görtz's great plan was furthered. Nevertheless, he negotiated with all the allied princes, the better to hide his secret intrigues. The tsar, too, distracted them all by continuing to offer them hopes of his fulfilling his commitments. Meanwhile, Charles was in Norway with his brother-in-law the Prince of Hesse, at the head of twenty thousand men; the country was guarded only by eleven thousand Danes, divided into several contingents, which Charles and the Prince of Hesse routed.

Charles advanced as far as Christiana, the capital. Fortune was beginning to favour him again in this part of the world, but never had the king been so hard put to it to feed his troops. An army and a Danish fleet were approaching to defend Norway. Charles was forced, from lack of provisions, to return to Sweden and await the outcome of his minister's vast enterprises.

This undertaking demanded profound secrecy and immense preparations, two somewhat incompatible things. Görtz sought as far as the seas of Asia for help, which, odious as it seemed, would have been none the less useful for an invasion of Scotland and which would at least have brought Sweden money, men and ships.

For a long while, pirates of all nations, particularly the English, had banded together and infested the seas of Europe and America. Relentlessly pursued everywhere, they had just retreated to the coast of Madagascar, a large island to the east of Africa. They were desperate men, nearly all of them famous for deeds which, had they been lawful, would have been heroic. They were looking for a prince who would be willing to take them under his protection, but international law closed all the harbours of the world to them.

As soon as they knew that Charles XII had returned to Sweden, they hoped that this prince, who had a passion for war and was being obliged to wage it without a fleet or sufficient soldiers, might come to a satisfactory arrangement with them. They sent a deputy to him, who travelled to Europe in a Dutch ship and approached Baron Görtz with the proposition that they should be admitted to the harbour of Gothenburg, to which they offered to bring sixty ships loaded with treasure.

The baron induced the king to agree to this proposal, and the very next year two Swedish noblemen, Cromstrom and Mendal, were sent to Madagascar to conclude the bargain with these pirates.

Later, Görtz found a nobler and more important source of help in Cardinal Alberoni, a powerful genius who had governed Spain long enough to establish his fame but not long enough to restore that country to its former greatness. He eagerly welcomed the project of putting the son of James II on the English throne. Nevertheless, as he had only just assumed the reins of government, and had to set Spain on a firm footing before thinking of overthrowing other kingdoms, it seemed that it would be several years before he could take part in this great scheme. But in less than two years he had changed the face of Spain, restored her prestige in Europe and, according to report, was advising the Turks to attack the Emperor of Germany, while at the same time plotting to deprive the Duke of Orleans of the regency of France and King George of the crown of England. So dangerous can one man be when he is in absolute control of a powerful state and has a great and courageous spirit!

Having scattered sparks in the Courts of Russia and Spain to be kindled into the great conflagration he was planning, Görtz went secretly to France, and thence to Holland, where he had interviews with the pretender's supporters.

He acquired as much detailed information as possible about their strength, the number and disposition of the disaffected in England, the money they could provide and the troops they could muster. The disaffected asked for only ten thousand men and were convinced that, with the aid of these troops, success was assured.

On Görtz's instructions, Count Gyllenborg, the Swedish ambassador in England, held several conferences with the leading Jacobites; he encouraged them and promised them all they wanted. The pretender's party went so far as to provide considerable sums of money which Görtz received in Holland. He negotiated the purchase of some ships, six of which he bought in Brittany, as well as weapons of all kinds.

He then secretly despatched several officers to France, among others the Chevalier de Folard, who having fought in thirty campaigns in the French army with little reward for his services, had since offered them to Charles XII, less from motives of self-interest than from the desire to serve under a king who had such an amazing reputation. The Chevalier de Folard hoped, moreover, that he could interest this prince in his new ideas on warfare; he had studied the art and theory of war all his life and later published his discoveries in his *Commentaries on Polybius*. His views appealed to Charles XII, who had himself waged war in a new way and had never allowed convention to influence him in anything: he destined the Chevalier de Folard to be one of the instruments he intended to use in the projected invasion of Scotland. This nobleman carried out Baron Görtz's secret orders in France. Several officers and a greater number of Irishmen entered into this new kind of plot, which was being woven simultaneously in England, France and Russia and whose strands extended secretly from one end of Europe to the other.

For Görtz, these preparations were still very sketchy, but the great thing was that they had begun. The most important matter, without which nothing could succeed, was to bring peace between Charles and the tsar; many difficulties remained to be smoothed out. Baron Osterman, the Russian minister of state, had not at first let himself be drawn into Görtz's schemes: he was as cautious as Görtz was enterprising. His slow and moderate policy was to let everything ripen gradually, whereas the other's impatient nature wanted to reap immediately after he had sowed. Osterman feared that the emperor, his master, dazzled by the brilliance of the project, might grant Sweden too advantageous a peace, so he delayed the conclusion of this affair by spinning out the proceedings and raising objections at every turn.

Luckily for Baron Görtz, the tsar himself came to Holland at the beginning of 1717. His intention was to go on afterwards to France; he had not yet visited that famous country which, for more than a century, had been criticized, envied and imitated by all its neighbours. He wanted to satisfy his insatiable passion for seeing and learning and at the same time pursue his political ends.

Görtz saw the tsar twice at The Hague and got further in these two conferences than he had done in six months with plenipotentiaries. Everything was turning out well: his great plans seemed veiled in impenetrable secrecy and he flattered himself that Europe would know nothing of them till they were carried out. However, at The Hague, he talked of nothing but peace: he openly proclaimed that he wished to see the King of England act as the peacemaker of the north; he even made a pretence of urging that a congress should be held in Brunswick, at which the differences between Sweden and her enemies could be settled amicably.

The first to discover these intrigues was the Duke of Orleans, the Regent of France, who had spies all over Europe. Men of this type, who make their living by selling their friends' secrets and subsist on accusations and even slanders, had multiplied to such an extent under his government that half the nation had become spies on the other half. The Duke of Orleans, who had personal obligations to the King of England, informed him of the plots which were being hatched against him.

At the same time, the Dutch, who had taken offence at Görtz's behaviour, communicated their suspicions to the English minister. Görtz and Gyllenborg were pressing on enthusiastically with their plans, when they were both arrested, one at Deventer in Guelders, the other in London.

As Gyllenborg, the Swedish ambassador, had violated international law by conspiring against the prince to whom he had been sent, the English had no scruples about violating the same law by laying hands on his person. But everyone was amazed that the States-General should be so incredibly obliging to the King of England as to put Baron Görtz in prison. They even instructed Count Welderen to interrogate him. This formality was yet another insult, and since it proved futile, only made them look fools. Görtz asked Count Welderen if he knew him. 'Yes,' replied the Dutchman. 'Well then,' said Baron Görtz, 'if you know me, you ought to know that I only say what I wish.' The interrogation proceeded no further. All the ambassadors, particularly the Marquis of Monteleon, the Spanish minister in England, protested against the offence committed against the persons of Görtz and Gyllenborg. The Dutch had no excuse: they had not only violated a sacred law in arresting the King of Sweden's prime minister, who had plotted nothing against them, but they were acting directly against the principles of that precious liberty which has attracted so many foreigners to their country and been the foundation of its greatness.

As regards the King of England, he had only done what was just in arresting an enemy. To justify himself he had the correspondence between Görtz and Gyllenborg, found among the latter's papers, printed. The King of Sweden was in the province of Scania when these printed letters were brought to him, with the news of the imprisonment of his two ministers. He asked, with a smile, whether they had not also printed his. He immediately ordered the English resident and all his family and servants to be arrested in Stockholm and the Dutch resident to be forbidden access to his court and kept under close watch. However he neither admitted nor disowned any responsibility for Baron Görtz. Being too proud to deny that he knew and approved of this enterprise, and too wise to admit being privy to a plot which had been discovered almost as soon as it was hatched, he maintained a disdainful silence towards England and Holland.

The tsar took quite another line. As he was not named, but only obscurely hinted at, in Gyllenborg's and Görtz's letters, he wrote a long letter to the King of England, full of congratulations on the discovery of the plot, and assurances of the warmest friendship. King George did not believe these protestations, but pretended that he did. A plot hatched by private individuals is annihilated when it is discovered, but a plot hatched by kings only gains new strength from discovery. The tsar arrived in Paris in the May of that same year 1717. He did not spend his time solely in seeing the beauties of art and nature, visiting academies and public libraries, experimental laboratories and royal palaces: he proposed to the Duke of Orleans, the Regent of France, a treaty, which had he accepted it, would have set the final seal on Russia's greatness. His plan was to ally himself with the King of Sweden, who was to cede larger territories to him, to deprive the Danes of their command over the Baltic Sea, to weaken the English by a civil war and to attract all the trade of the north to Russia. He even thought of stirring up strife again between King Stanislas and King Augustus, so that, having lit the fire in all these places, he could fan it into a blaze or extinguish it, as best suited his interests. With these ideas in mind, he proposed to the Regent of France that he should act as mediator between Sweden and Russia and moreover proposed an offensive and defensive alliance between these countries and Spain. This treaty, which seemed so natural and so advantageous to these nations and would put the balance of Europe in their hands, was nevertheless rejected by the Duke of Orleans. At that very time, he was making quite the opposite commitments and allying himself with the Emperor of Germany and George, King of England. Political motives were now making all the princes change their mind to such an extent that the tsar was prepared to abjure his former ally, King Augustus, and espouse the cause of his mortal enemy, Charles, while France, for the sake of the English and Germans, was going to make war on Louis XIV's grandson after having supported him for so long against those very enemies at the cost of so much money and bloodshed. All that the tsar obtained by indirect means was that the regent should use his good offices to secure the release of Baron Görtz and Count Gyllenborg. He returned to his own country at the end of June, after having presented France with the rare spectacle of an emperor who travelled in order to learn. But too many Frenchmen saw only the outward boorishness which was the legacy of his bad upbringing, and the great legislator who had created a new nation escaped their notice.

What he had looked for in the Duke of Orleans he soon found in Cardinal Alberoni, who had become all-powerful in Spain. Alberoni desired nothing more ardently than the establishment of the pretender on the English throne. He desired it both as the chief minister of Spain, which England had treated so ill, and as a personal enemy of the Duke of Orleans who was leagued with England against Spain, and lastly as a priest of the church for which the pretender's father had lost his crown.

The Duke of Ormond, who was as popular in England as the Duke of Marlborough was admired there, had left his country at the accession of King George and retired to Madrid. Armed with full powers by the King of Spain and the pretender, he went to meet the tsar on his journey home, at Mittau in Courland, accompanied by Irnegan, another able and enterprising Englishman. He asked the hand of the tsar's daughter, Princess Anna Petrovna,* in marriage for the son of James II, hoping that this alliance would attach the tsar more closely to the cause of this unfortunate prince. But this proposal set matters back for a while instead of advancing them. In Görtz's plans, this princess had long been destined to marry the Duke of Holstein, whom she did in fact marry later. As soon as Görtz heard of the Duke of Ormond's proposal, he was jealous of it and set out to thwart it. He left prison in August, as did Count Gyllenborg, without the King of Sweden having deigned to make the least apology to the King of England or show the slightest displeasure at his minister's conduct.

At the same time, the English resident and his family were released in Stockholm, where they had been treated far more harshly than Gyllenborg had been in London.

Görtz, set free, was an even more dangerous enemy, for he was

---

* Cardinal Alberoni himself has certified the truth of all these accounts in a letter of thanks to the author. Moreover, M. Nordberg, who is as ill-informed about European affairs as he is a bad writer, asserts that the Duke of Ormond did not leave England on the accession of George I, but immediately after the death of Queen Anne, as if George I had not been the immediate successor of this queen.

now inspired by vengeance in addition to his other powerful motives. He went post-haste to the tsar and gained more influence over him than ever with his insinuations. To begin with, he assured him that, with a single Russian plenipotentiary, he would remove all the obstacles which were delaying the conclusion of the peace with Sweden in less than three months. He took a map which the tsar had drawn himself, and, drawing a line from Viborg to the Arctic Ocean, skirting Lake Ladoga, he undertook to induce his master to cede everything east of that line, as well as Karelia, Ingria and Livonia. He then threw out the suggestion that the tsar should marry his daughter to the Duke of Holstein, dangling various tempting baits before him: the duke might cede his dominions to him in return for their equivalent, whereby he would become a member of the empire, opening up the distant prospect of the imperial crown, either for one of his descendants or for himself. By thus playing on the tsar's ambitions, he deprived the pretender of the Russian princess, while at the same time opening his path to England, fulfilling all his aims simultaneously.

The tsar decided that the conferences his minister of state, Osterman, was to have with Baron Görtz should be held on the island of Åland. He asked the Duke of Ormond to leave, so as not to give too flagrant offence to England with whom he did not wish to break until he was on the point of invading it. The only person he kept in St Petersburg was Ormond's confidant, Irnegan, who was charged to carry on the intrigues, and who took such precautions to conceal his presence in the city that he went out only at night and never saw the tsar's ministers except disguised as a peasant or a Tartar.

As soon as the Duke of Ormond had left, the tsar wrote to the King of England, expressing his satisfaction at having dismissed the greatest partisan of the pretender, and Baron Görtz returned to Sweden full of hope.

He found his master at the head of thirty-five thousand regular troops and the coast guarded by the militia. The only thing the king lacked was money; his credit was exhausted both at home and abroad. France, which had provided him with some subsidies during the last years of Louis XIV, had ceased to do so under the regency of the Duke of Orleans, whose policy was the very opposite. Spain had promised him some, but was not yet in a position to provide much. Baron Görtz now made free use of an expedient he had already tried before he went to France and Holland; this was to give copper the same value as silver, so that a copper coin whose intrinsic value was a halfpenny passed for forty pence when stamped with the king's head. Governors of a besieged town have often used much the same device by paying the soldiers and citizens with leather money while waiting to be able to obtain real coins. This inflated currency, which depends entirely on good faith to maintain its credit, is like paper money whose fictitious value can easily exceed the actual funds the state possesses.

These expedients can be employed to good purpose in a free country; they have sometimes saved a republic, but they are almost invariably disastrous to a monarchy, for the people soon lose faith in them and the minister is reduced to creating an atmosphere of false confidence by further financial jugglery. The inflated coins are minted in larger and larger quantities, individuals bury their gold and silver, and the whole economy breaks down in chaos, often with the most fatal results. This was what happened in the kingdom of Sweden.

Baron Görtz, who had at first prudently distributed only a restricted number of these new coins to the public, was soon forced to go far beyond his original limit by the rapid movement of events he could no longer control. All merchandise and provisions having risen to an excessive price, he was obliged to increase the number of copper coins. The more they were multiplied, the more they were discredited. Sweden, flooded with this worthless money, cried out with one voice against Baron Görtz. The people, still full of veneration for Charles XII, did not dare go so far as to hate him, but let the full weight of their resentment fall on his minister, whom, as a foreigner and as the man who controlled the country's finances, they had a double reason for loathing.

A tax which he wished to impose on the clergy made him universally execrated; the priests, who too often identify their cause with the Deity's, publicly denounced him as an atheist because he demanded money from them; the new copper coins had some of the pagan gods stamped on them and they took advantage of this to call these coins 'Görtz's gods'.

As well as being hated by the public, Görtz was also the object of the other ministers' jealousy, which was all the more implacable for being impotent. The king's sister and the prince her husband feared him because he was connected by birth with the Duke of Holstein and might one day endeavour to place him on the throne of Sweden. No one in the kingdom had ever liked him but Charles XII, but this universal detestation only served to make the king his firmer friend, for Charles's feelings were always strengthened by opposition. He now showed a confidence in the baron which amounted almost to deference: he gave him absolute power in the internal government of the kingdom and entrusted everything concerned with the negotiations with the tsar entirely to him. The thing he was most anxious for him to do was to hurry on the conferences to be held on Aland.

As soon as Görtz had finished dealing with the financial arrangements which required his presence in Stockholm, he left to go and meet the tsar's minister and complete the great work he had begun.

Here are the preliminary conditions of that alliance, which was to have changed the face of Europe, as they were found among Görtz's papers after his death.

The tsar was to retain the whole of Livonia and part of Ingria and Karelia and return all the rest to Sweden; he was to unite with Charles in restoring King Stanislas to the throne of Poland and to promise to return to that country with eighty thousand Russians in order to depose King Augustus, the very man on whose behalf he had waged war for ten years. He was to supply the King of Sweden with the necessary ships to transport ten thousand Swedes to England and thirty thousand to Germany; the combined forces of Peter and Charles were to attack the King of England in his Hanoverian dominions, particularly in Bremen and Verden; the same troops were to be used to re-establish the Duke of Holstein and to force the King of Prussia to accept a treaty which deprived him of part of his new acquisitions.

From then on Charles behaved as if his victorious troops, reinforced by the tsar's, had already carried out everything they had planned. He boldly demanded that the Emperor of Germany should implement the treaty of Alt-Ranstadt. The Court of Vienna scarcely deigned to reply to a demand from a prince from whom it believed it had nothing to fear.

The King of Poland did not feel so secure; he saw the storm gathering on all sides. The Polish nobility was leagued against him, and ever since his restoration he had perpetually been either fighting his subjects or negotiating with them. The tsar, who was a mediator to be feared, had a hundred galleys in Danzig Bay and eighty thousand men on the frontiers of Poland. All the north was rife with suspicions and alarms. Flemming, the most mistrustful of men and the one whom the neighbouring powers had most reason to mistrust, was the first to suspect the tsar's and the King of Sweden's designs in favour of Stanislas. He wished to have him kidnapped in the Duchy of Zweibrücken, in the way that James Sobieski had been kidnapped in Silesia. One of those adventurous and restless Frenchmen who go to try their fortune in foreign lands had recently enlisted, with some other Frenchmen of the same type, in the service of the King of Poland. He approached Flemming with a plan by which he undertook to go, with thirty determined French officers, and carry Stanislas off from his palace and bring him to Dresden as a prisoner. The plan was approved. Such enterprises were then quite common. Some of those who are known in Italy as *bravi* had made similar coups in Lombardy during the last war between France and Germany. Since then, some French refugees in Holland had even dared to enter the precincts of Versailles with the intention of kidnapping the dauphin and had captured an equerry almost under the windows of Louis XIV's palace.

The adventurer therefore got his men and his relays of horses all ready to seize and abduct Stanislas. The plot was discovered on the eve of being executed. Several of the conspirators escaped; a few were captured. They did not expect to be treated as prisoners of war but as bandits. Stanislas, instead of punishing them, contented himself with giving them a few kindly rebukes and even gave them money to help them on their way. His kindness and generosity proved that his rival, Augustus, had indeed reason to fear him.*

* This is what Nordberg calls lacking in respect to crowned heads, as if this truthful account contained an insult, and as if one owed anything other than truth to kings who are dead. Does he think history ought to be like sermons preached before kings, in which one pays them compliments?

Meanwhile, in October 1718, Charles set out for the second time to conquer Norway. He had planned everything so efficiently that he hoped to be master of that country in six months. He preferred to go and conquer rocks amidst snow and ice in a winter so bitter that it kills animals even in Sweden where the air is milder, rather than go and recapture his beautiful provinces in Germany from the hands of his enemies; this was because he hoped that his new alliance with the tsar would soon put him in a position to recapture all these provinces, but still more because it was more gratifying to his pride to wrest a kingdom from his victorious enemy.

At the mouth of the river Tistedal stands the town of Fredrikshald, an important stronghold regarded as the key to Norway. Charles laid siege to it in the month of December. Numb with cold, the soldiers could hardly shift the hardened earth under the ice; it was like digging trenches in rock. But the Swedes could not lose heart when they saw their king sharing their hardships. Charles never endured greater ones; his constitution had been so toughened by eighteen years of hard living that in Norway he slept out in the open in the depth of winter, on straw or a plank, and wrapped only in a cloak, without the least damage to his health. Many of his soldiers fell dead of cold at their posts, but the others, nearly frozen as they were, did not dare to complain when their king was suffering the same hardships. It was some time before this expedition that, while he was in Scania, he heard of a woman who had lived several months without taking any nourishment other than water. Having made a point all his life of enduring the utmost rigours human nature can bear, he decided to try how long he could bear hunger without any ill-effect, physically or mentally. He spent five whole days without eating or drinking; on the morning of the sixth he galloped two leagues and dismounted at the house of his brother-in-law, the Prince of Hesse, where he ate a great deal. His five days' abstinence had not lowered him nor did eating a large meal after so long a fast cause him any discomfort. With this iron body, governed by so bold and inflexible a spirit, no matter to what state he might be reduced, he had no neighbour to whom he was not a formidable menace.*

* Nordberg claims that it was to cure himself of a chest complaint that Charles XII tried this extraordinary fast; the confessor Nordberg is certainly a bad doctor.

On December 11th, St Andrew's Day [*sic*], he went at about nine o'clock in the evening to inspect the trench and, not finding it as far advanced as he hoped, he was extremely displeased. Mégret, the French engineer who was conducting the siege, assured him that the town would be taken in eight days. 'We shall see,' said the king, and he went on inspecting the siegeworks with the engineer. He stopped at a spot where the communication trench formed an angle with the parallel, knelt down on the inner ramp and, leaning his elbow on the parapet, stayed some while watching the men going on digging the trenches by starlight.

The least circumstances become important when they concern the death of such a man as Charles XII; therefore I must issue a warning that all the conversation which so many writers have reported between the king and the engineer Mégret is absolutely false. Here is what I know to be true about this event.

Nearly half the king's body was exposed to a gun-battery pointing directly at the corner where he was. The only people near him were two Frenchmen; one was M. Siquier, his aide-camp, an intelligent and energetic man, who had entered his service in Turkey and who was particularly attached to the Prince of Hesse; the other was this engineer. The cannon fired grape-shot at them, but the king was more exposed than the others. A few paces behind was Count Schwerin, who was in command of the trench. Count Posse, a captain in the guards, and an aide-de-camp named Kaulbar were taking orders from them. At that moment, Siquier and Mégret saw the king collapse over the parapet with a heavy sigh; they rushed to him, but he was already dead. A ball weighing half a pound had struck him in the right temple and had made a hole three fingers deep; his head had fallen forward over the parapet, the left eye had been staved in and the right was hanging out of its socket. The wound had killed him instantaneously, yet he had had the strength, even in that moment of sudden death, to make the instinctive gesture of grasping his sword, and he was still in that attitude. At this sight, Mégret, a strange and unfeeling man, merely remarked: 'The play is over, let us go and have supper.' Siquier rushed to alert Count Schwerin. Together they decided to keep the knowledge of this death from the soldiers until the Prince of Hesse could be informed of it. They wrapped the body in a grey cloak, and

Siquier put his hat and wig on the king's head. Charles's corpse, thus disguised and purporting to be that of Captain Carlsberg, was then carried through the troops, who saw their dead king pass by without suspecting it was he.

The prince immediately ordered that no one should leave the camp and had all the roads to Sweden guarded so as to give him time to take measures to ensure that his wife should succeed to the crown, and meanwhile prevent the Duke of Holstein, who might lay claim to it, from obtaining it.

Thus perished, at the age of thirty-six and a half, Charles XII, King of Sweden, after having experienced the greatest prosperity and the cruellest adversity without being softened by the one or shaken for one moment by the other. Nearly all his actions, even in his private life, had far exceeded the bounds of probability. He is perhaps the only man, and hitherto the only king, who has never shown weakness; he carried all heroic virtues to an excess where they are as dangerous as the opposite vices. His firmness which developed into obstinacy caused his disasters in the Ukraine and kept him ten years in Turkey; his generosity, which degenerated into extravagance, ruined Sweden; his courage, pushed to fool-hardiness, caused his death; his justice sometimes went as far as cruelty, and, in his last years, he exerted his authority to the point of tyranny. His great qualities, any one of which might have immortalized another prince, were a calamity to his country. He never attacked without provocation but he was immoderate and implacable in his vengeance. He was the first king who had the ambition to be a conqueror without wishing to enlarge his domin-ions; he wanted to win empires in order to bestow them. His passion for glory, war and vengeance prevented him from being a good politician, which a conqueror has always needed to be. Before a battle and after a victory, he was invariably modest, after a defeat invariably undaunted. As hard on others as he was on himself, as reckless of his subjects' lives and sufferings as of his own, he was a unique, rather than a great man, and to be admired rather than imitated. His life should teach kings that a peaceful and prosperous reign is infinitely preferable to so much glory.

Charles XII was tall and well-made; he had a very fine forehead, large blue eyes full of gentleness, and a well-cut nose, but the lower part of his face was disagreeable and too often disfigured by a frequent laugh which was no more than a grimace of the lips, and he had almost no hair or beard. He spoke very little and often replied only with this laugh which had become a nervous habit. At meal-times, a profound silence was observed at his table. In spite of his inflexible character, he was bashful and self-conscious. He would have been embarrassed if he had had to make conversation, because having devoted himself entirely to warfare and physical exertion, he had never mixed in society. Until his enforced leisure among the Turks, he had never read anything but Caesar's *Commentaries* and *The History of Alexander*, but he had written some reflections on warfare and on his campaigns from 1700 to 1709. He admitted this to the Chevalier de Folard, and told him that this manuscript had been lost on the ill-fated day of Poltava. Some people have tried to make out that this prince was a good mathematician; no doubt he had a very acute mind, but the proof they give of his mathematical knowledge is not very conclusive: he wished to change the practice of counting in tens, and proposed the number sixty-four instead, because this number contained both a cube and a square, and being divided by two could be finally reduced to unity. This idea merely proved that, in everything, he liked what was extraordinary and difficult.

As regards his religion, although the sentiments of a prince ought not to influence other men and the opinion of a monarch as ill-educated as Charles carries no weight in these matters, nevertheless the curiosity of those who take a keen interest in everything concerning this prince must be satisfied on this point as on the rest. I know from the person who has been my main source of information in writing this history that Charles XII was a strict Lutheran up to the year 1707. Then, in Leipzig, he met the famous philosopher, Leibnitz, who was a freethinker and expressed his views openly, and had already imbued more than one prince with his liberal ideas. I do not believe, as I have been told, that Charles lost faith in Lutheranism through talking to this philosopher, who had the honour of conversing with him only once and then only for a quarter-of-an-hour. But Baron Fabrice, who subsequently lived on familiar terms with him for seven years, told me that, during his sojourn in Turkey, where he came in contact with different religions, he lapsed much further from his own. Even La Motraye, in his *Voyages*, confirms this opinion. The Comte de Croissi thinks the same and has told me several times that this prince retained none of his original beliefs, except in that of absolute predestination, a doctrine which encouraged his boldness and justified his rashness.

I cannot refrain from mentioning here a slander which recurs all too often when a prince dies. Malicious and credulous people always claim that he has been either poisoned or assassinated. The rumour spread in Germany that it was M. Siquier himself who had killed the King of Sweden. This brave officer was for a long while driven to despair by this calumny: one day, when he was talking to me, he spoke these actual words: 'I could have killed the King of Sweden, but I had so much respect for that hero that if I had wanted to I would not have dared.'

I am well aware that Siquier himself had given rise to this deadly accusation which some Swedes still believe to be true. He admitted to me that when he was in Stockholm suffering from a raging fever he had cried out that he had killed the King of Sweden, and that in his delirium he had even opened the window and publicly asked pardon for this regicide. When, after his recovery, he was told what he had said during his illness he nearly died of grief. I did not wish to reveal this story during his lifetime. I saw him shortly before his death and I can definitely state that, far from having killed Charles XII, he would have laid down his own life for him a thousand times. If he had been guilty of such a crime it could only have been in the service of some power which would certainly have rewarded him well for committing it. He died in France very poor, and even needed the assistance of his friends. If these reasons do not suffice, another fact should be taken into consideration; the bullet which struck Charles XII could not have been loaded into a pistol and Siquier could not have fired this fatal shot except with a pistol he had concealed under his coat.

After the king's death the siege of Fredrikshald was raised, and the whole situation instantly changed. The Swedes, more conscious of the heavy price they had paid for their prince's glory than proud of it, now had only two desires; to make peace with their enemies and to put an end to the concentration of absolute power in the hands of one man. They were determined never again should the country experience what it had suffered under Baron Görtz. The diet freely elected Charles XII's sister as their queen, but made her solemnly renounce all hereditary right to the crown, so that she should hold it only by the assent of the people. She promised, with many oaths, that she would never attempt to re-establish arbitrary power: later she sacrificed her royal throne to her love for her husband, the Prince of Hesse, by yielding the crown to him. She persuaded the diet to elect him, and he mounted the throne on the same conditions as his wife.

Baron Görtz was arrested immediately after Charles's death and condemned by the senate to be beheaded in Stockholm at the foot of the public gallows: a sentence probably dictated by vengeance far more than by justice and a cruel insult to the memory of a king whom Sweden still admires.

APPENDIX

Voltaire's replies to certain allegations of inaccuracy
made against *The History of Charles XII.*

Letter from M. de Voltaire

Written from Paris, 25 April 1733

The great difficulty we have in France in obtaining books from Holland is the reason why I did not see the ninth volume of the *Bibliothèque raisonnée* until late; and, by the way, I must say that, if the rest of this journal is of the same standard as what I have so far read, men of letters in France are to be pitied for not knowing it.

On page 469 of this ninth volume, part II, I have found a letter against me in which I am accused of slandering the city of Hamburg in *The History of Charles XII*.

A few days ago a Hamburger, an estimable man of letters named M. Richey, who did me the honour to come and see me, renewed these complaints in the name of his fellow-citizens.

Here are the facts, and here is what I am obliged to state:

At the height of that disastrous war which ravaged the north, Count Stenbock and Count Welling, the King of Sweden's generals, decided, in the city of Hamburg itself, to burn Altona, a commercial city belonging to the Danes, which was beginning to do some damage to Hamburg's trade.

This decision was ruthlessly carried out on the night of the 9th of January. These generals slept in Hamburg that very night; they slept there on the 10th, 11th, 12th and 13th, and the letters they wrote to try and justify this barbarity were dated from Hamburg.

Again, it is certain, and the Hamburgers do not deny it, that several Altonese, including old men and pregnant women, who came to ask shelter in Hamburg were refused entry, and that some of these wretched people perished of cold and want amidst ice and snow under the walls of that city while their own was being burnt to ashes.

I was obliged to report these facts in *The History of Charles XII*. One of those who have written me their personal accounts of them insists very positively in one of his letters that the Hamburgers had given Count Stenbock money to induce him to exterminate Altona, as a rival to their trade. I have not endorsed such a grave accusation; however much reason I may have to be convinced of human wickedness, I have never been easy to convince that an alleged crime has been committed. I have effectively combatted more than one calumny, and I was the only one to vindicate the memory of Count Piper by stating the facts while the rest of Europe was slandering him by conjectures.

Instead, therefore, of adopting the opinions so firmly held by my correspondent, I have contented myself with reporting that *it was said* that the Hamburgers had secretly bribed Count Stenbock.*

This rumour was general and based on appearances: a historian may report rumours as well as facts, and provided he reports a public rumour merely as an opinion, not as a truth, he is neither responsible for it nor reprehensible for reporting it.

But when he learns that this popular opinion is false and slanderous, then it is his duty to declare it so and publicly to thank his informants.

I myself am now in this situation. M. Richey has convinced me of the innocence of his fellow-citizens. The *Bibliothèque raisonnée* has also very firmly denied the charge brought against the city of Hamburg. The author of the letter against me is reprehensible only in that he accuses me of having definitely said that the city of Hamburg was guilty; he ought to have distinguished between the opinion of part of the north, which I have reported as a vague rumour, and the affirmation he imputes to me. If I had indeed said: 'The city of Hamburg bought the ruin of the city of Altona,' I would most humbly beg his pardon, convinced as I am that there is nothing so shameful as not retracting when one is in the wrong. But I told the truth when I reported a current rumour and I am telling the truth when I say that when I investigated this rumour I found it to be entirely false.

I must furthermore state that contagious diseases were rife in

---

* In the 1732 edition to which the 'letter against him' in the *Bibliothèque raisonnée* referred, Voltaire had written: 'It was said that the Hamburgers had secretly given Stenbock a large sum in order to purchase the ruin of this town which was damaging their trade.' As will be seen at the end of his letter to the *Bibliothèque raisonnée*, he suppressed any mention of the rumour of bribery in the 1733 edition which was then in the press. (*Translator's note*)

Altona at the time of the fire, and that if the Hamburgers had no *lazaretti* (as I am assured), no places where the old people and women who were dying before their eyes could have been sheltered and isolated, they might well be excused for not having taken them in, for the preservation of one's own city must come before saving the lives of strangers.

I shall take great care to see that this passage in *The History of Charles XII* is corrected in the new edition now being printed in Amsterdam, and that it is restricted to the exact truth which I aim to convey and which I value above everything.

I also learn that letters from the poet Rousseau on the subject of the tragedy *Zaïre*, as insulting as they are ill-written, have been published in some weekly periodicals. This author of several plays, all of which have been hissed, sets himself up as judge of a play which the public has received with considerable indulgence, and this author of so many impious works publicly accuses me of having shown little respect for religion in a tragedy performed with the approval of the most virtuous magistrates, read by his eminence, Cardinal Fleury, and which is already being performed in some religious houses. People will do me the honour of believing that I shall not stoop to reply to the poet Rousseau.

Notes on La Motraye's *Remarques*

I. 'My admiration for everything that comes from your pen increases more and more.'

If that were so, M. de La Motraye would have communicated his remarks to M. de Voltaire instead of selling them to a bookseller.

II. 'Having for so many years had the honour of being in close touch with your hero and of continually conversing with his officers, I ought to know more about him than you do.'

The reminiscences which have been communicated to M. de Voltaire, and which he will depose in a public library, are written by ministers and general officers who may have seen many things which escaped M. de La Motraye's notice.

III. 'Everyone agrees that your book is very well written: that would suffice, they say, for a novel where imagination predominates, but it is not enough for a history where truth should reign supreme and where vigour and forcefulness are needed rather than grace and elegance.'

Vigour and forcefulness depend on style and not on truth. One can lie forcefully and tell the truth tediously.

IV. 'In the first book of your history . . . you make the Tsar Peter I win the battle of Azov against the Turks in 1697, and capture this town (the key to the Turkish Empire) from them, which surrendered on the 28th of July 1695; you make him leave Moscow on his great mission in 1678; he left on this mission in 1698.'

M. de La Motraye is mistaken. Azov surrendered on the 27th of June 1696. As regards the date 1678, everyone realizes that it is a printer's error. This error has been corrected in the latest editions of *The History of Charles XII*.

V. 'What surprises me, is that you have not corrected in this edition what you say of M. Le Fort, that he was the son of a French refugee in Geneva, and that he first sought employment in the Russian army.'

This error has been corrected in several editions. M. de La Motraye should have read them, since this criticism was printed after the fourth edition of M. de Voltaire's book published in France.

VI. 'M. Le Fort came from a legal and commercial Genevese family . . . His father sent him to stay with M. Franconis, a famous merchant of this town (Amsterdam).'

M. de Voltaire never had any intention of writing the history of M. Le Fort nor that of M. Franconis.

VII. 'This prince (the Tsar Peter) one day noticed how respectfully Le Fort stood behind the chair of his master (the Danish ambassador) during dinner, and, looking at him more closely, was struck by his good manners and good looks; and, as he acted as interpreter and spoke good Russian, his majesty asked him what his nationality was and where he had learnt this language, and plied him with other questions which he answered satisfactorily. The tsar was delighted with him and asked him if he would like to enter his service.'

It is for the reader to decide whether these details were very relevant to *The History of Charles XII.*

VIII. 'The tsar was so pleased (with Le Fort's clothes) that he said he wished to have similar ones for a company of fifty men, of which he would make him captain, and which he wished him to train in the manners of the courts he had told him about. Le Fort searched among all the foreign merchants established in Moscow for everything necessary to fit out this company, and, having hired all the tailors in the town, he asked the tsar for permission to have the measurements taken of the strelitzes* who had the best figures and the handsomest faces.'

It is an established fact that there was not one strelitz in this company of fifty men, but these little facts are trifles about which it hardly matters being right.

IX. 'What you treat as a popular rumour, or a falsehood, concerning the over-indulgence in wine which led Charles XII, before the war, to actions unworthy of a prince . . . is quite true.'

It is quite false. M. le Comte de Croissi once took the liberty of asking Charles XII himself if it was, and, whatever M. de La Motraye may say about it, the king replied that it was a slander. This is what I heard from the lips of M. le Comte de Croissi, the ambassador to that king.

X. 'Count Dahlberg having recaptured the fort of Dunamunden

* Special Russian infantrymen. (*Translator's note*)

from the Saxons by capitulation, after an attack by the besiegers as long and vigorous as the resistance of the besieged, this young hero (Charles XII) was all for his sending the prisoners back into it, so as to take it by assault, and without giving or receiving quarter.'

This is neither probable nor true. Such tales would disgrace a history.

XI. 'The accounts of the victory of Narva, besieged by the Russians in 1700, vary greatly; and, from what I have learnt of them . . . do not entirely agree with what you say about it. You make Charles land with 16,000 men, etc. . . .'

Such accounts do hardly more than copy M. de Voltaire's history; the only difference is in the style, and in details which a judicious writer omits.

XII. 'The officers whom I have just mentioned have told me, among other details, that the number of Russian prisoners was so great that, to get rid of them, they were sent back to their master, after the Swedes had taken everything from them down to a knife, and cut the belts of their breeches in two places, so that they were obliged to hold them up with both hands.'

It remains to be seen whether it is a very grave fault to have omitted the adventure of the Russians' breeches.

XIII. 'I will not quarrel with you over the etymology of the word *tsar* or *tsarafis*: I content myself with saying that I have never heard anyone called *tsar* but the sovereign of Russia, whose eldest son is always *tsarevitch*; but I do know that the Asiatics normally call the Prince of Georgia *gurgistanbey* . . .'

All this does not prevent the word *tchar* from meaning king and prince among the Scythians.

XIV. 'People also find that the account you have given of the siege and battle of Poltava does not tally with those they have had hitherto, nor with what they have heard from those who were present at it; but I will not dwell on that, and will revert for a moment to Narva . . .'

These critical opinions do not seem to be very consistent. As regards Poltava, M. de Voltaire still has the plan of the battle which was given to him by a highly experienced officer. As regards Narva and its consequences, M. de La Motraye does M. de Voltaire much honour by repeating what he has said about it in his history.

XV. 'You say that General Rehnskiöld had all the Russian prisoners brutally massacred six hours after the battle of Fraustadt, regardless of their surrender or their tears: some Swedish officers who were present have assured me that it was the king himself who ordered this massacre.'

M. de La Motraye was not there, and all those who were know that the king did not see Rehnskiöld until some days after. If Charles had had the Russians killed so long after they had been given quarter, he would have been guilty of the most unpardonable and incredible cruelty; but one knows that he had no part in it.

XVI. 'But, you will add, Charles XII violated international law by having Patkul handed over to him: I shall not make any reply to this objection.'

If you are not making any reply to this objection, it was not worth the trouble of raising it yourself.

XVII. 'It was Baron Stralheim, famous for his witty remarks, who said to Charles, the day after he returned from his visit to King Augustus, what you make General Rehnskiöld say.'

This mistake in the name had already been corrected.

XVIII. 'This hero, who was all-powerful in Saxony and Poland, would have done the most generous thing in the world if he had gone to visit King Augustus, or had invited him to his quarters immediately after the ratification of the treaty of Alt-Ranstadt, and had torn up this treaty and said: *I restore your crown to you: reign and be as sincerely my friend as I wish to be yours.*'

M. de Voltaire has contented himself with saying what Charles XII did: it is for M. de La Motraye to say what Charles ought to have done.

XIX. 'You say that, on his arrival in Leipzig, the Duke of Marlborough spoke secretly, not to Count Piper, but to Baron Görtz etc. . . . I have never heard any mention of this incident.'

You have heard it spoken of by Baron Fabrice, who was your patron when you were with the King of Sweden and who told me this fact, of which he was a witness.

XX. 'As soon as the duke saw him (Count Piper) standing at his door ready to receive him, he got out of the carriage and, putting on his hat, walked past him without greeting him, and drew aside, as if to make water.'

Whether the Duke of Marlborough pissed or not on alighting from his carriage may be irrelevant, but from this very coldness between him and Count Piper it seems quite plain that the Duke of Marlborough had spoken to Baron Görtz.

XXI. 'I had the honour of being received in private quite often by Charles XII during his stay in Bender; I never observed that he showed the least dislike of France.'

There are diplomatic messengers who are received in private by princes, who carry state secrets but do not know what they are.

XXII. 'The treaty in favour of the Silesian protestants which you make the Emperor Joseph break as soon as Charles was no longer in a position to impose laws continued to be implemented after that. Passing through Silesia on my return from Russia I saw a large number of these protestants still in possession of the privileges and the churches they had recovered by this treaty.'

Only very few of these churches were given back; this is a known fact.

XXIII. 'The ambassador whom you make the sultan send to the King of Sweden was an aga who had been sent to the republic of Poland, who, seeing that all the foreign ministers were congratulating Charles on his victories, and the new king on his accession, did the same.'

Since he returned the Swedish slaves, he presumably was sent on some mission to the King of Sweden.

XXIV. 'You say that gangrene set in in the king's foot immediately after his wound at Poltava: it was only at Bender that some symptoms of it appeared.'

If M. de La Motraye had read the last edition of the book he is criticizing, he would have read that they were already beginning to fear gangrene.

XXV. 'I have more than once heard the surgeon who embalmed Charles XII's corpse say that he had never seen a healthier body or one all of whose parts were more perfect, except that the skin lining the lower part of the abdomen was so thin, which he attributed to violent and frequent horse exercise, that if he had lived he would inevitably have had a rupture.'

Frequent horse exercise would have had the opposite effect, but this mistake is excusable.

XXVI. 'The whole chancery staff was not captured as you say, since M. Muller, Councillor Fief and several secretaries whom I ransomed at Bender from the hands of the Turks and Tartars were not.'

I said that most of the chancery staff was captured, which is true.

XXVII. 'This prince was put in a carriage which had been conveyed to the other side of the river, for he was not fit to ride, and General Hord, who was also wounded, got into it with him. They crossed the desert which lies between the Dnieper and the Bug and which forms part of the *Scythia parva* of ancient times, where I got lost and wandered for three or four days without finding either water or provisions, on my way back from Circassia in 1717.'

Nearly all this can be found in the history, except for the dearth of water from which M. de La Motraye suffered.

XXVIII. 'The king accepted the refreshments which this pasha had brought, received his apologies and did not reprimand him as you say.'

Count Poniatowski has written us the contrary.

XXIX. 'The king later wrote the sultan the letter you found in the appendix to my first volume, but you have altered the style and abridged it by half.'

This is not a fault of which readers will complain.

XXX. 'Count Piper, whom you make die in Moscow, died in Slutelburg.'

This quite unimportant error has already been acknowledged and corrected in an English and a Dutch edition.

XXXI. 'Moreover, the Lutherans, far from believing in predestination, abhor the Calvinists and other Christians who believe in it . . . But one can easily forgive you this error when one remembers that you have studied ancient mythology more than theological systems.'

When one has the bad grace to insult well-known men with malicious gibes, one should at least be guilty of no more than rudeness and not of being fundamentally mistaken. It is extraordinary to see M. de La Motraye affirming that predestination is not one of Luther's dogmas. Does not the whole of Europe know that it was one of the main articles of his creed? It is a known and undisputed fact that, in his books, Luther denies free-will and the merit of good works. The Lutherans have since deviated from this dogma, like all sects which have changed the religion of their founder. It is not only on predestination that Lutherans and Calvinists are divided, but on many other points. Moreover, M. de Voltaire knows ancient and modern mythologies and esteems them as he should.

XXXII. 'You say that General Poniatowski found means of conveying a letter from Charles XII to the Sultana Valida (or Sultana Mother). This letter and those which you make Valida write with her own hand to this general, as well as the account of this hero's exploits you make M. Brue give the chief eunuch . . . all this can only seem pure fiction to those who have some knowledge of the Turkish character.'

The author still has in his possession, and will depose in a public library, the letter from Count Poniatowski in which these actual words appear: 'If I can find some of the letters from the Sultana Valida, I will send them to you by Mme de . . .' M. de La Motraye may contradict Count Poniatowski if he wishes, in order to indulge himself in the pleasure of writing.

XXXIII. '. . . The sultans never married, and only took concubines who were not taught to write.'

This is entirely false. There was no woman who was not taught to read and write.

XXXIV. 'M. Brue was a good friend of mine and has provided me with some memoirs; he was too well aware of the Turks' indifference to what Christians do to have said that they were interested in discussing the subject.'

The Turks may be very indifferent about what Christians do in France and Rome but not about what a king who caused so many viziers to be deposed was doing in their own country.

XXXV. 'The rebels, who deposed Mustapha Achmet in 1703 and raised his brother to the throne instead, are said to have made it a condition that the new sultan should not allow the sultana his mother to play any part in the affairs of the empire; and I have never heard anyone say since that she meddled in them.'

Count Poniatowski, Baron Fabrice, M. de Fierville and M. de Villelongue may know things that M. de La Motraye does not.

XXXVI. 'It is as doubtful whether the tsar demanded Mazeppa from the Porte as it is that the vizier who could have forced him to hand over Cantemir, after the battle of the Prut, asked him to.'

This is quite certain. The proof of it is in the manuscripts which will be deposited.

XXXVII. 'The episode of the phial of poison, destined for General Poniatowski by the Russians, which you say was conveyed to the sultan, has no more foundation; at the very most it was no more than an invention to make them odious to the Turks.'

M. de La Motraye, who was not there, again contradicts Count Poniatowski, and will be very surprised when he sees his letter.

XXXVIII. 'You attribute to Charles XII, with equally little foundation, the deposition of all the viziers whom he believed hostile to him.'

It is untrue that M. de Voltaire attributes the deposition of all the viziers to Charles XII and his party.

XXXIX. 'You make Baltagi Mehemet vizier through an intrigue of his wife's, you depose him through another, and have him made vizier again through a third intrigue of the same woman's. Nevertheless he was vizier only once.'

He was vizier twice. He was Pasha of Aleppo after his first viziership, as all our merchants in Aleppo know and attest.

XL. 'You make him say to the sultan, when he receives the sabre: "Your Highness knows that I was brought up to use an axe to chop wood, not a sword to command your armies: I will try to serve you well, but if I do not succeed, remember that I have begged you not to hold it against me." The sultan, you add, assured him of his friendship, and the vizier prepared himself to obey. This dialogue is as conjectural as the following reply you make the deposed Grand-Vizier Couprougli Oglou give to the sultan . . .'

We have proofs in writing of everything we have asserted in *The History of Charles XII*. The doubts expressed by M. de La Motraye, who was not able to see or hear everything and who only saw or heard from a distance, are not enough to destroy the validity of the most authentic memoirs.

XLI. 'You make the Turkish army destined to fight the tsar, who was then in Moldavia, assemble at Belgrade, which would mean a détour of more than a hundred leagues. This army was assembled in the plain of Adrianople, which is on the direct route.'

It is certain that the greater part of the army did assemble at Belgrade, because there were many troops in Hungary. It is about a hundred of our leagues from Belgrade to Yassi, and a hundred and fifty from Adrianople to Yassi.

XLII. 'Sultan Ibrahim, whom Osman Aga and the former Vizier Chourlourli Ali Pasha had planned to put on the throne, by deposing Achmet, was not Sultan Mustapha's eldest son, as you say, but the only son of Soliman, the uncle of both of them.'

This is corrected in the last Dutch edition.

XLIII. 'Baltagi Mehemet was not banished for the reason you allege, nor for any other, but, on his return from Adrianople with the army, he asked the sultan to accept his resignation on account of his great age, and recommended Jussuf Pasha, then a janissary, as his successor to the viziership. This request was granted and he voluntarily chose to retire to Lemnos.'

Count Poniatowski definitely says the opposite.

XLIV. 'M. Gluck, in whose house the lady Catherine was a servant, and whom you call a local administrator, was the minister in charge of the principal church of Marienburg.'

He is described as a Lutheran minister in four editions.

XLV. 'To make one believe the Turks capable of the treachery you attribute to them (of wishing to hand over Charles XII to his enemies in Poland) one would have to assume that the tsar and the King of Poland had bribed not only the khan, the pasha and the emissaries from the Porte, but all the troops of the escort.'

No treachery was attributed to them; the Tartars were suspected, not the Turks.

XLVI. 'You say that, when I was sent to Constantinople to borrow money for the King of Sweden, I put this prince's letters of authorization in a book from which I had removed the pages and passed through the midst of the Turks with my book in my hand; it was in my valise, mixed up with other books.'

It is true that this important error was left in.

XLVII. 'The sultan ordered twelve hundred purses for the king only after this prince had written to him that he was resolved to return immediately to his own kingdom, and asked him for a thousand.'

This is stated word for word in the history.

XLVIII. 'You say that the Swedes' interpretation of Count Flemming's alleged letters in cipher to the khan induced them to believe that King Augustus was negotiating with the khan and the pasha to deliver the King of Sweden into his hands; you add that Charles XII's suspicion of this was confirmed by the hurried departure of Count Sapieha. All this has seemed fanciful and could have been a pretext for delaying the departure of the king, who, having seen the ease and generosity with which the sultan had given twelve hundred purses instead of the thousand he had asked, asked him for still another thousand. This suspicion, which has been made to serve as a reason for this prince's refusal and resistance at Varnitza, could not have been confirmed by the hurried departure of Sapieha, who did not leave Bender till some weeks after the Varnitza affair, when His Majesty had already arrived in the vicinity of Adrianople. Here is what is certain beyond question about this count. He had impoverished himself in Poland in order to serve this monarch, and had been no more favourably regarded by him there than at Bender, where he said that his compatriots and rivals had warned his majesty against him, as they did King Stanislas, he added, when he arrived there. Finding himself without money and without credit, he thought of making his peace with King Augustus, as so many of these same compatriots did later. What treachery do you see in that?'

What is certain beyond question throughout this passage, is that M. de La Motraye knows nothing about the matter.

XLIX. 'I have never heard any mention of the words: "We will fight *pro aris et focis*" which you put in the mouth of this prince.'

It is what we heard from the mouth of Baron Fabrice and several other witnesses.

L. 'Some servants . . . told me that they thought Frederick (Charles XII's valet) had been burnt to death, because they had seen a large part of the floor collapse in blazing embers just at the spot where he was firing at the Turks through a window.'

A man who had been his servant affirms that he was cut in half by the Tartars.

LI. 'They did not disarm him (Charles XII) as you say; he flung his sword away to forestall them.'

They wrenched his sword from him as he was raising his arm.

LII. 'Nothing is easier than presenting requests to the sultan: no vizier has ever forbidden anyone to do so.'

This had been expressly forbidden. It is very strange that M. de

La Motraye, who was not there, claims to know more about it than M. de Villelongue himself. The author has M. de Villelongue's original letters, which may serve to confound rash judgements.

LIII. 'It was not Sultan Galga (as the eldest sons of the khans are called) but Carplan Gherei, brother of the deposed khan, who was put in his place.'

So, in the new Dutch edition, you will find Carplan Gherei.

LIV. 'I am well aware that M. Désaleurs also persuaded some merchants to lend him a sum of money. I cannot say how much, but he lent nothing himself and only guaranteed the loan.'

This again is quite untrue. M. Désaleurs' children have the relevant documents which show that he lent twenty thousand crowns and guaranteed a similar sum.

LV. 'Mr James Cooke . . . not only advanced him further sums, but opined that his majesty would not be offended by the offer . . . of what he and his brother possessed in the way of silver plate etc.'

Any judicious reader will see that the story of Mr Thomas Cooke's payments ought not to take up two pages in the history of Charles XII.

LVI. 'You assert that there was no Dutch minister at the Court of Sweden when the king had the English resident arrested in Stockholm in reprisal for the arrest of Count Gyllenborg in London, and that therefore he could not avenge the arrest of Baron Görtz by the Dutch. Nevertheless, there was one in Sweden at the time.'

This minister did not arrive in Sweden till more than four months after Baron Görtz had been released in Holland.

LVII. 'You say, speaking of the circumstances of the king's death, that what so many writers, including myself, have reported about the conversation between this prince and the engineer Mégret is totally false.'

Yes, we say so and we are right to say so. M. Siquier, who was the only person near the king, has repeatedly told the author, in the presence of witnesses, that all this conversation was entirely mythical. Siquier is in Paris; you can get the information from the man himself.

LVIII. 'Those who, not knowing all this, thought and still think that the king was killed by one of his own men, did not suspect M. Siquier till some years later.'

The whole of Europe is quite convinced of the absurdity of this slander, and M. de Voltaire has only reported it in order to make people realize its absurdity. He hopes that this example may serve to check the unbridled imagination of those who invariably impute the death of a prince to the ambition of his successor.

LIX. 'We think that, instead of rating the English of our age so far below those of the days of Cromwell, you might very well have compared them to your heroes . . . Various London weekly periodicals have rebuked you very sharply . . . I am sorry for you . . . for having unwittingly incurred the hatred of nearly all the nations you have had to mention.'

By what right, and on what grounds, do you dare have the effrontery to say that M. de Voltaire has incurred the hatred of the nations he has mentioned? It is true that his history has long been the subject of some discussion in the English papers. But it is easy to see from these papers that *The History of Charles XII* served as a pretext for party writers to air their political views. Everyone knows how much M. de Voltaire owes to the English and also how sincerely attached he is to that country.

LX. 'In another place in this same *errata*, in meaning to correct an alleged error, you make a real one. You say that one should read Achmet II, instead of Mahomet IV.'

This list of *errata* was not compiled by the author of *The History of Charles XII*. It is very imperfect and very incorrect. The majority of the mistakes have been corrected in the last Dutch edition, and the order of succession in the Turkish Empire is faithfully observed in it.

LXI. 'You say . . . that Baron Görtz went from Sweden to France and Holland, which is true. But you add "and England, to test the feasibility of the means he intended to employ". He did not go to England, at least not after the King of Sweden's return to his dominions.'

People who talked to him during his secret journey to England are still in Paris.

LXII. 'These duchies (Bremen and Verden) were not the reasons of the animosity Charles may have felt against King George of England. The King of Denmark was the one whom he always appeared to hate most.'

M. de La Motraye will permit us to believe the memoirs of the best-informed ministers.

LXIII. 'You make the Duke of Ormond go to Madrid some years before he went there. You send him to meet Tsar Peter I in Courland . . . He did not go to Courland, any more than he went to the congress of Aland which began in 1717.'

These facts are so well known that one can only marvel at the boldness with which you deny them. There is not an Englishman in Paris who does not know that the Duke of Ormond left Loches for Spain at the end of 1716.

LXIV. 'It is only at that time, to wit in 1717, that you place the complete execution or the free extension of the plan to give a little copper coin, intrinsically worth half a sou in France, the face value of thirty-two sous. This project was planned in Stralsund, and carried out in Sweden as early as 1715, as is shown by the first print of one of these fictitious coins which I reproduced in my second volume as well as prints of those of 1716, 1717, 1718 and 1719. This last was struck and circulated in 1718 and the greatest number of them appeared that same year and excited the greatest popular feeling against Baron Görtz.'

By your own words, you establish the fact that this money was not always used to the same extent. The period of its widest circulation was in fact in 1717 and 1718, not in 1719. For it was then that it began to be abolished.

LXV. 'One is surprised, sir, to see you make so many blunders about things so close to us and consequently so easy to investigate, and to find so many anachronisms in so modern and so brief a history.'

The anachronisms and errors are in these brief *Remarques*. We have felt obliged to reply to them out of respect for the public.

Letter to Marshal Schulenburg
General of the Venetians

Sir,

I have received, via a courier from his excellency the French ambassador, the journal of your campaigns of 1703 and 1704, which you have been so good as to send me. I will say of you as of Caesar: *eodem animo scripsit quo bellavit* [he wrote in the same spirit in which he fought]. You must have known, sir, how greatly such an account would interest me and would lead to requests for further favours. I beg you to communicate to me any information you can give me concerning the wars of Charles XII. I have the honour to send you a journal of the campaigns of this king, who was worthy of being your adversary. This journal goes up to the battle of Poltava inclusive and is written by a Swedish officer named Adlerfelt. The author seems to me very well informed, and as accurate as anyone can be. It is not a history – it falls far short of that – but it provides excellent material for composing one, and I may well have to revise many things in my own in the light of this officer's memoirs.

Moreover, I admit to you, sir, that I have been delighted to see many details in these memoirs which agree with the information on which I have worked. Sceptical as I am about everything, especially anecdotes, I was beginning to accuse myself of credulity and inaccuracy in many facts I had alleged. For instance, I no longer ventured to believe that M. de Guiscard was in Charles XII's ship on the expedition to Copenhagen; I began to repent of having said that the cardinal-primate, who was so instrumental in the deposition of King Augustus, was secretly opposed to the election of King Stanislas; I was almost ashamed of having alleged that the Duke of Marlborough had an interview with Baron Görtz before seeing Count Piper when he went to see Charles XII. M. de La Motraye had contradicted me on these facts with an assurance which convinced me he must be right; nevertheless they are all confirmed by M. Adlerfelt's memoirs.

I also find in them that the King of Sweden did sometimes dine, as I had said, with this King Augustus, whom he had dethroned, and that he gave him the place of honour. I find that King Augustus and King Stanislas met at his court and saluted each other without speaking to each other. The extraordinary visit which Charles XII paid to Augustus in Dresden is not omitted. Even Baron Stralheim's witticism is quoted in them word for word, just as I had reported it.

Finally, here is what is said about all this in the preface to M. Adlerfelt's book:

'As to M. de La Motraye, who has presumed to criticize M. de Voltaire, the reading of these memoirs will only serve to confound him and to point out to him his own errors which are far more numerous than those he attributes to his opponent.'

It is true, sir, that I see clearly from this journal that I have been mistaken about the details of several military events. I had indeed rightly stated the number of Swedish and Russian troops at the famous battle of Narva, but on many other occasions I have been wrong. Time, as you know, is the father of truth; I do not even know if one can ever hope to know the whole of it. You will see that on certain points M. Adlerfelt does not agree with you, sir, on the subject of your wonderful crossing of the Oder; but I would rather believe the German general, who must have known all, than the Swedish officer who could have known only part of it.

I shall revise my history in the light of your excellency's memoirs and those of this officer. I am still waiting for an extract from the Swedish history of Charles XII, written by his chaplain M. Nordberg.

Frankly, I fear that this chaplain may have sometimes seen things with very different eyes from those of the ministers who have provided me with my materials. I shall respect his enthusiasm for his master: but I myself, who have been chaplain neither to the King of Sweden nor the tsar, and who have sought only to tell the truth, shall always declare that Charles XII's stubbornness at Bender, his obstinacy in staying in bed for ten months, and many of his actions after the disastrous battle of Poltava strike me as more eccentric than heroic.

If one can make history serve a useful purpose, it seems to me it is by pointing out the good and the evil kings have done to mankind. I think, for instance, that if Charles XII, after having dethroned his enemy Augustus, given Poland a king, and defeated the King of Denmark, had granted the tsar peace as he asked him; if he had returned home as the conqueror and peacemaker of the north, and applied himself to making trade and the arts to flourish in his country, he would then truly have been a great man: instead of which, he was only a great warrior, finally defeated by a prince whom he did not esteem. It would have been well for the happiness of mankind if Peter the Great had been less cruel, and Charles XII less stubborn.

I infinitely prefer to either of them a prince who regards humaneness as the greatest of virtues, who only goes to war out of necessity, who encourages all the arts and has a knowledge of all of them, in short a philosopher on the throne; such is my hero, sir. Do not think he is an imaginary being; this hero really exists in the person of a young king whose reputation will soon reach you;* you will see that it justifies my conviction; he deserves such generals as yourself. To write the history of such kings is a pleasure, for then one is writing that of the happiness of mankind.

But if you search through M. Adlerfelt's diary, what will you find in it except such things as this: on Monday, April 3, so many thousand men were slaughtered on such and such a field; on Tuesday, whole villages were reduced to ashes and women were burnt in the flames along with the children they were holding in their arms; on Thursday, a thousand bombs shattered the houses of a free and innocent town which had not paid a hundred thousand crowns in ready money to a foreign conqueror who was passing near its walls; on Friday, fifteen or sixteen hundred prisoners died of cold and hunger?

Have you not often thought, sir, that your illustrious profession is a dreadful, although necessary one? I see that M. Adlerfelt sometimes glosses over cruelties which ought indeed to be forgotten, so as never to be imitated. For example, I have been assured that, at the battle of Fraustadt, Marshal Rehnskiöld had twelve or fifteen hundred Russians massacred in cold blood when they were begging for their lives on their knees six hours after the battle: he claims that there were not more than six hundred of them, and he also says that they were killed immediately after the action. You, sir, must know

---

* Voltaire refers to Frederick II of Prussia (Frederick the Great) who, when he wrote this letter to Schulenburg in 1740, had been on the throne for two months. (*Translator's note*)

if this is so, since you were there on that unlucky day and the manner in which you drew up your forces was admired by the Swedes themselves, so be so kind as to tell me the truth, which I revere as much as your fame.

I await with the greatest impatience any other information which you would be willing to do me the favour of imparting to me: permit me to ask you what you think of Charles XII's march into the Ukraine, of his retreat to Turkey, and of the death of Patkul. You could dictate many things to a secretary which will help to make known truths for which the public will be grateful to you. By giving it information, sir, you would reward it for the admiration it has for you.

I am, sir, with the most respectful esteem, and with sincere wishes for the preservation of a life which you have so often risked losing,

Your very obedient and humble servant

DE VOLTAIRE

The Hague, 2 August 1740

As I was finishing this letter, I learnt that the French translation of *The History of Charles XII* by his chaplain, M. Nordberg, is being printed in The Hague; this will provide me with a fresh palette into which I shall dip my brushes when I have to repaint my picture.*

---

* The 1756, 1768 and 1775 editions add this footnote: 'The palette could not be used. We know that, up to 1709, the *History of Charles XII* by Nordberg is only an undigested mass of ill-reported facts and, after 1709, only a copy of the history composed by M. de V.'

Letter to the *Journal des savants*

Sirs, having seen in the *Journal* an extract from some *Remarques d'un seigneur polonais* on *The History of Charles XII*, I have the honour to inform you that the person who was kind enough to give himself the trouble of making them, did so for me alone, so that I should profit from them in a new edition. I still have the manuscript which this Polish nobleman* gave me in Brussels, and I have been unable to discover how a copy of it fell into the hands of the bookseller Adrien Motients who has published it.

Everyone is doubtless as aware as I am of the difference between the conduct of this nobleman, who only wrote for my information, and that of the many critics who only write in order to contradict and humiliate an author, to vaunt themselves at his expense; in fact, to sell a pamphlet. It is certain that if these critics' sole aim were to enlighten a writer and do the public a service, as nearly all of them boast, they would imitate the behaviour of the estimable man who gave me these comments; a person who informs us of the truth in that way does so for our benefit, but one who publicly reveals errors which he might have pointed out in private seems to have no object other than to harm us. I am most sincerely convinced that there are many errors in my *History of Charles XII*, and I can only thank those who reprimand me for them, from whatever motive. I have long been collecting memoirs in order to rectify this work, some of them written by persons deserving of the utmost respect, and if I am asked why I have so long delayed in making use of them it is because I wish to use them better.

When I composed this history of the most extraordinary monarch who has ever reigned in Europe, I intended to write no more than a simple essay; in a way, I was in the same state of mind as when I wrote the *Henriade*. I had had the privilege of spending some months in the country in 1716 in the company of the late M. de Caumartin, the man who knew more anecdotes about Henry IV than anyone in France. He taught me a thousand things about this great king,

* Count Poniatowski.

which were so touching and sublime, and which so fired my imagination that I ventured to conceive the idea of an epic poem, which, unworthy as it is of the hero and the nation, has nevertheless been received by that nation with some indulgence.

In the same way, finding myself in the country with Baron Fabrice, who had spent seven years with Charles XII, he told me such extraordinary things that I could not resist the desire he inspired in me to write about them. He let me see his memoirs, I consulted others as well, and I wrote this essay which has only too often been reprinted. But, just as it was only after ten years that I produced the version of the *Henriade* more or less as it stands today, it took me even longer to revise and correct *The History of Charles XII*. A poem demands a continual study to find new embellishments, a history demands an assiduous search for fresh truths, and both these tasks are the work of time.

Two years ago, four volumes of a very accurate journal of Charles XII's campaigns from 1700–1709 were published, but the material did not suffice me. I waited until I could have access to the complete history written in Swedish by M. Nordberg, formerly chaplain to the King of Sweden, a history which will probably be the most faithful one that we can have of this kind. M. de Valmod, a talented young Swede who knows our language extremely well, has just translated M. Nordberg's book, which is at this moment being printed in The Hague in four volumes, the first of which is due to appear immediately.

I shall wait till the whole book is published in order that, out of so many materials, I may finally build an edifice which may last for a while.

I have no doubt that M. Nordberg will often contradict the memoirs I have in my hands. I have all the more reason to think so, since these memoirs themselves differ from each other as much as the minds of those who communicated them to me, and no doubt the chaplain of Charles XII will have seen things in quite another light than the ministers of the Tsar of Russia.

I think one must despair of ever knowing all the exact details. Judges who interrogate witnesses never know all the circumstances of a case, and a historian, whoever he may be, has far more reason for not knowing them. It is quite enough that he should record great events and have acquired a general knowledge of human behaviour. This is the most important thing and luckily what is easiest to know. Provided the great figures in the picture are truly drawn and stand out strongly in the foreground, it matters little if the others are not wholly seen. The laws of perspective do not permit it, neither does the perspective of history permit us to know every minute detail accurately.

I need no further proof of this than the different reasons each one gives for the abstinence from wine which the King of Sweden imposed on himself from his early youth. A French ambassador at his court has assured me that this austerity was only one more of the king's virtues, and that he had renounced wine, as he had renounced love, without ever having been overcome by either, solely in order never to allow himself to be mastered by them, and to set new examples in everything. The Polish nobleman whose *Remarques* have been printed says, on the contrary, that Charles XII deprived himself of wine in order to punish himself all his life for having once got drunk. Both of these motives are praiseworthy, the second perhaps more so than the first, in that it implies a propensity that had been overcome. A circumstance that at first made me believe the ambassador's account is that Charles XII later gave up beer, and that thus it seemed probable that he renounced beer and wine only as part of the austere régime which was one feature of his heroism.

I know that it may seem very puerile to scruple to investigate whether a Swede who lived nearly thirty years ago did or did not drink wine, and for what reason he did not drink it. But so petty a detail ceases to be trivial when it concerns a hero. Moreover, a historian who is scrupulous about the smallest truths deserves more credence on great ones.

I have recorded contrary opinions about many events so as to leave the reader free to judge. My impartiality cannot be doubted: I am merely a painter who tries to apply true colours to the drawings he has been given. Everything about Charles XII and Peter the Great is indifferent to me, except the good the latter has done to mankind; it is not my purpose either to flatter them or to denigrate them; I speak of them with the respect one owes to kings who died in our own day and with that which one owes to truth. This desire to know and to tell the truth obliges me to issue a warning to booksellers who wished to produce a new edition of this history which they ought to defer for a long while. I also wish that they had been less hasty in producing some editions of my works. Permit me, above all, sirs, to protest more particularly against two of these new editions* into which a great many pieces have been inserted which are not by me at all, such as the beginning of a novel, an apotheosis, and I know not what other writings of this nature. In fairness one should be responsible only for one's own mistakes but authors are often made responsible for those of others by reason of their having been made in a book bearing their name.

I have the honour to be, etc.

---

* They bear the imprint of the *Compagnie des libraires d'Amsterdam* and are full of ridiculous mistakes and pieces falsely supposed to have been written by me.

Letter to M. Nordberg

Chaplain to King Charles XII of Sweden and author of a history of
that monarch

Permit me, sir, after having undertaken the task of reading what has
so far been published of your *History of Charles XII*, to address some
just complaints to you, both about the manner in which you deal
with this history and that which you use in your preface towards
those who have dealt with it before you.

We love' |the truth, but the old proverb 'Not all truths are suit-
able to be told' applies most of all to irrelevant truths. Deign
to remember this passage in the preface to M. de Voltaire's
history: 'The history of a prince,' he says, 'is not everything he
has done, but only what he has done worthy of being transmitted
to posterity.'

Perhaps there are readers who will like to see the catechism
which was taught to Charles XII, and who will be delighted to
learn that, in 1693, Doctor Peter Rudbekius conferred a doctor's
degree on Aquinus (master of arts), on Samuel Virenius, Ennegius,
Herlandus, Stukius, and other persons who were no doubt very
estimable, but who had little connection with the battles, triumphs
and defeats of your hero.

Perhaps it is important for Europe to know that the chapel of the
palace of Stockholm, which was burnt fifty years ago, was in the
new wing on the north side, and that it contained two pictures by
the incumbent, Kloker, which are now in the church of St Nicholas;
that the seats were covered in blue on solemn occasions; that some
were of oak and others of walnut; that, instead of chandeliers, there
were little flat candlesticks, which nevertheless produced a very fine
effect; that it contained four plaster figures and that the floor was of
black and white tiles.

We should also like to think that it is of the utmost consequence
to know that there was no imitation gold in the daïs used for the
coronation of Charles XII; to know the width of the canopy;
whether the church was hung with red or blue cloth and how high

the pews were. All this may have its value for those who like to learn anything concerning princes.

You tell us, after detailing all these great matters, at what hour Charles was crowned, but you do not tell us why he was crowned before the age prescribed by the law; why the queen mother was deprived of the regency; how the famous Piper won the confidence of the king; what was Sweden's military strength at that time; what was the size of its population; who were its allies, how it was governed, what were its deficiencies and resources.

You have given us a part of M. Adlerfelt's military diary; but, sir, a diary is no more a history than building materials are a house. Permit us to say that history does not consist in enumerating petty facts and producing manifestos and rescripts. It was certainly not thus that Quintus-Curtius composed the history of Alexander; it was certainly not thus that Titus-Livius and Tacitus wrote Roman history. There are a thousand journalists, but we have hardly two or three modern historians. We only wish that all those who grind the colours would give them to a painter to create a picture with them.

You are not unaware that M. de Voltaire has published the following statement, which your translator quotes:

'I love truth, and I have no other aim and no other concern but to know it. The passages in my *History of Charles XII* where I have been mistaken will be altered. It is very natural that M. Nordberg, a Swede and an eye-witness, should be better informed than myself, a foreigner. I shall revise my work in the light of his memoirs and shall be delighted to correct my errors.'

You see, sir, with what courtesy M. de Voltaire spoke of you, and with what deference he awaited your work, although he had reports on his from many ambassadors, with whom you do not seem to have had much contact, and even from more than one crowned head.

You have replied to this French politeness in a manner which seems in somewhat barbarous taste.

You say, in your preface, that the history written by M. de Voltaire is not worth the trouble of translating, although it has been translated into nearly all European languages and eight editions of the English translation have been published in London. You then very politely add that a Puffendorf would treat him, like Varillas, as an arch-liar.

To give proofs of this highly flattering supposition, you do not fail to put, in the margins of your book, all the major errors into which he has fallen.

You explicitly note that Major-General Stuart did not receive a small wound in the shoulder, as the French author rashly states on the authority of a German one, but a rather severe bruise. You cannot deny that M. de Voltaire has faithfully recorded the battle of Narva, which at least produced an interesting description from him; you ought to know that he was the first writer who dared to affirm that Charles XII engaged in this battle with only eight thousand men. All the other historians gave him twenty thousand: they said what seemed probable, but M. de Voltaire was the first to tell the truth about this important matter. Nevertheless you call him an arch-liar because he makes General Liewen wear a scarlet gold-braided uniform at the siege of Thorn and you point out this huge mistake by definitely affirming that the background of this gold braid was not red.

But you, sir, who, for such grave reasons as this, freely bestow the fine name of arch-liar not only on a man who is a great lover of truth, but on all the other historians who have written the history of Charles XII, what would you wish to be called yourself after the letter you report to have been written to this monarch by the sultan? Here is the beginning of this letter:

'We, Sultan Bassa, to King Charles XII, by the grace of God King of Sweden and the Goths, greetings, etc.'

You who have lived among the Turks, and who seem to have learnt from them not to mince your words, how can you be ignorant of their style? What Turkish Emperor has ever entitled himself Bassa? What letter from the divan has ever begun thus? What prince has ever written that he will send plenipotentiary ambassadors at the first opportunity in order to learn the circumstances of a battle? What letter from the sultan has ever ended with the words: 'May God keep you'? Finally, where have you ever seen a dispatch from Constantinople which was dated from the year of the creation and not from the year of the hegira? The august sultan's imam who will write the history of this great emperor and his grand-vizier may well say some very insulting things about you, if Turkish politeness permits him.

After producing such a piece, which would so grievously distress this Baron de Puffendorf, it hardly becomes you, does it, to cry 'liar' over a red uniform?

Furthermore, are you such a zealous partisan of the truth when you suppress the harshness exercised by the chamber of liquidations under Charles XII? Or when you pretend to forget, in speaking of Patkul, that he had defended the rights of the Livonians, who had charged him to do so; those same Livonians who nowadays live in peace under the mild rule of the illustrious Semiramis of the north? This is not merely to betray the truth, sir, it is to betray the cause of the human race; it is to fail your illustrious country, the enemy of oppression.

Cease then, in your hotch-potch of plagiarisms, to lavish vandal and abusive epithets on those whose duty it is to write history; cease to justify yourself with the barbarous pedantry which you impute to this Puffendorf.

Do you know that this Puffendorf is an author sometimes as inaccurate as he is fashionable? Do you know that he is read because he is the only one of his kind who was tolerable in his day? Do you know that those whom you call arch-liars would blush if they did not know more of the world's history than your Puffendorf? Do you know that M. de La Martinière has corrected more than a thousand mistakes in the last edition of his book?

Let us open this well-known book at random. I come upon the section on the popes. He says, speaking of Julius II, that 'like Alexander VI, he had left a shameful reputation'. Nevertheless, the Italians revere the memory of Julius II; they see in him a great man who, after having presided over four conclaves and commanded armies, pursued till his death the splendid project of driving the barbarians out of Italy. He loved all the arts, he laid the foundation of that church which is the finest monument in the world; he encouraged painting, sculpture and architecture, while at the same time reviving the long-lost valour of the Romans. The Italians rightly despise the ridiculous manner in which the majority of ultramontanes write the history of the popes. One must know how to distinguish the pontiff from the sovereign; one must be able to esteem many popes, even if one has been born in Sweden; one must remember what the great Count de Medici said, 'one does not govern states with paternosters'; in short, one must have no nationality and strip oneself of all partisan spirit when one writes history.

I find, on reopening Puffendorf's book, at the section on Queen Mary of England, the daughter of Henry VIII, that 'she could not be recognized as a legitimate daughter without the authority of the pope'. How many crass errors in these words! She had been recognized by parliament; and besides, how could she have needed Rome to legitimize her since Rome had neither been able nor wished to declare her mother's marriage invalid?

I read the section on Charles V: I see in it that, 'even before the year 1516, Charles V had ever before his eyes *ne plus ultra* [perfection]:' but at that time he was fifteen years old, and this motto was not adopted till long afterwards.

Shall we say on that account that Puffendorf is an arch-liar? No, we will say that, in a work that covers so wide a range, he can be excused for having erred; but we beg you, sir, to be more accurate than he, better informed than you are about the epistolary style of the Turks, more polite to the French, and, finally, more impartial and discriminating in the choice of the documents you quote.

It is a misfortune inseparable from the benefits we reap from the invention of printing that this host of scandalous documents should be published to the shame of mind and morals. Wherever there is a host of writers, there is a host of slanders; these wretched works, often originating in France, find their way into the north, just as our bad wines are sold there as burgundy or champagne. People drink the latter and read the former, often with as little discrimination, but men who have any true appreciation of wine or literature know better than to accept what France rejects.

You quote, sir, from works very unworthy of being known by the chaplain of Charles XII. Your translator, M. Walmoth, has had the fairness to state in his notes that these are bad and disreputable satires which it is not permissible for a respectable man to quote.

A historian has many duties. Permit me to remind you here of two of them which are of some importance: that of never slandering and that of never boring. I can forgive you for the first, because your work will be little read; but I cannot forgive you for the second, because I have been obliged to read you. I am, however, as far as it is possible for me to be, your very obedient and humble servant.

The Necessity of Doubt

Explanatory comments on *The History of Charles XII*

Scepticism, let us remember, is the foundation of all wisdom, according to Aristotle. This is an excellent maxim for anyone who reads history, especially ancient history.

What absurd facts, what a conglomeration of fables that shock commonsense you find in it! Well then, do not believe them.

There were kings, consuls and decemvirs in Rome. The Romans destroyed Carthage; Caesar defeated Pompey; all that is true. But when you are told that Castor and Pollux fought for that nation; that a Vestal refloated a stranded ship with her girdle; that a chasm closed up when Curtius threw himself into it; do not believe a word of it. You will read everywhere of prodigies, fulfilled prophecies, miraculous cures wrought in the temple of Aesculapius; do not believe a word of them. Yet a hundred witnesses have signed the report of them on metal tablets; and the temples were filled with *ex-votos* attesting cures. Believe that there were fools and knaves who attested what they had not seen; believe that there were pious folk who gave presents to the priests of Aesculapius when their children had been cured of a cold. But as for the miracles of Aesculapius, do not believe them for a moment. They are no truer than those of the Jesuit Xavier, to whom a crab brought his crucifix back from the bottom of the sea, and who was in two ships at once.

But the Egyptian priests were all sorcerers, and Herodotus admires their profound knowledge of witchcraft: do not believe everything Herodotus tells you.

I mistrust everything miraculous. But ought I to extend my incredulity to facts which belong to the natural order of human things, but are nevertheless highly improbable?

For example, Plutarch affirms that Caesar threw himself, fully armed, into the Mediterranean, holding aloft papers he did not want to get wet in one hand, and swimming with the other. Do not believe a word of this tale Plutarch tells you. Rather believe Caesar, who does not say a word of it in his *Commentaries*; and be quite certain that if one throws oneself into the sea holding papers in one's hand, they get wet.

You will find, in Quintus-Curtius, that Alexander and his generals were quite amazed when they saw the ebb and flow of the tide in the Atlantic Ocean, which was something they did not expect: do not believe it.

It is very likely that Alexander, when he was drunk, killed Clitus; that he loved Ephestion in the way Socrates loved Alcibiades. But it is highly unlikely that the pupil of Aristotle did not know there were tides in the Atlantic. There were philosophers in his army. It was enough to have been on the Euphrates, which has tides at its mouth, to be aware of this phenomenon. Alexander had been in Africa, whose shores are bathed by the Atlantic. Could his admiral, Nearchus, have been so ignorant as not to know what every child on the banks of the Indus knows? Such idiocies, repeated by so many authors, bring too much discredit on historians.

Père Maimbourg will repeat to you, after a hundred others, that two Jews promised the empire to Leo the Isaurian, on condition that, when he was emperor, he would destroy all the images. What interest, I ask you, could these two Jews have in preventing Christians from having pictures and statues? How could these two wretched creatures promise anyone the empire? Is it not an insult to one's reader to present him with such fables?

One must admit that Mézerai, in his harsh, vulgar, uneven style, mingles similar absurdities with the ill-digested facts he records. Now it is Henry V, King of England, crowned King of France in Paris, dying of piles, as a result, he says, of having sat on the throne of the French kings. Now it is St Michael appearing to Joan of Arc.

I do not even believe eye-witnesses when they tell me things that commonsense refuses to accept. It is no use the Sire de Joinville, or rather the person who has translated his memoirs of the crusades from the medieval French, affirming that the Egyptian Emirs, after having assassinated their soldan, offered the crown to their prisoner, St Louis: I would as lief be told that we offered the crown of France to a Turk. What likelihood is there that the Mahomedans would have thought of making a man their sovereign whom they could only regard as a barbarian chief whom they had captured in a battle, who knew neither their laws nor their language, and who was the greatest enemy of their religion?

I have no more faith in the Sire de Joinville when he tells me this tale than when he tells me that the Nile overflows after the feast of St Remigius, at the beginning of October. I just as boldly call into question the story of the Old Man of the Mountain, who, on the rumour of St Louis' crusade, despatched two assassins to Paris to kill him, but, on hearing of his virtue, sent two couriers off the next day to countermand their orders. This episode is too much like something out of the *Arabian Nights*.

I say boldly to Mézerai, Père Daniel, and all the historians that I do not believe for a moment that a hailstorm made Edward III examine his conscience and procured peace for Philippe de Valois. Conquerors are not so pious and do not make peace because it rains.

Nothing is more certain than that crimes are committed, but they must be verified. In Mézerai's book you will find over sixty princes who were 'foully done to death'. But he says so without proof, and a popular rumour ought not to be reported except as a rumour.

I do not even believe Livy when he tells me that Pyrrhus's doctor suggested to the Romans that he should poison his master, in return for a monetary reward. At that time the Romans had hardly any money, and Pyrrhus had enough to buy the republic if it had been willing to sell itself; the post of Pyrrhus's head physician was probably more lucrative than that of a consul. I shall only believe such a tale when someone manages to convince me that the head physician of one of our kings proposed to a Swiss canton that it should pay him for poisoning his patient.

Let us also mistrust anything that seems exaggerated. That an innumerable army of Persians should have been halted by three hundred Spartans at the pass of Thermopylae does not shock me; the lie of the land makes it credible. Charles XII, with eight thousand seasoned men, defeats about eighty thousand ill-armed Russian peasants: I marvel at it, but I believe it. But when I read that Simon de Montfort beat a hundred thousand men with nine hundred soldiers divided into three companies, then I say once more: I do not believe it for a moment. I am told it was a miracle. But is it really true that God worked this miracle for Simon de Montfort?

I should question the truth of Charles XII's fight at Bender, if I did not have the testimony of several eye-witnesses, and if the character of Charles XII did not make this heroic folly credible. This scepticism with which we ought to regard particular facts should be extended to the manners and customs of foreign nations. We should refuse to believe any historian, ancient or modern, who reports things contrary to nature and normal human feelings.

All the first accounts of America spoke only of cannibals. To hear them, it would appear that the Americans eat men as commonly as we eat sheep. The best evidence they can produce in support boils down to the case of a few prisoners who were eaten by their conquerors instead of being eaten by worms.

The new Puffendorf, as inaccurate as the older one, says that, in the year 1589, an Englishman and four women, who had escaped from a shipwreck on the way to Madagascar, landed on a desert island, and that the Englishman worked so efficiently that, in the year 1667, visitors found this island, Pines, populated with twelve thousand sturdy English protestants.

The ancients and their innumerable and credulous plagiarists tell us repeatedly that in Babylon, the most civilized city in the world, all the women and girls prostituted themselves once a year in the temple of Venus. I have no difficulty in believing that, in Babylon, as elsewhere, people sometimes bought sexual pleasure for money. But nothing will ever convince me that in the city that was at that time the most civilized in the world all the fathers and husbands sent their daughters and wives to a market of public prostitution, and that the legislators ordered this fine commerce. Every day a hundred similar nonsensical things are printed about the customs of the Orientals; and, for one traveller like Chardin, how many travellers there are like Paul Lucas and Jean Struys, and like the Jesuit Avril, who baptized a thousand people a day in Persia, where he did not understand the language, and who tells you that the Russian caravans went to China and back in three months!

It is otherwise with *The History of Charles XII*. I can definitely state that if ever a history has deserved the belief of the reader it is this one. I composed it, at first, as people know, on the basis of the memoirs of Baron Fabrice, MM. de Villelongue and de Fierville, and on the reports of many eye-witnesses. But as witnesses do not see everything, and sometimes see wrong, I fell into more than one error, not in essential facts, but in some anecdotes which are quite unimportant in themselves, but over which petty critics exulted.

I have since revised this history in the light of M. Adlerfelt's military diary which is very accurate and which served to rectify some facts and some dates.

I have even made use of the history written by Nordberg, Charles XII's chaplain and confessor. It is true that it is a very ill-digested and ill-written work in which one finds too many petty facts which have no relevance to his subject and in which great events are so badly reported that they become small. It is a hotch-potch of rescripts, declarations and proclamations which are normally issued in the name of kings when they are at war. They are useless to the soldier and the politician and boring for the reader. A writer may consult them occasionally when he needs to extract some information from them, as an architect uses rubble in a building.

Among the official documents with which Nordberg has overloaded his wretched history, there are even some false and absurd ones like the letter from Achmet, the Emperor of the Turks, whom this historian calls 'Sultan Bassa by the grace of God'.★

This same Nordberg makes the King of Sweden say something about King Stanislas which that monarch never said or could have said. He pretends that, in replying to the primate's objections, he told him that Stanislas had made many friends during his travels in Italy. Nevertheless, it is quite certain that Stanislas was never in Italy, as this monarch has assured me himself. After all, what does it matter whether or not a Pole in the eighteenth century travelled in Italy for pleasure? How many irrelevant facts must be excluded from a history, and how thankful I am that I condensed that of Charles XII!

Nordberg had neither brilliance nor wit nor a knowledge of worldly affairs, which is perhaps why Charles XII decided to choose him for his confessor. I do not know whether he has made this prince out a good Christian, but he certainly has not made him out a hero, and Charles XII would be ignored, if he were known only from the writings of Nordberg.

★ See M. de Voltaire's letter to M. Nordberg.

It is well to draw attention here to a little pamphlet, published a few years ago, entitled: *Historical and critical comments on the History of Charles XII by M. de Voltaire*. This little work is by Count Poniatowski and consists of the replies he had made to some fresh questions I put to him on his last visit to Paris, but his secretary made a duplicate copy of it which fell into the hands of a bookseller, who did not fail to take advantage of this to publish it. A Dutch proof-reader entitled this information from Count Poniatowski *Criticism* in order to sell it better. This is one of the least frauds practised by booksellers.

La Motraye, Baron Fabrice's servant, has also published some comments on this history. Among the errors and pettinesses of which this criticism of La Motraye's is full, there are however some true and useful things in it, and I have been careful to make use of these in the last editions, especially in that of 1739. For, as regards history, nothing must be neglected, and one must consult, if one can, both kings and valets.

Important Statement

on *The History of Charles XII*

We feel obliged, out of respect for the public and for the truth, to publish a piece of unimpeachable evidence to the trustworthiness of *The History of Charles XII*.

Not long ago, the King of Poland, Duke of Lorraine, had this work re-read to him at Commercy. He was so struck by the truth of certain facts of which he had been a witness, and so indignant at the impudence with which they had been contested in some lampoons and newspapers, that he wished to confirm the credit the historian deserves by adding the seal of his own testimony. Being unable to write himself, he ordered one of his high officials to draw up the following statement:*

We, lieutenant-general in the king's army, marshal of the household of his majesty the King of Poland certify that His Polish Majesty, after having heard the reading of *The History of Charles XII*, written by M. de Voltaire (last Geneva edition), after having praised the style . . . of this history, and having admired those features . . . which characterize all the works of this illustrious author, did us the honour to tell us that he was prepared to give M. de Voltaire a certificate to attest the exact accuracy of the facts contained in this history. This prince added that M. de Voltaire has not forgotten or displaced any fact or any interesting circumstance; that everything is true and that everything is in its correct order in this history; that he has written about Poland and about all the events which occurred there as if he had been an eye-witness of them. We certify, moreover, that this prince ordered us to write then and there to M. de Voltaire to give him an account of what we had just heard, and to assure him of his esteem and friendship.

* We are obliged to publish it; we have only taken the liberty of sparing the reader some too laudatory words. We are quite aware that we owe them only to indulgence and kindness, and we restrict ourselves solely to the testimony given on behalf of the truth.

The lively concern we have for M. de Voltaire's fame and that which every honest man must have for one who asserts the truth of the facts in contemporary histories, urged us to ask the King of Poland's permission to send M. de Voltaire a formal certificate of everything his majesty had done us the honour of telling us. His majesty not only consented to this but even ordered us to send it to M. de Voltaire with a request that he should make use of it whenever, and in whatever way, he considered appropriate, whether by showing it to people, or by having it published, etc.

Written at Commercy, this 11th day of July 1759.

Le Comte de Tressan.